An Introdu[ction to]
Hotel and Catering
Economics

CHRIS RYAN
Lecturer, Clarendon College of Further Education, Nottingham

Stanley Thornes (Publishers) Ltd

© C A Ryan 1980

All rights reserved. No part of this publication may be reproduced, stored in a retrieval system, or transmitted in any form or by any means, electronic, mechanical, photocopying, recording or otherwise, without the permission of the copyright holder.

First published in 1980 by Stanley Thornes (Publishers) Ltd
Educa House, Liddington Estate, Leckhampton Road,
Cheltenham, Glos, GL53 0DN

British Library Cataloguing in Publication Data
Ryan, Chris
   An introduction to hotel and catering economics.
   1. Hotels, taverns etc.—Great Britain
   2. Caterers and catering—Great Britain
   I. Title
   338.4'7'6479441   TX910.G7

ISBN 0 85950 424 7

Typeset by Quadraset Ltd, Combe End, Radstock, Bath
Printed and bound in Great Britain by The Pitman Press, Bath

Preface

This book results from teaching economics to students on catering courses. It applies economic theory to a description of the industry and will meet the requirements of students on the new TEC National and Higher National courses in catering studies, the BEC National and Higher National tourism courses and the new Part B of the HCIMA syllabus. These are all new courses relating to the industry, which is also in a situation of change. The tourist, hotel and catering industries have emerged into the public view much more in recent years and this book records their growing importance, and their current problems.

Finally I would like to thank Sue Davies for typing the manuscript, Roger and Linda Michell for proof-reading, many people in the industry for giving me some of their valuable time, Don Manley of the publishers for his friendly support, and an especial thank you to my loving wife Anca, who has supported me in the writing of this book and has shown exceptional patience over the last year.

Nottingham, 1980 Chris Ryan

Acknowledgments

Thanks are due to the following who provided useful information used in this book: M. Beckley, Holiday Inns of Canada; *Birds Eye Review*; *Catering Times*; Clarendon College, Nottingham; English Tourist Board; *Fast Food Magazine*; Pannel, Kerr, Forster & Company; Her Majesty's Stationery Office; Hotel and Catering Industry Training Board; Howarth & Howarth; Richard Kotas; A. C. Neilsen Ltd; Greene, Belfield & Smith Ltd; Tourism Society; Trent Polytechnic; the Universities of Edinburgh, Nottingham, Stirling, Surrey, Wales; D. Welch of Trusthouse Forte; C. York of Embassy Hotels; and M. York of Ladbroke Hotels.

We apologise to any person or institution inadvertently omitted from this list.

Contents

Preface iii

Acknowledgments iv

Chapter 1 **INTRODUCTION** 1
A Period of Change: 1946 to the Present 1
The Industry Defined 5
The Demand for Hotel and Catering Services 15
Types of Catering Establishments 18
The Industry as an Employer 19
The Industry as a Purchaser of Services 20
The Industry and Economic Policy 21
The Industrial Structure of the Industry 22
The Importance of the Hotel and Catering Industry 23

Chapter 2 **CONCEPTS OF DEMAND** 32
Introduction 32
The Theory of Demand 32
The Demand Curve 33
Shifts in Demand 35
Revenue and the Demand Curve 36
The Determinants of Demand 36

Chapter 3 **THE DEMAND FOR ACCOMMODATION** 46
Introduction 46
Types of Demand 47
The General Pattern of Demand 48
The Foreign Visitor 50
The British Holiday-maker 53
Business and Conference Demand 58
The Composite Demand for Hotel Accommodation 61
Problems and Prospects 71

Chapter 4	**THE DEMAND FOR FOOD AND DRINK**	**74**
	Expenditure on Food	74
	Expenditure on Drink	75
	The Patterns of Eating Out	79
	The Socioeconomic Framework of Demand	82
	Levels of Activity	83
	The Elasticities of Demand	86
Chapter 5	**THE DEMANDS OF THE INDUSTRY**	**89**
	Introduction	89
	The Industry's Demand for Capital—Investment Finance	91
	The Sources of Finance	95
	The Value of Investment	102
	The Demand for Capital Equipment and Convenience Foods	103
	The Demand for Labour	108
	Labour Demand in Different Sectors of the Industry	110
	The Geographical Pattern of Labour Demand	113
	The Nature of the Jobs	114
	The Self-employed	117
	Unemployment	118
	Labour Turnover	122
	Levels of Pay	126
Chapter 6	**THE SUPPLY OF SERVICES IN THE HOTEL AND CATERING INDUSTRY**	**130**
	Theoretical Concepts	130
	The Supply of Accommodation	134
	Industrial and Welfare Catering	139
Chapter 7	**THE MARKET STRUCTURE**	**143**
	Perfect Competition	143
	Imperfect Competition	147
	Oligopoly, Duopoly and Monopoly	147
	The Theories and the Hotel and Catering Industry	150
	Concentration Curves	151
	Summary	172

CONTENTS

Chapter 8	**OPERATING COSTS AND PROFITABILITY**	**175**
	Capital Costs	175
	Operating Costs: 1. Hotels	177
	Operating Costs: 2. Catering	185
	Economies of Scale	188
Chapter 9	**PRICING POLICIES**	**193**
	Marginal Costing Techniques	193
	Cost-Plus Pricing	200
	Target Rate of Return Pricing or Backward Pricing	203
	Contribution Analysis of Pricing	204
	Profit Sensitivity Analysis	207
	The Importance of Price—A Case Study: Weekend Breaks	208
	Current Problems in Tariffs and Marketing	211
Chapter 10	**GOVERNMENT ECONOMIC POLICY AND THE CATERING INDUSTRY**	**217**
	The Aims of Government Economic Policy	217
	The Industry, Its Employment Policy and Relations with the Government	222
	The Industry and Inflation	234
	The Industry and the Balance of Payments	234
	The Industry and Economic Growth	237
	Miscellaneous Contributions	239
Chapter 11	**AGENCIES INVOLVED IN THE HOTEL AND CATERING INDUSTRY**	**240**
	Introduction	240
	The Catering Industries Liaison Committee (CILC)	240
	The British Tourist Authority and the Regional Tourist Boards	243
	The Hotel, Catering and Management Association	247
	The British Hotels, Restaurants and Caterers Association	248
	The Hotel and Catering Industrial Training Board	248
	The Wages Council	250
	Trades Unions	253

Chapter 12 **FUTURE TRENDS: A BRIEF NOTE**   **256**

       QUESTIONS   **262**

       OUTLINE ANSWERS   **263**

       APPENDIX ON SOURCES OF STATISTICAL INFORMATION   **275**

       INDEX   **277**

1
Introduction

A Period of Change: 1946 to the Present

There have been considerable and significant changes in the catering industry since the immediate post-war years, when having a bottle of wine with a meal in a restaurant meant you were definitely of the 'posh' class of society, or aping the posh, or having something very special to celebrate. Today, every town has its restaurants and in a diversity that was unknown 30 years ago. Then a cup of tea would be served at the ABC or the Lyons Corner Houses, with their gold ornate scrolled lettering and utilitarian tables; or at an English Tea Shoppe complete with cakes and scones, waitresses in lacy aprons and black dresses, and a background of gentility with the gentle hum of chatter. But in 1955 Lyons introduced Wimpy Houses, and now Wimpys, Golden Egg and Pancake Houses have replaced the ABC's and offer a background of pop, French fries, and plastic decor that is both bright and easy to clean; and while there have been imitations of an American catering style, the 'king' of the real American hamburger, McDonald's now stands poised for an onslaught on the British market. Motorway building has meant motorway catering, and with the cost of hiring and transporting staff to locations that are only on the map because of motorway planners, self-service has become a normal factor in this and other catering.

The towns have also seen other changes. The fish and chip shop has had an embattled existence in the face of cod wars and potato shortages which combined to create high prices, and as they have retreated their place has often been taken by Chinese take-aways. Restaurants of many nationalities are found in many of Britain's towns. Indian, Pakistani, Chinese, Italian, French and Greek restaurants and bistros provide a touch of the exotic and compete successfully with the English restaurant offering traditional fare. And whilst the Italian restaurant was known before the Second World War, it is primarily the last 30 years which have seen this influx of different nationalities contributing to the British gastronomic scene. In 1951, Raymond Postgate's *Good*

Food Guide was launched and at that time 'eating out' meant primarily eating in a hotel. Egon Ronay's *Restaurant Guide* did not begin until four years later, and it was not until 1959 and the Mario and Franco trattorias that 'trendiness' instead of the formality of severe head waiters began to create a new style. The growth of Chinese restaurants began in the 1960s, and by the late 1960s it was the turn of the Indian restaurants to expand and flourish.

Yet some traditions have maintained themselves. The 'ploughman's lunch' of the pub is familiar, and pubs have become not only a place for drinks but for steak sandwiches, shepherd's pie and of an ingenuity revealed in brewers' competitions for anything ranging from the best pub sandwich and snack to a full-blown, stomach-gurgling, mouth-watering meal. Less happy traditions also continue, such as poor service and over-brewed cups of tea.

At the higher end of the market, expensive eating out still entails going to a hotel restaurant, and it is here that the grand tradition of the master chef is perpetuated and maintained. Yet, even the grand restaurants have partaken in a technological revolution of freezers, microwave ovens and special catering size packs of any food one cares to mention. And over the last 30 years large hotel chains, such as Trusthouse Forte and Grand Metropolitan, have grown from humbler beginnings such as ice-cream parlours. Furthermore, not only do these chains dominate the British scene, but they venture abroad with a new-found confidence in British cuisine being superior to the much vaunted continental snails and sauces.

But, at the same time, foreign intrusion into the most sacred of British institutions has occurred in the hotel industry and following the new world of haves and have-nots created by the 1973 oil crisis, the Dorchester Hotel is now in Arab ownership.

The invasion of the Continent by British hotels is, however, comparatively new compared with the invasion by the British holiday-maker. British holidays just after the war meant a week by the seaside, safe in the arms of buxom boarding house ladies of cheery disposition; or for the gregarious, the hearty, knobbly knees contests of the new holiday camps set in coastal resorts, often in converted army camps and barracks. Entrepreneurs, such as Billy Butlin and Fred Pontin, were starting to create and later to recreate a new image in British holiday-making, initially with the image of a 'wakey, wakey, campers' appealing to those who were stoically after a 'good time'. More recently, there has

INTRODUCTION

been the development of 'Pontinental', seeking to emulate the sophistication of Mediterranean resorts. British tourism overseas was to increase by leaps and bounds as, in the early 1960s, the sun shone on Clarksons, Horizon Holidays and others, for a holiday in Spain for a week; and later a fortnight was as cheap if not cheaper than a holiday in Blackpool. By the middle 1960s seven million British visitors overseas spent £300 million and for many, January became a month of yielding to the comfortable pages of holiday brochures. Indeed, such was the boom that concern was expressed by the tourist offices of coastal towns, and reports of landladies and small hotels closing down percolated through the British Isles. But, by 1967, a new reality was created by a devalued pound sterling and limits of £50 being imposed for spending money overseas, and by the beginning of 1974, the package holiday became a fraught affair with the collapse of holiday companies (including the largest, Clarksons, brought low by troubles in the holiday trade and in its parent company, Court Lines Ltd.). In addition, surcharges existed to increase holiday charges by 10% or more. At the same time, the floating of the pound against a background of a weak balance of payments was to create an opportunity for the British holiday trade. In 1976, about 10 million overseas visitors came to Britain compared with 11 million British going overseas; and it was no longer news to see Arabs, Germans and Japanese in Oxford Street or Stratford-upon-Avon. At the same time, a new framework of regional tourist authorities 'sold' Britain more effectively than before, not only to overseas visitors but to the British themselves. Tourism was now big business. This had a significant impact on hotel and catering, as hotels had to improve their standards. People on holiday are not willing to accept standards markedly lower than those they enjoy at home, and consequently an increasingly larger proportion of British hotels have full bathroom facilities with each bed-unit; yet there are considerable regional variations. At the same time increasing prices have also led to an increase in self-catering holidays.

So far we have concentrated on the hotel and restaurants; but as we will see, this is but a part of the total catering industry. Other aspects of the industry have also undergone change, but often from a technological basis. Industrial catering and the school meals service, by and large, serve a captive clientele and their growth is determined in a large part not by their own activities, but by industrial, economic and population trends. But behind the chatty exterior of the lady ladling out the soup, a revolution has taken place that has affected this part of catering just as surely as it has affected hotels and restaurants. Today, industrial and schools catering is not simply a matter of feeding hungry stomachs but of ensuring a variety of food to avoid 'menu fatigue' whilst maintaining dietary standards. The kitchens and canteens are now supplied with special catering packs. There is a food manufacturing industry, and food is no longer simply the province of agriculture. Packs of dehydrated, frozen, tinned and powdered foods line the shelves in sizes of pre-ordained portion control. The food is prepared in special equipment not yet found in the housewife's kitchen; although within the last ten years or so, private ownership of freezers has no longer become unusual. Microwave ovens are an unexceptional part of catering today and are being introduced to the private home. Specialized firms have grown to meet specialized needs and firms supply services such as overnight oven cleaning and ventilation and temperature control. Science in the form of diets and vitamins on the one hand and technology on the other, has invaded the sacred confines of Mrs Beeton.

Thus, the industry has been emerging from its Cinderella position to one which justifiably attracts the attention of the press, television—and of the Government. Just after the war Government interest was of a welfare nature, ranging from the setting of minimum wage levels to the setting of dietary standards for schools and hospitals. To some extent this 'consumer protection' has continued with recent fire legislation, but increasingly tourism has been viewed as a foreign exchange earner second only to North Sea Oil. Government interest has spawned the Tourist Boards, experimental development areas—and sometimes even money. Yet it can still be argued that there has been less official support for the United Kingdom hotel industry than has been the case in some continental countries. None the less, the success and growth of the industry has made it an important factor in this country's economy.

Yet the industry is far from homogeneous, ranging as it does from the transport cafés to the Savoy, from the unskilled, untrained and poorly paid part-time waitress to the renowned chefs of the grand London hotels. It is an industry of many facets and faces, combining a queer mix of self-abasement with claims of prestige. As we will later note, NEDC reports reveal an industry with a labour force of low morale, and yet such is the importance of the industry that it has had a National

Economic Development Committee (or 'Little Neddy') to itself and has emerged as an important invisible trade earner for the United Kingdom. Let us now view its diversity by adopting the official classifications and definitions that exist.

The Industry Defined

The range of activities covered by the industry are indicated by the 1968 Standard Industrial Classification which defines the hotel and catering industry as:

> Establishments (whether or not licensed for the sale of intoxicating liquors) providing meals, light refreshments, drink or accommodation. Included are the Hotel and Catering Services Division of the British Transport Commission; NAAFI and School Canteens; Canteens run by Catering Contractors; Social and Political Clubs; Residential Clubs; Hostels; Holiday Camps; and the letting of furnished apartments for short-term vacancies. Canteens run by industrial establishments for their own employees are excluded as are Sports Clubs.

The sheer diversity of activities, coupled with the fact that many enterprises are very small, makes it almost impossible to achieve statistical accuracy about the industry. Even the 1968 definition is ambiguous.

For example, if you work in the canteen of John Player and Sons, who provide their own catering for their own employees, you will be listed as being employed in the tobacco industry. If, however, you were employed by a firm of contract caterers who were providing the catering services for a firm such as Player's, you would be counted as being employed in the catering industry. In both cases the services of catering for people is provided, but only in one case are the returns duly seized upon by the statisticians of the Civil Service as belonging to the catering industry. The reason for this is that in classifying industries firms get categorized by their main activities, and so, for example, the main activity of a firm like John Player is not the provision of good meals to staff, however much the staff enjoy the meals! Yet in spite of the obvious statistical difficulties involved, those statistics made available in the NEDC reports *Trends in Catering* indicate that at least 90 million meals a week are eaten outside the home at a cost of over £30 million. A lot of food, and a lot of money!

In attempting to indicate the scope of the industry one can try and classify the various types of establishment—but this again is a task with many pitfalls as establishments can provide more than one service. However, the following is a generally accepted classification, and is based on the 1968 Standard Industrial Classification.

The Standard Industrial Classification (SIC) was first issued in 1948 and was an attempt to secure uniformity, and so one could compare the growth of industries and activities, one with another, and over time. So, for example, one can look up the turnover of the 'hotel sector' in 1971 and compare it with that of today to work out its growth, or one can compare the respective turnovers of the catering industry and the chemical industry. The SIC had a revision in 1958 which regrouped industries, particularly in engineering, and which transferred some industries such as garage repairs from manufacturing to service sectors. This means that in comparing present statistics with those prior to 1958 you must be aware that the figures are based on different classifications.

The problem of definition is a very important one. First you must try and create a definition that covers the most common form of activity of that type, listing, as it were, the characteristics of that activity. Then you apply the definition by taking various firms and seeing whether their activities correspond with your definition. Too wide a definition encompasses many firms with great differences; too narrow a definition means too small a sample. Try defining a 'hotel'. Have you included its restaurant services and its areas of relaxation or have you merely considered the provision of beds for the night? Did you lay down a minimum size? If not, how do you distinguish between a boarding house and a hotel? What have the following companies in common: Rank, EMI, Trusthouse Forte, Ladbrokes and Grand Metropolitan? Yes, the answer is 'hotels'—but are they truly hotel companies, since their activities together not only include hotels but self-catering holidays, guided missiles, photocopiers, casinos, fast-food outlets and so on? If a company issues what are known as consolidated accounts, in other words figures for the group as a whole, then we may know it is a large hotelier, but its hotel division may only account for 10% of its activities. Do we define it as a hotel company? Can we estimate the turnover of the hotel industry as a whole? The answer is probably no in both cases. When one also considers that figures such as tax returns may be a year or so late in preparation, that people are busy and may not fill in forms accurately, but may only 'estimate' figures, that some will not give a full disclosure of facts, then one can see that the statistics are far from accurate. This is not to say they are without value. First they quantify an item. There is little point in saying hotels are big business—your concept of big may be different from mine, and a figure will solve that difficulty. Also, if that figure is prepared in the same way year after year, then, whatever the shortcomings of that method of preparation, it will reveal the underlying trends in the industry. However, one cannot begin to collect and classify information unless you have defined the basic units of information—hence the Standard Industrial Classification. This applies to the hotel and catering industry as follows:

Hotels (SI Classification 884)

According to statutory definitions for liquor licensing, a licensed hotel is one that has *four or more letting bedrooms with, in addition, cleaning services and, if required, the provision of meals*. But other definitions are also used. In the English Hotel Occupancy Survey, the English Tourist Board define a hotel as *an establishment listed in one or more guide books, having five or more bedrooms, and not calling itself a guest-house or a boarding house, and not being listed as providing bed and breakfast accommodation only*.

Other planning bodies use in their planning much wider definitions, such as that provided by the Hotel Proprietors Act of 1956, where a hotel is *an establishment held out by the proprietor as offering food and drink and if so required, sleeping accommodation without special contract, to any traveller presenting himself, who is willing to pay a reasonable sum for the services and facilities provided and who is in a fit state to be received*.

This lack of an 'official', generally accepted definition accounts in part for the varying statistics as to the number of hotels that exist. Other 'counting' problems arise from the fact that many hotels are not open the whole year round; for many of them in coastal resorts close during the off-season period. The 1968 DEP Manpower Study estimated there were about 34 000 hotels and guest-houses in the UK, and the 1973 Hotels and Catering EDC report *Hotel Prospects to 1980* gave a figure of 35 585 hotels. The total bed-space provided by these hotels is approximately 858 000 in 457 000 rooms, but this is by no means uniformly distributed throughout the country. In addition there are considerable differences between hotels; in their age and the facilities provided. Thus it is still more common that British hotels do not provide private bathrooms, yet of course the newer hotels tend to be built with private bathrooms as living standards and expectations rise. Yet, even today only about 25% of the rooms provided have private bathrooms (in licensed hotels); though this is not to mean that only 25% of hotel guests are clean!

Unlike many European countries, the UK has no official grading or classification for hotels, or indeed, as has been noted, categorization. Thus, while many package holiday-makers to Spain will be acquainted with the grading of hotels by 1–5 stars, 1–3 for hostels, paradors, albergues and refugios, which are classified on the basis of facilities provided, no such official classification exists here. The nearest to it are the schemes run by the AA and RAC with, for the AA a star rating of 1–5 with rosettes for cuisine. Other criteria of excellence for restaurants which hotels have can be found in publications such as *The Good Food Guide*. As tourism becomes increasingly important it is possible that such a grading may become operative, and provision for such a policy was made under The Development of Tourism Act (1969) at the discretion of the Minister. At the time of writing the Minister has not seen fit to exercise that discretion. Indeed the question of hotel registration schemes has been a hotly debated subject until quite recently, with Sir Mark Henry (former chairman of the English Tourist Board) a strong advocate of a compulsory registration scheme and the British Hotels, Restaurants and Caterers Association fiercely opposing such ideas, even though accepting the need for a register of hotels.

The advantages of a grading system include:

(i) the gaining of knowledge about accommodation facilities—its distribution, size and type;

(ii) the improvement of the availability and reliability of information to the consumer.

Consequently the consumer will know what to expect and has an indicator of quality and can judge whether a hotel represents 'good value for money'.

There are however some disadvantages to the system:

(i) Many grading systems are based on the physical features of a hotel, such as the possession of a swimming pool, size of lounges, etc., and these are not always a good indicator of quality.

(ii) If attempts are made to assess quality then a uniform system is required nationally, since local systems may simply lead to differing sets of local criteria which may simply serve to confuse. Could we be sure that the criteria used in Bournemouth are the same as those of Rhyl? However, a national system would become expensive, require an inspectorate, and may turn out to be far too bureaucratic.

Consequently the whole issue was referred to a Consultative Committee on Registration of Tourist Accommodation under the chairmanship of Professor John Beavis, and in July 1979 it rejected the case for statutory registration. While the English Tourist Board accepted its findings, the Welsh and Scottish Tourist Boards were certainly disappointed though the economic recession of 1979 and 1980 has made it unlikely that they will pursue their own schemes.

This is not to say that registration will not occur however. One factor in the Beavis report which contributed to the final decision was the success of voluntary registration schemes (Table 1.1), of which the Southern Tourist Board's is perhaps the best known. Launched in 1978, by July 1979 it covered 57% of known establishments in its area, and 70% of bed-space. The scheme categorizes accommodation as services accommodation (covering hotels, motels, inns and guesthouses), bed and breakfast and farmhouses, and also lists self-catering accommodation, camping and caravanning centres and holiday centres for groups and young people. The scheme has been supported by local government authorities and is based on the voluntary completion of a questionnaire by hoteliers, and the information is published in a booklet, *Where to Stay in the South*. It is seen as a move towards the setting of minimum standards. One could also argue that such information is also a necessity if package holiday schemes in the UK are to be created

TABLE 1.1 **How registration has grown—number of establishments**
(ETB Voluntary Registration Scheme)

Year	In guide	Not in guide	Total
1975	7 300	—	7 300
1976	7 925	460	8 385
1977	8 349	881	9 230
1978	9 686	1 269	10 955
1979 (estimate)	11 300	1 700	13 000

and sold in the high street in competition with overseas holidays, whether that high street is in Bromley or Munich.

Motels (SI Classification 884)

The motel (or motor lodge or motor inn) is an establishment for an overnight stay that is very common in the USA and becoming less uncommon in the UK. At the same time, changes are occurring that confuse the originally clear distinction between a 'hotel' and a 'motel'. Initially motels were generally establishments offering self-contained units of double-bed space and private bathrooms with little or no common facilities such as guest room or restaurant. Then, the more successful chains such as Holiday Inn in the USA offered motel units with common facilities such as a restaurant and swimming pool. At the same time, increasing building costs have led to designs of repetitive bedroom units of precast and fabricated design. These are then arranged in a single- or two-storey formation around a service area that offers communal facilities such as a restaurant. Such establishments may be completely new, as in the case of Travelodge in the USA, owned by Trusthouse Forte, or the new units may be a form of expansion to an existing older hotel, as at the Norfolk Capital Hotels site of The Angel Hotel, Chippenham. Certainly the standard of finish tends to be good, with private bathrooms, television and radio in each unit. But obviously such a development blurs the distinction between hotel and motel.

Holiday Camps (SI Classification 884)

Holiday camps began in the inter-war years, but their real growth was in the post-war period up to the early 1960s. Today, there are about 109 holiday camps, and they account for about 3–5% of the accommodation used by British resident holiday-makers, which was approximately 25 million bed-nights in 1975. This compares with 16 million bed-nights in 1967. The holiday camp provides a complete package holiday with accommodation, meals and most of the entertainment provided at an inclusive price, although self-catering facilities are now common. Such a trend is in part a response to demand, in part a marketing exercise to become more price competitive, and in part a reflection of increased labour costs. Rather than close units and lose revenue, it remains possible to maintain some revenue whilst offering a reduced service which lowers costs, and so presents an attractive price to the holiday-maker.

At the same time the combined factors of increased self-catering on the one hand and the extension of dining facilities on the other has meant that single-sitting meals are now possible with a subsequent saving on labour costs and less rush for the holiday-maker. One by-product of this has been the disappearance of the infamous bugle call in Butlin's holiday camps. The last 'wakey-wakey' was called in their Ayr holiday camp on 14 September 1979 when Mr Butlin ceremoniously broke the infamous record. But such proceedings were made possible only by a £2 million modernization of the catering facilities at Ayr. While holiday camps have continued to hold a steady share of the market in the last five years, some of the organizations have not been without their difficulties with consequent takeovers of companies. Thus Butlin's is today a wholly owned subsidiary of the Rank Organisation Limited.

Boarding Houses, Guest-houses, etc (SI Classification 884)

The collecting of information on boarding and guest-houses is incomplete by the very reason that so many of the units are small, often family run, and only open during peak season in seaside and country areas. Yet, they are none the less an important part of the British holiday scene and, for example, certain types of holiday such as on farms have their devoted customers who return year after year. Thus the current copy of the annual *Farm Holiday Guide* runs to over 600 pages with well over 3000 establishments. Their share of the holiday market has declined slightly in the last five years, and the need to meet higher standards of fire precautions that became necessary in 1977 has meant that some establishments have reduced their accommodation. None the less, this category still accounts for about 10% of the holiday demand for bed-space in the UK, though this is a decline from 1968 when it was estimated that the unlicensed hotel, guest-house, boarding house group supplied 16% of the bed-space used.

Restaurants, Cafés, Snack Bars (SI Classification 885)

The NEDC reports on the patterns of eating out indicate that every week at least 22 million people are eating on average four meals a week outside the home. Various estimates indicate that eating out accounts for about 7% of total domestic expenditure in Britain. Not all of this expenditure is in restaurants, cafés and snack bars, of course, as there are also clubs and works canteens, schools and colleges. However, it is thought that 'take-away' establishments account for about 16% of the total meals, and store restaurants, cafés, hotel restaurants provide a further 25%. There is, of course, great diversity of types and standards involved in this category, as it includes motorway restaurants, catering on railway stations, fish and chip shops, Chinese and Indian take-aways, cafés, snack bars, and sandwich bars, tea-rooms and licensed restaurants which can cater for the well-to-do in opulent surroundings, or the utilitarian approach of the restaurant catering for office workers in London.

As with hotels and motels, the question of definition is becoming increasingly difficult. For example, we all know the difference between a pub and a restaurant. But into which of these categories would you classify a Berni Inn? Again there are many examples where the standard distinctions no longer apply as firms diversify their activities to meet consumer demand (or indeed to generate demand) and thereby increase their profits. One such example is the policy of Clifton Inns of developing a full restaurant within a pub, such as Magog's in London's Russia Row. For £10 000 in 1979 a former basement bar was converted into a 400 square feet traditional English-style restaurant, a deliberate policy aimed at increasing revenue by changing the purpose of previously under-utlilized available space. This diversification of purpose is, of course, nothing new. Country hotels have long served a triple function of being a pub, and a restaurant as well as being a hotel, but sometimes the problem of definition becomes a serious matter in law as well as for the compiler of statistics. When the Hotel and Catering Industry Training Board was established in 1966 it was not until a House of Lords' Judgement in 1969 that the HCITB knew whether, for example, its powers would extend to restaurants in clubs and department stores.

Clubs (SI Classification 887, 882, 883)

There are, of course, almost as many clubs as there are interests: political, social, tennis, theatrical, YMCA and YWCA—you name it, and there is probably a club for it. Not all of course, serve meals or drinks, but those which do serve alcoholic drinks need a licence which is obtainable from the local magistrates which lays down the conditions for the serving of alcohol. Consequently it is possible to check the number of licensed clubs, and in total there are just under 30 000 such establishments, selling, it is thought, about 20% of the total beer consumed in the UK.

Catering Contractors (SI Classification 888) and Welfare Catering

This category covers a range of activities from the provision of the proverbial strawberries and cream at Wimbledon, the caviar and bubbly at Ascot, to the tea-vending machine in the office, to the hungry schoolboy (or schoolgirl) demanding a second helping of chips. In the private sector contract catering can be of the permanent nature of a works canteen, to the once-in-a-lifetime requirements of the arrangements for a wedding. As an industry it has its share of both large firms and small, in that on the one hand it has large organizations such as Bateman's Catering with a turnover of over £20 million, whilst on the other hand, there are several family businesses, perhaps connected with a small bakery or similar retail business. In the public sector catering has expanded enormously since the end of the Second World War, and the establishment of a 'welfare system' of free education and free hospital services. Today nearly every school, college, polytechnic and university has its canteen, as does every hospital. Since there are approximately 33 000 schools, 600 colleges, 50 universities, and 2600 hospitals in the country, it can be imagined that the turnover in these canteens is large. Thus the annual canteen budget of a medium-sized College of Further Education could easily be over £100 000. The expenditure on school meals in England and Wales in 1977 was over £500 million. At the same time it is estimated that about 40% of the total manpower employed in the hotel and catering industry is employed in the hospitals/education sector, although this is a rough estimate due to the problems of definition in the statistics. However, the Department of Employment estimate that in 1970 private catering contractors employed about 55 000 whilst a total of 450 000 were employed in industrial and welfare catering, representing approximately 2% of the total labour force. One facet of this sector of catering is that it is often subsidized, and this is equally true of both the public and private sector. Yet, as will be seen later, especially in the public sector institutional caterers often have to work within a very tight budget whilst having to avoid what has been aptly termed *menu fatigue*, i.e. repetitive serving of the same old thing day after day. On the other hand, children often seem to like chips with everything!

Yet another aspect of contract catering which can be separately identified is that of 'travel' catering. Again, this is a term covering a multitude of sins, or rather, situations. It can cover both the gastronomic delights of a cruiser at sea holidaying in warm, romantic areas of the world and the famed British Rail cup of tea on a high-speed train. One such type of catering which has an ambiguous image is airline catering, which has been castigated as the ultimate in plastic provision and taste but which has been one of the main means of competition between airlines resulting in some good food. The common feature between rail and air travel has been the comparatively limited space in which to prepare, and indeed, to serve meals, and thus the advent of the pre-cooked, pre-packed meals has been important.

Another form of contract catering with its own peculiar set of problems is outdoor catering, a specialized area of activities meeting the needs of those at race-courses, motor-racing circuits, dances, garden parties and so on. Often the caterer provides more than just the food in that all the associated trappings of, for example, tables and chairs and indeed, even marquees and hangings may be provided. At permanent sites of outdoor events, such as race circuits, permanent buildings might exist. Some firms specialize in this form of catering, and an example would be Ring and Brymer Limited (a subsidiary of Trusthouse Forte Limited), who specialize in racecourse catering.

Like other areas we have examined, contract catering has been undergoing a change. The large contract caterers have long discarded the image of the chips with everything syndrome and have been in the forefront of the utilization of technology and bulk purchasing methods, with the result that their activities have diversified into non-catering areas as they help to equip all types of institutions in overseas markets.

Further Problems with the Standard Industrial Classification

As you are by now aware, the industry presents the statistician with a bewildering mix of activities difficult to define. None the less, the SIC is the major base for collecting statistics but it must be remembered that it is not an exhaustive basis for all of the industry. In comparing the employment figures for the industry as produced by the Hotel and Catering Industry Training Board and the Central Statistical Office one can see that the SIC covers only about 64% of those employed in the industry. Specifically the SIC does not cover catering activities in industrial and staff canteens, education, hospitals, transport, the armed forces and institutions unless those activities are carried out by contract caterers, and as we have seen contract caterers employ only about 10% of the personnel involved in this area. It also means that the SIC applies primarily to the commercial sector of the industry, and of course the methods of budgeting and price fixing might vary between, let us say, a commercial restaurant and a hospital providing meals for its patients and staff. Both have a common objective, the provision of meals, but the one is concerned with profit, the other with the provision of a service within a partially subsidized budget. The fact that the SIC does not cover such an important part of the catering industry means that information is relatively scarce about institutional catering.

The Demand for Hotel and Catering Services

Introduction

The scope and importance of the industry is only seen in part by looking at the supply of its services—however rich is its pattern of diversity. Yet obviously the supply is a reflection of a demand, and so the scope of the industry may be looked at from the demand viewpoint. In a sense the demand is a simple one, to eat and to sleep somewhere, but in a sophisticated and complex society, such as ours, such a statement, whilst true, is also a simplification. It is even a simplification to say how many meals are eaten outside the home, or how many hotel bedrooms are used. The estimated 858 000 bed-spaces fall into various categories, each category being indicative of a degree of luxury. Yet, what is a luxury to one person is a necessity to another, and what is the dream of one person is the commonplace of another. In short, when looking more closely at the demand for food and accommodation, as we will do later, it is necessary to indicate how much was demanded at a particular price in what period of time. Only then would an entrepreneur in the hotel or catering business be able to supply the required service in the right amounts. However, to satisfy the curious, and using an annual average bed-space occupancy of 45% p.a. it can be estimated that 70 million beds are occupied in hotels in a year. The pattern of expenditure is however far more complex as already indicated, for prices vary between hotels and between high and low season. For example the Exp-o-tel survey of London hotel prices for April 1977 found that the cheapest single room was £6.20 and the most expensive was £47.20. (By 1979 the top tariff had risen to over £60.) And, as will be seen, not everyone away from home spends his time in a hotel.

There are various reasons why people stay away from home; the two most common being for pleasure whilst on a holiday, or for business. It is also worthwhile distinguishing between a demand for accommodation and a demand for food and drink, which latter can cover a meal at the works canteen, or at a restaurant in the evening. A number of demands can be distinguished, some of which are indicated below.

Business Demand

This term can cover the sales representative staying at a hotel whilst visiting customers and the demand made by business on hotels for conferences and exhibitions. It may mean a firm making a block booking for their personnel whilst they attend an exhibition at, say, Olympia or the National Exhibition Centre; or the hotel itself provides the facilities for the conference and so on. Business demand for this type of usage is not confined to hotels, for universities may also offer similar facilities during the summer months, as may some stately homes. An example of a stately home being used in this way was the 1977 EEC meeting of ministers at Leeds Castle in Kent.

Holiday Demand

Holiday demand is obviously important to hotels at coastal resorts, and they may have a definite seasonal pattern, whereas hotels in cities may have a more even demand. Even those hotels in resorts can go some way to lessening the seasonal impact of the holiday trade by appealing to the conference and banqueting business. Holiday demand for accommodation also extends to hostels, camping and caravan sites, staying with relatives or friends, houseboats, guest-houses, bed and breakfast accommodation, and holiday camps.

Home and Foreign Demand

In looking at total demand it has become increasingly important to distinguish between demand by British residents, and demand by overseas residents. The two are not always complementary. For example, in 1977 there were yet even more foreign visitors than in 1976, and an estimated 12 million overseas visitors visited the UK in Jubilee year. Yet at the same time British coastal resorts indicated business as much as a third down in some cases compared with 1976. In the middle of the tourist boom of 1977, Harvey Powell of the British Hotels, Restaurants and Caterers Association was making a plea to *save our dying resorts*. Part of the problem, and it is certainly not a new one, is that overseas visitors tend to converge on certain areas, notably London and Stratford-upon-Avon, and not on others, although there are increasing efforts by the Tourist Boards to attract overseas demand to other regions with growing success. In addition British demand is in part determined by current economic considerations. Increasing economic affluence in the 1960s led to an increase in overseas holidaying by the British, an increase that both made and was made easier by, package holiday firms. To some degree this growth was made at the expense of the traditional British seaside hotel, but with the 1971 floating of the pound sterling and high inflation rates, overseas travel became more expensive, whilst even holidaying at home likewise became more costly. In 1976 and 1977 overseas package holiday companies were reporting aircraft vacancies and were using 'airfare schemes only' to fill their aircraft. However, this did not mean that the British were switching wholesale to holidaying in the UK. Surveys reported that the lower and higher income groups were simply deferring holiday plans, and that hoteliers' main custom would come from the middle income groups of up to £4500 p.a.; who, on intentions surveys, still planned a main holiday.

Institutional Demands

Such demands can clearly be differentiated. In 1976 there were 295 000 students at universities, of whom well over a third were staying in halls of residence. At the same time nearly all would have regularly had a meal on the campus. Whilst accommodation is the exception outside of higher education, there was, of course, the demand of 13 million schoolchildren and students at sixth-form colleges, tertiary colleges and further and technical colleges for meals. Likewise there was the demand for meals and accommodation of 42 000 prisoners in 1975, and over 320 000 people are patients at any one time in hospital. Also hospital catering does not end with the patients, for about 35 000 hospital doctors and 400 000 nurses require meals and of course many nurses live in accommodation provided in nurses' homes. The standard of institutional catering has undoubtedly improved over the years because of the provision of convenience foods and fast-food preparation equipment on the one hand, and a public unwillingness to accept low standards on the other. Many institutions have their canteen committees. The King Edward's Hospital Fund for London has undertaken surveys of the patients' degrees of satisfaction of food and has generally found high degrees of satisfaction. However, one is tempted to a wry smile by learning that from one survey of 2000 inmates of nine mental hospitals that 75% were satisfied with their food! More seriously, it is perhaps noteworthy that most complaints are from short-term patients who tend to have the greater experience of alternative catering.

Private hotels are not entirely unaffected by local authority demands. For example, local authorities may temporarily place the homeless in private hotels and guest houses, and for example, in 1976 Kent County Council was reported to have spent £40 000 on bed and breakfast in such accommodation for the homeless.

Types of Catering Establishment

A demand for food and drink obviously exists outside of a demand for accommodation, and apart from the home there is a diversity of places where one can eat, varying in their style, prices, atmosphere—indeed, varying in almost any way one cares to name. For the purpose of the NEDC reports 'eating out' outlet types for food and drink are described as:

(i) **Take-away**—This covers Chinese take-aways, fish and chip shops, some sandwich and coffee bars; in short anywhere where the main purpose is the provision of cooked and prepared food not eaten on the premises.

(ii) **Pubs and pub restaurants**—This term, of course, covers your favourite 'local' and its ploughman's lunch or Lancashire hotpot.

(iii) **Store restaurants**—There is yet again a wide range of styles of catering for the public found within stores, from the self-service style of some of the chain stores to the waitress services of the department stores. Department stores tend to an ethos of service and more luxury compared with the perhaps more utilitarian style of the chain stores, though not all can emulate the famed roof-top gardens and restaurant of Derry and Toms. The demand is almost entirely from shoppers.

(iv) **Cafés, snack bars**—At times it is difficult to distinguish between a café and a restaurant but differentiating features are the variation and choice of menu, the type of service, the surroundings, and possibly the price, in that cafés are generally cheaper than restaurants.

(v) **Hotels and restaurants**—Hotels often find that their restaurant is an important revenue earner, and this can be significantly important in the off-peak holiday periods if they have established a good local reputation, for then people will visit the hotel for a meal out. This is especially true of rural hotels where there may be limited choice as to restaurants.

(vi) **Place of work**—Obviously people need to eat whilst at work, and therefore this is the most common place to eat outside the home.

(vii) **Educational and hospital**—As indicated in the discussion on 'institutional demands', this is an important part of the catering industry and one facing considerable change in the 1980s as local authorities are forced to reconsider education budgets.

The Industry as an Employer

The scope of the industry cannot really be simply assessed by simply listing its services and the demand for those services. It is traditionally a labour intensive industry and in many ways continues to be so in spite of increasing wage costs. While it is true that the industry looks at means of reducing costs it none the less remains essentially a service industry, and therefore offers a choice. To the traveller in a hurry, or the person not wishing to spend much, it can offer the self-service style of catering, the vending machine, and the motel room. To the person on a holiday wishing to take things more leisurely, there is the facility of waiter service, a fully stocked bar; all the requirements of a lazy luxury can be provided—at a price. In that it is a service, labour-intensive industry, the hotel and catering industry has similarities with retail distribution and education. Table 1.2 indicates that in 1970, the industry was the seventh largest employer in Britain, and remained so in 1977, with an increase of 304 000 employees.

TABLE 1.2 **Ten largest employment groups (in thousands)**

Employment group	1970	1977
1. Retail distribution	1 877	1 857
2. Educational services	1 832	1 820
3. Construction	1 322	1 228
4. Medical and dental services	1 008	1 260
5. Insurance, banking, finance	954	1 110
6. Local government service	842	948
7. Hotel and catering	568	872
8. National government scheme	549	635
9. Wholesale distribution	516	535
10. Motor vehicle manufacturing	512	476
Total number of employees	23 446	24 887

(Source: *Annual Abstract of Statistics*, 1979)

The industry accounts for 3.6% of the employed population of Britain. There is, however, one distinctive feature about the industry, and that is the number of people who are self-employed within it: about 20% of the total. Opinions as to the significance of this vary, but it does create an industry that is comprised of the widest possible range of business sizes, from the giants to the proverbial one-man business.

The Industry as a Purchaser of Services

The industry provides employment directly as well as indirectly. The service side of the industry is made possible only by the work of other sectors of the economy: agriculture, construction, and the manufacturers and suppliers of the specialized equipment that the hotel and catering establishments use. There is a multiplier effect, for as the industry grows, so too it provides employment for many who would not necessarily see themselves as part of the hotel and catering industry. It has even been argued that for parts of the catering industry there will come about a distinction between the provision of the service and the preparation of the food. According to Birds Eye, in 1977 the catering industry used £140 million of frozen foods, whilst firms specializing in the preparation of items for the restaurant trade have grown. A dynamic example is Alveston Kitchens Ltd. formed in 1969 to provide high quality frozen entrées. Just prior to its take-over in 1977 by United Biscuits, Alveston provided 150 000 dishes a week to 1000 restaurants, and from a turnover of £48 000 in 1969 had attained £3 million in 1977.

The building of a new hotel is a major and costly enterprise, and can provide employment in the construction industry for many months. Estimates for building a city-centre hotel in 1977 of a multi-storey nature are in the region of £25 000–30 000 per room. As the industry changes in response to economic conditions, technology and demand, so do the fortunes of the suppliers of catering equipment. In 1976 the Catering Equipment Manufacturers Association indicated a 30% increase in sales to £76.6 million. Thus, to assess the scope and size of the industry it is not sufficient simply to look at the turnover of hotels and restaurants, and this is something of which we must be continually aware.

The Industry and Economic Policy

Since the middle 1960s the industry has attracted increasing government attention for a number of reasons, including:

(i) Better organization of the industry with its various associations and boards informing government of its activities—a task of communication made considerably easier by the setting up of the Hotel and Catering Economic Development Committee in 1966 which served as a meeting place for government officials, trade unionists and firms in the hotel and catering industry.

(ii) The work of the Tourist Boards in attracting tourists to their various parts of the country and getting industry and commerce 'tourist-minded'. As a result, Britain now has an important tourist industry that makes a significant contribution to this country's balance of payments. Tourism has been a growing positive factor in the British balance of payments in a time of economic uncertainty, and government is naturally drawn to any growth point in a relatively ailing economy.

(iii) As a major employer the industry attracts government attention at a time of increasing unemployment, particularly as the industry is comparatively labour-intensive, relatively successful, compared with much of British industry, and is active in development areas where government is seeking to initiate business activity.

(iv) And this is a mixed blessing, the industry has been comparatively cheap for the Government to support, whilst creating employment and creating wealth by tourism. Thus, in the financial year of 1976–77 the Government made a £20 million grant towards the Tourist Boards, which is comparatively small compared with the investment ploughed into British Leyland.

The industry has emerged in the 1970s as an important element in national economic thinking for the immediate reasons indicated above. At the same time its emergence has been against a background of some increase in leisure time, certainly over the long-term, and an increase in wealth to enjoy that leisure time. It has been estimated that in 1978 61% of the British population had a holiday of some sort, and indeed over half had at least two holidays away from home. As yet, there is no Ministry of Tourism in the United Kingdom, but the impact of tourism can be such as to attract planning bodies and research, and it is not inconceivable that in the next five years government may take a more active planning role in the industry.

The Industrial Structure of the Industry

The size of establishments varies considerably in the industry, ranging from the very large corporation to the one-man business. The leading hotel operator in the UK is Trusthouse Forte, with, in 1978, a turnover of £613 million, whilst the foremost restaurant operator is Grand Metropolitan with sales of over £500 million in its hotels, entertainments, catering and public houses divisions. On the other hand, the largest private unquoted company appears to be Yate's Brothers' Wine Lodges who had a turnover of less than £5 million in the same period. However, while the industry possesses these extremely large companies and complex interlocking company situations with major firms owning industrial contractors (e.g. Bateman Catering is a subsidiary of Grand Metropolitan), vending machine companies (e.g. Mars Limited own the company that use the Vendepac trade name), the industry retains a high degree of competition. This is due to two factors. The first is the large number of small businesses that can operate effectively and competitively because hotel and catering is a service industry, so that large corporations do not have the monopoly of a willingness to help or an ability to be friendly and get on with people. While small businesses may not be able to cater for conferences or banquets of large numbers, or build 200-room hotels, they can, and do, effectively compete for the number of guests and diners that their capacity permits. The other factor is the large degree of delegation and autonomy that is apparently allowed to subsidiaries by the large companies—of which the ultimate example is the franchising system. In part the very nature of the industry demands this delegation because a customer awaiting service in (say) Leeds will not wait for an official go-ahead to descend from on high in the form of a memorandum from Head Office in Bristol or London. The customer, whether a person in a restaurant, a firm seeking a staff restaurant, or conference facilities, rightly expects immediate service, and thus it is the caterer or hotelier on the spot who provides the service. Indeed large firms in the industry often attempt to encourage competition between their own regional divisions by awarding prizes to those of their staff who get the most orders or create the best menus. Consequently the industry displays many of the facets of a highly competitive situation, and the largest four firms in the hotel business account for only about 6% of the total bed-space capacity, whilst the four largest restaurant chains possess less than 3% of the total number of restaurants in the UK—although this is a volatile section of the industry. It is symptomatic of highly competitive situations that there is considerable advertising, competition in service, and even price competition. This is true of the hotel and catering industry, although it has been already noted that it is a far from homogeneous industry in the services that its establishments offer. To categorize both the London Savoy and the Chinese take-away as caterers is perhaps like saying that the Mini and the Rolls-Royce are both cars. Yet there is the equivalent of the 'special offer' in the schemes that are being created for 'weekend breaks' and similar activities in that they offer the public the same services at a cheaper price on certain conditions compared with the normal circumstances. The result is a wide choice of service to the public, and in that sense again, the hotel and catering industry is the epitome of the economist's concept of competitive industry.

The Importance of the Hotel and Catering Industry

In attempting to assess the importance of the industry it is necessary to establish a framework of comparison and criteria of importance. We have stated that the industry is important to the national economy, so why not let the economy be our framework, ambitious though that may seem. The economy may be divided into three sectors:

(i) **The Primary Sector**—In essence this means the gaining of the raw materials and foodstuffs. It thus covers all the extractive industries such as coal mining and obtaining North Sea Oil, and agriculture, fishing and forestry.

(ii) **The Secondary Sector**—In essence, changing the raw materials to the desired end-product. It thus covers any form of manufacture that you care to name—e.g. cars, tinned goods, books, buildings, etc. This sector has sometimes been called the 'manufacturing sector', but this term perhaps tends to restrict our notion of what can be included because of our common tendency to falsely equate manufacture with heavy industry.

(iii) **The Tertiary Sector**—This sector distributes the goods that are made, and aids the making of the goods in the widest possible sense. It therefore, covers not only services such as transport, insurance, warehousing and such activities but also the leisure, educational and health services, so that from a perhaps cynical viewpoint, we may all be better producers because we are healthy, educated and relaxed!

As society develops the inter-relationship between these sectors change (Table 1.3). Prior to the Industrial Revolution in the late eighteenth century the primary sector, and particularly agriculture, was the most important and most people were employed in that sector. Indeed, land was a very important criterion of wealth. Since the Industrial Revolution people have progressively left the land for employment in the secondary and tertiary sectors of the economy.

TABLE 1.3 **Distribution of manpower between sectors of the economy**

Sector	1921	1964	1977
Primary	13.1	6.1	1.7
Secondary	39.0	43.9	41.3
Tertiary	47.9	50.0	57.0

(Source: *DEP Gazette*)

However, the main growth of urban population has been not at the cost of rural depopulation but primarily because of the faster natural growth of the urban population. In 1881 agricultural workers accounted for over 12% of the working population; by 1911 that figure was down to 8%; and today it is less than 2%. At the end of the First World War the distribution of population between the sectors was basically determined for the next 60 years. However, this is not to say that the pattern of employment has remained unchanged since 1921. There have, of course, been tremendous changes within manufacturing. In 1921 textiles were still very important; shipbuilding likewise; the motor-car industry was only just preparing for its tremendous growth of the 1930s; and the electronics industry was the dream of only a few. Likewise there have been tremendous changes in the tertiary sector, to which, as if you had not already gathered, the hotel and catering industry belongs. The tertiary stage had developed considerably in the latter part of the nineteenth century, and by 1881 even that stand-by of female occupation—domestic service—was beginning to decline slowly in relative importance. The growth of the tertiary sector continues today, and more recently there has been a notable growth of employment within the public sector of central and local government.

In 1970 central and local government employed about 6% of the working population, whereas by 1976 this figure had increased to 7%, an increase of nearly 200 000 employees.

In assessing the importance of the hotel and catering industry, therefore, we can note how large an employer it is, what proportion of the total workforce it employs, and look at its position within the tertiary sector. Has it, for example, grown in importance in the tertiary sector, or has its rate of growth simply been a reflection of general trends within the tertiary sector? Table 1.4 answers these questions. In 1976, the industry employed 816 000, which is an increase of 44% over 1970. As the seventh largest employer it employs 3.6% of the total working population and has achieved a faster growth rate in employment than has occurred in the economy generally, and in the tertiary sector particularly.

As we will see on examining the pattern of labour in the industry in Chapter 5, this increase of labour has been uneven between the sectors of the industry; for example, public houses have achieved a growth rate in employment of nearly 200% in the same period. The hotel and catering industry has therefore taken full advantage of the trend of

TABLE 1.4 **Employment growth between economic sectors (Great Britain)**

	1970 Number (thousands)	% of total*	1977 Number (thousands)	% of total*	Change in numbers (thousands)
Primary	391	1.7	395	1.7	+4
Secondary	10 765	48.1	8 969	40.2	−1796
Tertiary	11 183	50.2	12 951	58.1	+1768
Total	22 339	100.0	22 315	100.0	−24
Hotel and catering	568	2.5	882	3.9	+314
Distribution	2 702	12.0	2 735	12.2	+33
Local government	857	3.8	956	4.3	+99
Central government	559	2.5	672	3.0	+113

*Percentages do not add up to 100% due to rounding.

(Source: *DEP Gazette, Annual Abstract of Statistics*)

employment from the secondary to the tertiary sector, which trend in part is a reflection of increased leisure time.

A second approach to assessing the importance of the hotel and catering industry is similar to the first, only in this instance instead of looking at employment we can look at expenditure, and therefore indirectly at sales revenue. Because there are so many small firms in the industry it is not possible to estimate accurately the turnover of the hotel and catering industry since only limited liability companies need to file accounts for public inspection at Companies House. However, based on surveys it becomes possible to calculate the total turnover of the industry. For example, if the largest five companies accounted for 10% of the total business in that survey and should one in ten people go to those companies, then you could estimate the industry turnover by multiplying those companies' turnover as given in their annual accounts by ten. A check on the resultant figure could be gained by analysing the expenditure patterns of firms and individuals in that their expenditure is someone else's revenue. Theoretically it does not matter whether you look at expenditure or revenue in total—they are simply two ways of looking at the same flow of money. In practice, the two sets of figures never match because there are time lags involved in, for example, recording transactions. But enough of these outline explanations—essentially the moral of the homily is that these, like other figures, are but estimates and are far from accurate to the *n*th decimal place. They exist as a guide to comparative importance, not to absolute certainty.

From Table 1.5 it can be seen that the hotel and catering industry has a turnover of 5% of the National Product, and has achieved a growth rate of 137% in money terms in the period covered. All the figures are in money terms and therefore do not take inflation into account Yet, in spite of this growth, the industry has lost way compared with the growth in National Income generally, and the growth of the tertiary sector more particularly. In part, this is due to the complex growth situation in which the industry finds itself at present. International tourism is growing, as will be noted, but as far as the UK is concerned most foreign tourists tend to go to certain areas with the result that other parts of the country do not obtain the same proportionate benefit from this trade. At the same time the domestic demand for the industry's services is affected by the state of the economy and possibly wage inflation in particular. It is possible to argue that when wages increase rapidly there is a tendency for the British to book a foreign holiday, and when wage restraint is imposed, then, in times of economic recession, there is a deferment of holidays by British residents.

This is a concept that will be examined in Chapter 2. If this is so, then the traditional coastal resorts are faced with a falling demand even

TABLE 1.5 **Gross National Product by industry sector by factor cost (at current values)**

	1970 £ million	%*	1977 £ million	%*	1970–77 % change
Primary	1 880	4.2	7 074	5.6	+276
Secondary	18 634	41.3	43 341	34.1	+133
Tertiary	24 618	54.5	76 646	60.3	+211
Total**	45 132**	100.0	127 061**	100.0	+181
Hotel and catering	2 735	6.0	6 484	5.1	+137
Local authority educational services	1 320	2.9	5 054	3.9	+282
Public admin and defence	2 840	6.3	9 159	7.2	+222

*Percentages do not add up to 100% due to rounding.
**Before adjustments for stock appreciation and residual errors.
(Source: *National Income and Expenditure Tables, Annual Abstract of Statistics*)

at a time when the industry is catering for more foreign visitors and earning more foreign exchange than ever before.

On the other hand, it can be argued that the statistics in Table 1.5 tend to underestimate the performance of the hotel and catering industry because the above average growth in the tertiary sector comes from an increase in government activity, and the governmental share of the National Income has increased rapidly in the last decade—though by how much is a matter of contention by economists because of debate about whether or not to include things such as social security payments and pensions; which are technically termed *transfer payments*. As Table 1.5 shows, an example of this growth of government expenditure has been of spending on education.

Probably both factors play a role in 'explaining' Table 1.5, and certainly the mixed profit fortunes of the companies in the industry in the period 1974–77 indicate that while demand has grown, it has done so unevenly. Yet, whatever the position as to growth, any industry that has a turnover of 5% of the Gross National Product can only be considered as being important.

Mention has been made of the industry's contribution to the balance of payments. This contribution is in two direct ways. First there is the expenditure of foreign visitors to Britain, and secondly the expenditure by British tourists. Obviously tourist expenditure is not wholly on the services offered by the hotel and catering industry, and it is incorrect simply to equate hotels and catering with tourism. Tourism covers additional facets such as the mode of travel and tourist attractions (be they stately homes, beautiful countryside or the British heritage). The items on which tourists spend their money (whether Jubilee mugs or plastic Welsh dolls) are all part of the pattern of tourism. However effectively we may sell Britain to the British and the rest of the world, one thing is certain: a lack of good accommodation and good food would prejudice that sales drive. Consequently the hotel and catering industry has a vital role to play in tourism. The scale of tourism can be simply shown by a few figures. In 1976 10 million overseas tourists visited Britain, compared with a British population of approximately 55 million. In the Jubilee Year of 1977 the number of tourists was about 12 million. Of course this imposed a strain upon facilities, especially in London, which is always a focal point and was even more so during the Jubilee celebrations. Sir Alexander Glen, a former chairman of the British Tourist Authority, made a preliminary estimate in July 1977

INTRODUCTION

that, at the height of the Jubilee celebrations, the population of London was swelled by an additional 5 million tourists. This influx of people into London is not without its benefits, as estimates show that 65% of foreign tourist expenditure is in London, and indeed about 6% of all foreign tourist expenditure is in the shops of, and around, Oxford Street, which in 1977 represented about £125 million for these retailers! What these figures imply in hard cash terms can be seen from Fig. 1.1 which indicates the contribution of travel to the British balance of payments.

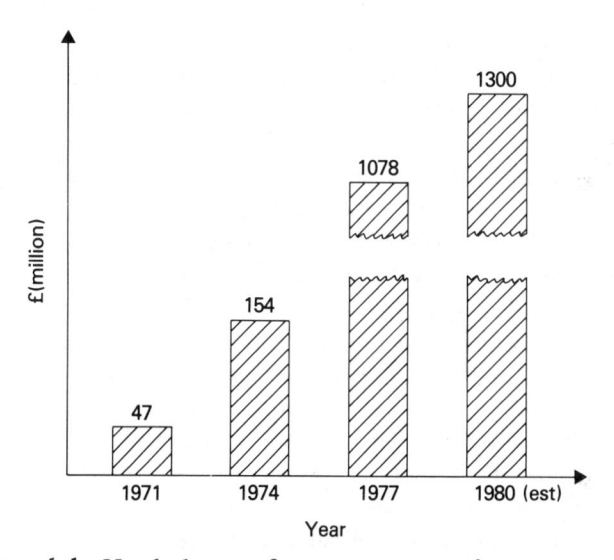

FIG. 1.1 **Net balance of payments—tourism account**
(Sources include *Annual Abstract of Statistics*)

The hotel and catering industry also benefits from the overseas visitors in that surveys on behalf of the BTA and other bodies indicate that about 25% of foreign tourist expenditure is on hotels, and a further 25% on restaurants. This is not, of course, uniform across the country as for example, whilst about 18% of foreign visitors visit friends and relations in the UK there are regional variations. For example, in the East Midlands 30% of overseas tourists visit friends and relations, and consequently one would expect hotels in that area to receive a lower proportion of overseas residents' expenditure. None the less, the hotel and catering industry is a major contributor and beneficiary of the tourist industry.

If we compare the earnings from overseas visitors with the total income from abroad, we find that tourism is becoming increasingly important in that in 1971 tourist receipts were 5.2% of total exports, 5.4% in 1973, 5.5% in 1975 and about 5.7% in 1977. The potential of tourism in the economy of a country has already been shown in other parts of the world. Spain is a European example of where tourism has contributed greatly to that country's economy, and many emergent African countries have attempted to develop a tourist industry as a means of earning foreign currency that can then be used for the purchase of required products.

The industry is, therefore, important as an employer, as a significantly large industry in terms of turnover, and as an earner of foreign revenue. But the importance of the industry does not stop at that. With every transaction there is a multiplier effect. For example, a restaurant might order equipment from a manufacturer, and so create jobs in the manufacturing sector of the economy; it will purchase food and so create another flow of money. Its employees will spend their wages and so another flow of revenue into different industries will be created. The hotel and catering industry spent approximately £3000 million in 1973 and is now spending considerably more than that, with estimates ranging from £8000 million to £10 000 million.

Not all sectors of the industry are equally important, and the industry is not equal in its importance throughout the various parts of the country. For example, the industry is relatively more important as an employer in the South-west of England in the summer than it is in London, although there are more employees in the industry in London. This is simply a reflection of the alternative employment opportunities that exist, and it also points out the need for a relative approach to statistics. Finally, Table 1.6 shows the turnover of the constituent parts of the industry. Over the period of 1966–78 the industry's turnover more than doubled in money terms. The fastest growth in the industry was in the licensed hotel and the public house sectors, and indeed public houses account for 56% of the industry's turnover. The smallest section of the industry is the canteen section providing meals at places of employment, and as the leisure industries expand, the canteen catering section will almost inevitably become relatively less important. This is not to say, however, that it cannot record any growth of

TABLE 1.6 **Turnover of sectors of the industry**

	1966 (£ million)	% of total	1978 (£ million)	% of total	% change
Total all caterers	2231	100	287	100	228
Licensed hotels and holiday camps	345	15	365	17	255
Restaurants, cafes, take-aways, etc.	567	25	248	21	195
Public houses	1180	53	288	56	241
Canteens	143	7	236	6	177

(Source: *Business Monitor*)

turnover in real terms, for it may be that as the public get used to a greater variety and better food, they will demand such from staff restaurants, who in response, can create a situation of growth in demand for their services.

2
Concepts of Demand

Introduction

At first sight it might seem easy to discuss the demand for the services of hotels and restaurants, in that all we need do is ask how many meals are served, how many people go on holiday and so on—and certainly these questions are asked. But if we ask comparatively simple questions, then we are likely to get relatively simple answers. From the viewpoint of someone who may be responsible for planning a hotel in an area or with attracting tourism, the questions of demand get increasingly complex. The simple question of 'what is the demand for hotel services?' becomes one of 'the demand of whom, for what type of service?' Consequently, it is useful to have a framework within which to develop the questioning, and for that reason we will first examine the economist's concept of demand. This should help us to formulate the right type of questions. So we embark upon some simple economic theory and then apply it to the practical problem, in the hope that we can gain some questions if not answers. It may turn out that in asking certain questions the answers are not known! In such cases the questions may lead to research which can help the marketing drive of the industry.

The Theory of Demand

In economic theory demand is important as it is a key factor in the allocation of resources. At the same time it is used in a very specific manner. It does not refer to desires, dreams or fantasies. You may like to drive down to your villa in the South of France in your Ferrari, but a simple factor such as the lack of cash may be holding you back. And so it is with most demands. What the economist is concerned with is the translation of the desire into an economic transaction, and in a society where money is the means of exchange, he looks at demand in terms of the number actually purchased. But, as we all know through everyday experience, the actual number purchased can depend on the price. The more expensive something is, the less will be purchased; the less expensive an item, the more will be purchased. That, anyway, is the normal pattern of events. Consequently, when he is being precise, the economist will speak of the number purchased at a given price. But that is still not the end of the story. There is a world of difference between saying 'I bought six Minis at £1500 each today', and 'I have bought six Minis at £1500 each over the last year'. The first implies greater wealth than the second. And so, in measuring demand there is a time element.

Consequently, for the economist there are three elements to demand:
(i) the number actually purchased,
(ii) the price at which they were purchased, and
(iii) the time in which they were purchased.

The Demand Curve

Traditionally the economist illustrates the way in which demand can aid in the allocation of resources by using a *demand curve*. Demand can vary as the price varies, and it is therefore possible to plot these combinations of price and quantity, within a given time period, on a graph. For example, a hotelier may consider opening a new hotel and wonder how much bed-space he should provide. He might therefore ask people how likely they would be to book a room at various tariffs or price levels and so arrive at Table 2.1 and Fig. 2.1. This table is often called a *demand schedule*. The demand curve is simply a diagrammatic representation of the demand schedule. The demand curve can therefore be defined as *a series of points joined together, each point representing the number purchased at a given price by a certain group of consumers within a certain period of time.*

It is usual for the demand curve to slope down from left to right, and this reflects the commonsense viewpoint stated earlier that the cheaper the goods, the more will be purchased if people are satisfied as to their quality. However, a demand curve is essentially a series of price/ quantity relationships, and therefore could conceivably take many forms. Generally, the longer the period of time involved, the more variable the shape of the demand curve may be because various factors discussed below can change. Before we look at these variables, one further point can be made about the economist's classic demand curve.

If we refer back to our original demand schedule we find that it was based on the response of people to various tariffs. In other words the final demand curve shows that 41 people would take up rooms at £4,

TABLE 2.1 **Hypothetical demand schedule for bed-space**

Tariff	Number indicating use of bed-space
£7.00	18
£6.00	24
£5.00	32
£4.00	41
£3.00	57

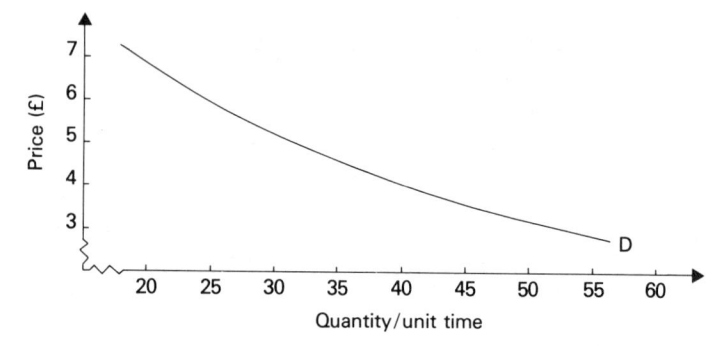

FIG. 2.1 **A demand curve for the demand schedule in Table 2.1**

or, if the price were £7, only 18 people would take up rooms. In other words the demand curve shows a series of alternative possible arrangements (Fig. 2.2). It therefore differs from the demand curve that traces actual sales at various prices. If this curve is a record of historical data, it is called a *statistical demand curve*, and is really a record of past sales; the type of graph that cartoonists always illustrate managers as possessing in their offices!

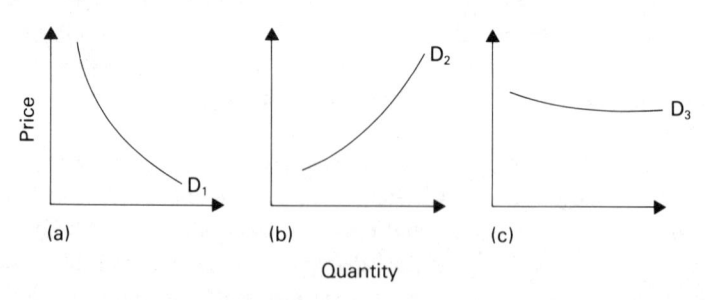

FIG. 2.2 **Possible demand curves**

Shifts in Demand

In normal conversation we may often refer to an increase in demand but in doing so we may fail to distinguish between a situation where more is purchased at the existing price, or more is purchased because the price is lower. The difference between these two is important, if only because of the possible difference in the total revenue that accrues to the seller. All of these points are illustrated in Fig. 2.3.

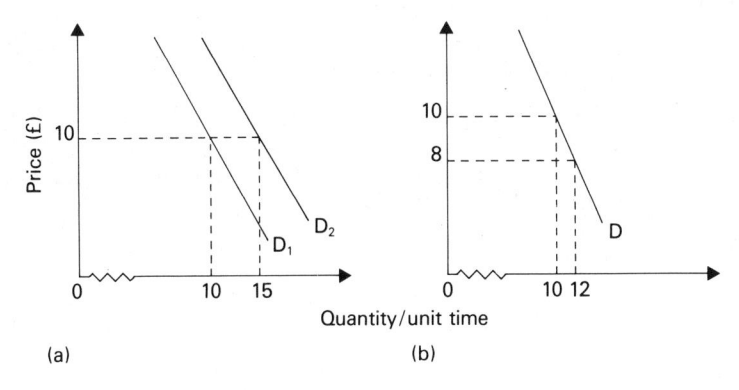

FIG. 2.3 (a) **A shift in the demand curve**
(b) **A move along the demand curve**

In the first instance ten items are sold at £10 each; and then demand increases, perhaps because of an increase in incomes, and so fifteen items are now demanded at £10 each. Total revenue (the number of items × price of each item) has now increased from £100 to £150. In the second example there has again been a situation of more being purchased, but this is due to a fall in price to £8. We have, therefore, moved to an alternative point along the *same* curve, and not moved to a new curve as in the former case. What has happened to the revenue in this new instance?

When the economist talks of an increase in demand he refers to the situation where the demand curve shifts to the right. So an increase in demand may be defined as occurring when 'more is sold at the same existing price'; likewise a fall in demand means that 'less is sold at the same existing price', and diagrammatically this is illustrated by drawing the new demand curve to the left of the original. If therefore a hotelier says that the bed or room occupancy has increased our next question could be 'did you lower your tariffs?' for if he did then we could guess that his clients were responding to his change of prices. But if he did not, then we would need to find other reasons. And if tariffs were reduced, could we automatically assume that his income went down? Think about this, for this could be important.

Revenue and the Demand Curve

Before considering the answers to these questions we can return to our diagram for one more point. You will have noted that in calculating total revenue the price was multiplied by the quantity purchased. In looking at Fig. 2.4 where the price is Oa and the quantity purchased is Oc; then total revenue is Oa × Oc; that is the area Oabc. If the price increased to Od, then total revenue will fall from Oabc to Odef; and indeed the area of the latter is smaller than that of the former.

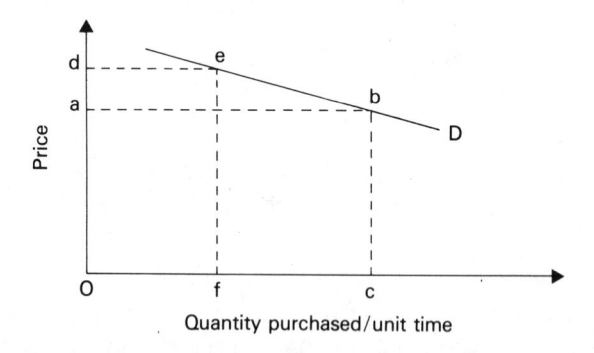

FIG. 2.4 **The demand curve and revenue**

The Determinants of Demand

It has been said that a hotelier may find that the demand for his services change without any change of policy on his part. A number of reasons may cause this. The economist usually has a general list of such reasons, which can be applied to any given situation. The general list, or *the determinants of demand* as they are usually called, include for the individual:

(i) **The price of the item demanded**—For example, if a caterer changes the prices he charges for a meal, he may attract or lose customers.

CONCEPTS OF DEMAND

(ii) **The price of other items**—This can include many things—for example, the prices charged by a competitor, but also such things as a person's rent, bus-fare and so on. If a person's income remains unchanged, but his rent, gas and electricity charges increase, then he correspondingly has less money to spend on holidays or eating out.

(iii) **Income**—If, on the other hand, none of his expenses change, but his income increases, then he can afford more expensive holidays.

(iv) **Taste and fashion**—The economist uses this 'catch-phrase' to cover the subjective elements of demand. So, whilst a person's income increases he may not spend more on his holidays for he might prefer to buy a bigger car, or a colour television set. In other words, a whole range of personal tastes and preferences make up and are affected in a person's demand schedule.

These four determinants of demand cover in fact a wider number of considerations than might at first sight appear. You could argue that supply and advertising are important considerations for people to demand something. But at what price is the good or service being supplied? And does not advertising seek to change a person's taste? In other words, it is aimed at the subjective element that makes up demand, and items such as tax changes, pensions, etc. change a person's disposable income. However, the four factors affect a single person's demand, and to look at the larger picture we must add together the demand of many.

This demand of the many is given the name *aggregate demand* by economists, and is part of the *macro-economics*—the prefix *macro* deriving from the Greek for 'many'. These considerations include:

(i) **The size of the population**—The more people there are, the more is demanded!

(ii) **The age distribution of the population**—The young have different tastes and preferences to the old, and indeed marketing men speak of a 'teenage market'.

(iii) **The sex distribution of the population**—This is about 50–50—but obviously if (say) young males were the numerically dominant section then their demand patterns would possibly be a dominant feature of that society.

(iv) **The total income**—A richer society is more likely to have leisure time involving high expenditure patterns.

(v) **The distribution of income**—Expenditure patterns between societies in part differ depending on whether or not there is equal income distribution. One can conjecture that a society, where, for example, 10% of the population has 50% of the wealth has a different demand pattern from one where income is more evenly divided.

(vi) **The degree of urbanization**—A rural population would tend to have some different demand schedules from a mainly city-dwelling population.

(vii) **The availability of raw materials**—A country without raw materials will need to import them, with various implications for its balance of payments and for the costs of producing final items.

(viii) **The state of technology**—It can be argued that the more sophisticated is the state of technology, the richer is the society and the more sophisticated are its demands.

(ix) **The sociopolitical structure of the country**—The demand schedules of various countries can be different as a result of different philosophies and systems. It can be readily envisaged that the holiday industry as we know it in the UK is different in some details from that of East European countries, even while many of the same considerations may apply in both systems to things such as kitchen layout and design, food preparation, etc. Likewise a less materialistic society, such as an Islamic state, would have a different economic system. For example, a few Islamic banks do not charge a rate of interest on bank loans.

(x) **The tax structures**—A system which taxes income can create some differences in detail from one that taxes expenditure in the sense that the price of a good includes an element of tax. Obviously tax systems affect disposable income, and the rate of tax or subsidy can affect the price of articles and thus the demand for them—e.g., a subsidy on butter will maintain demand for butter.

The implications of these factors for the hotel and catering industry can be seen in many ways. The demand for eating out is in part affected by the price of meals, a person's income, and the prices between various

CONCEPTS OF DEMAND

establishments. The relationship between the price charged and a group's income is an intimate one—for example, the transport café is not aiming at the regular diner at the Savoy Grill. As society becomes wealthier, the demand for holidays increase, but cost of labour also increases. The age distribution of society is important if it can be shown that the young travel more frequently but require cheaper accommodation. In short, we must begin to distinguish between *types* of demand. The demands of the businessman and the holiday-maker are different and neither can we assume that each demand is homogeneous. An increasingly complex society that has the income to enjoy leisure time creates sophisticated means of employing that leisure time. So there are many types of holiday now on offer, from camping to interest holidays of painting, Open University courses, as well as the traditional sunbathing. In the open spaces of America it is possible to leave the twentieth century (at least in part) as you go on a hunting holiday with flint-lock and musket. So, too, business demand for conferences can vary enormously with regard to factors such as presentation equipment, computer simulation exercises, etc.

The purpose of looking at the theory of demand was to see whether or not it could help us identify features of which we must be aware in estimating the demand for the industry's services. From the previous discussion a number of factors emerge. In analysing demand it becomes necessary to look at the demand for various price categories of accommodation and meals. This is of real concern to the businessman, for it may be that while he may serve fewer meals at high prices, he may make a greater profit than in catering for a mass market with lower-priced meals or accommodation. On the other hand, the size of the market and the type of market must be clear. Are you aiming for an older or younger clientele? Is the demand uniform throughout the UK—or are there regional differences? Is the demand for accommodation or restaurant meals affected by changes in price or income? In other words, the aggregation of numbers is insufficient; we must separate and redefine the aggregates.

We need also pay some further regard to economic theory. How do we measure the importance of changes of income or prices on the demand for a given service? Once again the economist can help by loaning us another of his ideas: the concept of *elasticity*. There are in fact different types of elasticity: *price-elasticity, income-elasticity*, etc. But whatever the type we are essentially measuring the responsiveness of demand to changes of some other variable. And so, to some more definitions:

Price-elasticity of demand is the responsiveness of demand to changes in price of the item or service demanded.

Income-elasticity of demand is the responsiveness of demand for an item or service to changes in income of the consumer.

Cross-elasticity of demand is the responsiveness of demand for one product or service to changes in the price of an alternative product or service.

Since these various elasticities operate on the same basic principle we can concentrate on price-elasticity of demand to see how we can apply the definition in practice. A verbal account of how to calculate price-elasticity is that:

$$\frac{\text{Elasticity}}{\text{of demand}} = \frac{\text{Proportionate change in quantity demanded}}{\text{Proportionate change in the price of the service demanded}}$$

Figure 2.5 indicates what this means in practice.

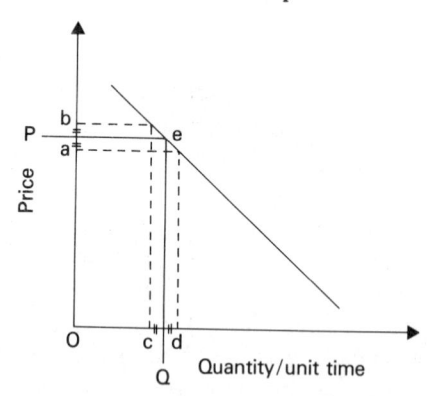

FIG. 2.5 **Calculating elasticity of demand**

In Fig. 2.5 Ob represents the original price at which Oc was demanded. The price then falls to Oa, whereupon demand reaches Od. The change in price is ab, and the change in the quantity demanded is cd. You might say these changes indicate the responsiveness of demand to a change in price—but is this the full picture? ab could be a change of say £1.00—but it makes a considerable difference if the price change was from £2.00 to £3.00 or £1001 to £1002. Likewise, the change

CONCEPTS OF DEMAND 41

in the quantity demanded could be 5 units; but there is an important relative difference between demand changing from 5 to 10 units, and 1005 to 1010 units. In other words, the absolute changes do not give a true picture of the degree of responsiveness of demand to changes of price, and that is why the economist uses the formula he does. But this presents us with a second problem. If we are to look at the relative changes of price and quantity, do we take, for instance, the change in price as a proportion of the old price (Ob) or the new price (Oa)? There is obviously a difference. If Ob equalled £5.00 and Oa £4.00, then it would obviously make a difference in the formula if we used $\frac{1}{5}$ or a $\frac{1}{4}$ in the calculation. One way around this problem is to use what is termed *point price-elasticity*. This calculates the elasticity of demand at point 'e' on the demand curve in Fig. 2.5, where OP is the half-way point between Oa and Ob and OQ is the half-way point between Oc and Od.

Taking our verbal definition of price-elasticity of demand we can now write that:

$$\text{Elasticity of demand, } E_d = \frac{ab}{OP} \div \frac{cd}{OQ}$$

To generalize the formula we can borrow from the mathematician the symbol Δ (delta) which means 'a change in'. So ΔP is a change in price, and ΔQ a change in quantity. So

$$E_d = \frac{\Delta Q}{OQ} \div \frac{\Delta P}{OP}$$

This can be rewritten as

$$E_d = \frac{\Delta Q}{OQ} \times \frac{OP}{\Delta P}$$

or when we put the Δ's on the same side

$$E_d = \frac{\Delta Q}{\Delta P} \times \frac{OP}{OQ}$$

So far, so good! But what does it all signify? Let us take some simple examples. First, we can suppose that a restaurant offers a set price of £1.50 and at that price 70 meals are purchased a day. Now, let us suppose the price increases to £1.70, and we now find that 60 are purchased. How responsive is this demand to the change in price? Well, applying our formula so that $\Delta P = 20p$, $\Delta Q = 10$, $OQ = 65$ and $OP = 160p$ we have

$$E_d = \frac{10}{20} \times \frac{160}{65} = 1.23$$

Now, where the value of elasticity of demand is greater than one we say that the demand is *elastic*; that is, the demand is responsive to the change in price. People take note, cut back on their spending, and consequently in our case the restaurant owner can expect a reduction in income. Whereas his original income was £105 (£1.50 × 70) per day, it is now £102 (£1.70 × 60) per day. (Of course, his profits may be bigger due to a fall in costs in supplying 10 less meals, but that is part of a fuller story.) Should the elasticity of demand be greater than one, and the price falls, then total expenditure will increase. Let us suppose that our restaurant owner was facing a situation where the demand was not very responsive to the change in price—perhaps his clients liked the premises a lot, or had nowhere else to eat. So, for example, we could say originally the meals were £1.50 and 70 people dined, and then the price increased to £1.70 and 66 people dined. In this case, $\Delta P = 20p$, $\Delta Q = 4$, $OP = 160p$, and $OQ = 68$; and thus,

$$E_d = \frac{4}{20} \times \frac{160}{68} = 0.47$$

Where elasticity of demand is less than one in value, the demand is described as *inelastic*; that is, not very responsive to the change in price. And now we find that the restaurant's revenue will have increased with the increase in price, for now the new revenue is £112.20 (£1.70 × 66), compared with the original £105. To complete the picture, when elasticity of demand is equal to one, then it can also be said to be equal to unity, and in this case total revenue remains the same after the price change as it was before the price change. A simple example of this is where the price of a meal was originally £1.20, and is now £1.50; where initially 125 people dined and now 100 dine. The revenue remains £150, and hence elasticity of demand equals one. If you do not believe me, here is the calculation:

CONCEPTS OF DEMAND

$$\Delta Q = 25, \quad \Delta P = 30p, \quad OQ = 112.5, \quad OP = 135p$$

$$E_d = \frac{\Delta Q}{\Delta P} \times \frac{OP}{OQ} = \frac{25}{30} \times \frac{135}{112.5} = 1$$

These relationships between elasticity, prices and revenues are important, so it is worthwhile summarizing them as follows.

> When E_d is greater than one, demand is *elastic*:
> If the price goes down, revenue goes up;
> if the price goes up, revenue goes down.
>
> When E_d is less than one, demand is *inelastic*:
> If the price goes down, revenue goes down;
> if the price goes up, revenue goes up.
>
> When E_d equals one, this is *unit elasticity*, and the total revenue remains the same with a change in price.

A moment's thought will show that if one bears in mind these relationships it becomes easy to know if demand is elastic or inelastic. All you do is see what happens to total revenue when the price changes. If the price increases and total revenue increases then the price-elasticity of demand is . . . ? Right, inelastic! And what if the price falls and total revenue increases? The importance of all this is quite considerable to both the individual in the industry and to the industry as a whole. If the individual hotelier or caterer can create an inelastic demand then, as he raises his prices to cover increased costs in inflationary times, he will not frighten away his customers and his revenue will increase. The means of creating an inelastic demand are primarily the correct identification of the customer's wants, so as to make him want to return again, even at higher prices. Other industries found this out long ago, and try to influence those wants by advertising, which therefore has a dual aim: not simply to sell more, but also to create an inelastic demand. If you believe that one restaurant is better than another then you will go to it even though it may be marginally more expensive, even if that belief is based purely on advertising. Yet, while Londoners know that the Savoy Grill is better than a snack bar, they do not always go to the former. There is the question of income, and of income elasticity. For example, some may still go on holiday, even though the cost has increased because their income has increased too. On the other hand, some people will still attempt to take the same type of holiday, even though their income remains unchanged and the cost of the holiday increases. In their case they have an income inelasticity of demand. The value of income elasticity becomes important when the hotel and catering industry is operating in an economic recession, as it has been for the last few years now. In part the industry has done well, because for the first part of the period wages increased with prices, and in the latter part from 1974–77, under various income policies, there was an increase in the number of foreign tourists. However, parts of the trade that cater for the British holiday-maker in areas where foreigners rarely go have suffered from an income elasticity; that is, people have cut back on their holidaying with the fall of real income.

In analysing the demand for the services of the hotel and catering industry it is therefore important to identify not only those income and age groups who tend to holiday most, or use restaurants most, but also try to estimate the degree of income and price-elasticity that exists, for these elasticities may indicate the long-term prospects of the industry. Experience of the 1920s and 1930s showed that the industry withstood the recession comparatively well and recovered quite quickly from the depth of the recession. However, this was in part due to circumstances that might not apply today. Holidays-with-pay legislation was introduced in the late 1930s, the motor-car industry became a mass industry offering far greater mobility than before, while public transport expanded also. Between 1935 and 1937 a new catering outlet, the milk-bar, grew in number from a very few to 900, and by 1937 many served food. Likewise, after the Second World War the industry recovered rapidly as people were free to holiday for the first time in peace-time conditions for six years, whilst during the war employee catering had come to stay. This experience seems to imply a relative income-elasticity of demand, in that while people cut back on holidays, or the type of holiday in times of economic recession, when their incomes increase, the services of the industry are given a reasonably high priority.

Cross-elasticity of demand would refer not only to a possible competitive demand between firms offering the same service, but also to demand between different services. The importance of cross-elasticities at work was evident during the expansion of the package holiday business—due, in part, to price competition between firms in the period prior to the collapse of Horizon and Clarksons. Business zoomed in the

CONCEPTS OF DEMAND 45

sense that increasing numbers took advantage of cheap Mediterranean holidays, and although tour operators did run into financial difficulties a habit was formed and many who took their first foreign holiday in that period around 1973 have gone on to take more at higher prices (implying therefore a lower price-elasticity of demand!).

These above points are the factors which we must analyse in determining the demand for the hotel and catering industry, and this is the subject of the next chapters.

3
The Demand for Accommodation

Introduction

Apart from institutional demand such as hospitals, colleges and universities the demand for accommodation arises from those on holiday and those on business. In looking at statistics relating to demand from various sources one must bear in mind that their definitions slightly vary. For example, some authorities define *domestic tourism* as 'holidays of four or more nights away from home', whilst others include the 'day-tripper' in their calculations of *number of visits*. This alone makes comparison difficult between countries, or even between different statistics relating to the UK. At the same time there is an element of double-counting in statistics of *visits*, as distinct from *visitors*, as people may visit a place more than once within a year for all sorts of reasons. Anyway, since most of the statistics used in this section are derived from the British Regional Tourist Boards, it may be worthwhile defining the terms as used by the ETB.

A tourist trip is defined as a stay of one or more nights away from home for holidays, visits to friends or relations, business conferences or any other purpose, except such things as boarding education or semi-permanent employment.

A tourist night is a night spent away from home on a tourist trip, staying in any type of accommodation.

Tourist spending is expenditure while away from home on a tourist trip, or advance payment for such things as fares and accommodation. Expenditure by the tourist on other people (for instance, children) is included. Hire purchase or mortgage or interest payments on equipment owned by the tourist are excluded.

Holidays are trips described by the tourist as holidays. They also include visits to friends and relatives which are considered by tourists to be mainly holiday visits.

Types of Demand

In discussing the demand for accommodation there are four classifications that can be identified:

(i) **Domestic non-business demand**—This means a demand for accommodation by British citizens within Britain. Such a demand arises primarily from holidaying but also includes visits to relatives, being away from home for affairs such as weddings, shopping in London, visits to exhibitions, and so on. The determinants of this demand will include social and psychological attitudes to travel and leisure in general, and such attitudes may be determined by one's own personality, occupation and the income it creates, and social class. Holiday entitlement is also important, as is the cost of travel. It has been argued that aircraft fares will become a more important determinant of tourism demand, and should they rapidly increase international tourism may suffer whilst domestic non-business demand would increase.

(ii) **Overseas non-business demand—or international tourism** —This term would include non-British citizens holidaying in Britain. The factors listed above and in the last chapter would be applicable to this category also as determinants of demand, but also of some importance would be items such as exchange rates and currency and other government restrictions. In 1979 the decline of the value of the dollar against the pound sterling allied with increased London hotel prices meant a fall in American tourism in the UK. In 1968 British holidaying overseas was limited by currency restrictions permitting only a maximum of £50 being taken out of the UK for holiday expenditure overseas. And, of course, in the final resort a government could try and stop its citizens from visiting another country, such as, for example East Germans being forbidden to holiday in West Germany in the 1960s.

(iii) **Business demand—domestic**—This term covers the demand by British businessmen travelling through Britain. A determinant of their demand for accommodation is the structure and organization of industrial and commercial activity within the UK, and the patterns and volumes of trade. The cost of travel would also be a factor.

(iv) **Business demand—overseas**—Whether or not foreign businessmen come to Britain will depend on the volume of trade between this and other countries. Business interests can be influenced by exchange rates, political decisions and the level of multinational companies' activities. For example, if Ford decides to assemble a car in its Belgium factories which includes parts made in Dagenham, those parts will be exported to Belgium whatever the rates of exchange. Thus, the volume of trade becomes independent of the price of the item, at least within a given range of prices. The amount of business travelling will be determined by the multinational's own organization.

One must also consider alternative means of communication as being a determinant of foreign business travel. Many international transactions can be completed by people sitting in their own offices, and consequently the need for travel is obviated. However, as long as there is a preference for face-to-face contact, business travel will continue, assuming that the costs of travel do not become prohibitive.

The General Pattern of Demand

There has been a considerable growth in the number of trips in Britain since the 1950s; and in the period following the end of rationing after the Second World War there was an air of tremendous confidence, and a 1966 National Catering Inquiry spoke of the possibility of the industry becoming 'one of the most explosive growth industries of all in the next twenty years'. As the figures in Table 3.1 show, early confidence has been realized in that the number of trips made by the British in Britain increased by over 400% in the decade 1965–75, and in the same years the number of trips by foreign visitors rose by over 310%. On the other hand, the economic problems of the 1970s are reflected by a fall of about 10.6% in the number of trips of the British within Britain between 1972 and 1975. As the number of trips has increased, so too has expenditure. In 1951, the British on holiday spent £320 million. By the beginning of the 1960s and the dawning of the 'age of affluence', expenditure had risen by £120 million to £440 million; and by 1978, and the 'age of inflation', expenditure in Britain was £2800 million. To this can be added a further £1700 million spent by overseas tourists in Britain. The expenditure by the British in 1975

TABLE 3.1 **Holidays in Britain—the number of trips in millions**

Year	Trips by British in Britain	Trips by British overseas	Trips to Britain by overseas residents
1951	25	0.8 (est)	0.6
1956	27	2.2	1.1
1962	32	4.25	2.0
1966	31	5.1	3.2
1972	132	10.5	7.5
1973	132	11.5	8.1
1974	114	10.4	8.5
1975	117	11.6	9.5
1976	121	11.1	10.8
1977	121	11.0	12.2

(Sources: *BTA British Home Tourism Survey, National Catering Inquiry* (1966), *International Passenger Survey*)

did represent a small growth in real terms over the previous year's figure of £1800 million, but the period from 1972 to the present has seen a reversal of the long-term path of expansion. The reasons for the fall in the number of visits are easy to spot: post-war records of unemployment, and some restrictions arising from industrial disputes, a threatened petrol shortage, an air of uncertainty as to spending plans with inflation rates of 10–20%—all of these factors led to a reduction of short holidays and second holidays. These factors are seen more clearly in Table 3.2 for nights spent away from home rather than the number of visits made, and over the period 1972–77 the British stayed away for

TABLE 3.2 **Nights away from home in Britain in millions (all trips)**

Year	Total nights away from home	Britain	Abroad	Overseas residents in UK
1972	725	605	120	108
1973	705	590	120	116
1974	640	535	110	119
1975	665	550	115	128
1976	655	545	110	134
1977	655	545	115	148

(Sources: *BTA British Home Tourism Survey, International Passenger Survey*)

fewer nights at both home and abroad, the total falling from 725 million nights to 655 million. On the other hand, the increasing number of foreign visitors to this country is reflected by the additional 15 million nights spent in this country by overseas residents in 1975 compared with 1972.

From previous experience it does seem that the trend of 1972–77 will be reversed when the economic recession comes to an end, although with the ending of that recession and the consequent improvement of the pound sterling against other currencies, one would expect an increase in holidaying abroad and a slowing down in the growth of foreign tourism unless the marketing of Britain proves effective against the movement of currencies. Any marketing effort overseas is however considerably aided by the fact that English is one of the major languages of the world.

The Foreign Visitor

Over the past ten years the number of visitors to Britain has climbed from four million to about 12 million. This has not been a steady growth in that there have been variations in the trend, and between 1973 and 1974 the growth rate was less than average at 3% because the number of visitors from North America fell by 15% due to adverse movements in currency markets against the US dollar. On the other hand, the number of visitors from EEC countries increased, and now accounts for over 45% of the total number of visitors as against 19% from North America. The relative decline in the importance of North American visitors is shown by the fact in 1973 they accounted for 27% of all visitors but in 1974 only 22%. None the less the USA is the country which tops the 'league' of country of origin of visitors to Britain, with Canada in fifth place. While traditionally most tourists to the UK come from North America and EEC countries, the fastest growth rates in 1975 were a 19% increase in overseas visitors from non-EEC countries compared with 1974, and a 16% increase in the same period from visitors from other parts of the world. In 1977–78 the number of visitors from outside of Europe and North America was increasing faster than from anywhere else, and they now equal the North American countries as a source of our overseas visitors. The figures in Table 3.3 hide certain differences in the pattern of holidays between various groups. For many Americans a visit to the UK may be

TABLE 3.3 **Overseas visitors to Britain—number of visits (thousands)**

Area	1965	1975	1978
N. America	879	1817	2475
W. Europe (EEC)	{1472}	3599	6163
W. Europe (non-EEC)		1128	1660
Other areas	1246	1597	2309
Total	3597	8141	12607
Average length of stay (nights)	17.8	13.6	12.3
Total nights (millions)	64	130	148

(Source: *International Passenger Survey*)

only part of a longer European trip and their consequent length of stay, at just over ten nights, is shorter than the average. Consequently, whilst Americans account for about 17% of the total number of visitors, their demand for accommodation is about 13% of overseas demand.

Visitors from European countries not geographically close to Britain (e.g. Austria) and those from Commonwealth countries tend to spend three weeks or more. Naturally, those coming to visit family and friends tend to stay longer, and about 16–20% of overseas visitors to this country come precisely for this reason. The other reasons for overseas visitors are indicated in Table 3.4 which also gives an indication of the regional differences that exist in the UK for attracting overseas visitors.

The implication is that for areas outside of the usual overseas tourist areas of London (which attracts over 65% of all foreign tourists) and Stratford-upon-Avon, an important cause of a visit is the existence of friends and relatives in that region. At the same time the creation of

TABLE 3.4 **Purpose of visit of overseas visitors, 1975**

Purpose	East Midlands %	UK %	UK numbers (thousands)	% change 1974–75
Holiday	36	47	3795	12
Business	22	21	1541	—
Visiting friends and relatives	30	18	1440	12
Other	12	14	1365	35
Inclusive holiday	2	15	n/a	n/a

(Source: *Industry and Trade Journal*, East Midland Tourist Board)

inclusive holiday tours to attract visitors to the area could obviously help certain regions. About a third of all American visitors, for example, come to the UK on an inclusive tour. Scotland attracted only 1 000 000 overseas visitors in 1977, yet they spent over £130 million, which accounted for about one third of all tourist spending in Scotland even whilst they are only 8% of all visitors. The tourist industry is as important to Scottish economy as agriculture and mining!

Whilst the average length of stay has tended to fall from 15 days in 1970 to 12.3 days in 1978, the average expenditure has increased considerably from £3.1 per day in 1967 to £7.5 per day in 1974. Preliminary estimates for 1977 show another doubling of expenditure from 1974 to 1977, whilst a radio report of a survey of Arab visitors shows expenditure of £500 per day (Radio 4, 28 July 1977)! In 1978 overseas tourists' spending rose a further 8% to £2323 million, and in 1979 a similar increase was expected. These figures exclude the fares paid to and from the UK and reflect expenditure within the UK on arrival. Apart from the Arabs, other large spenders tend to be Australians, New Zealanders and South Africans who may be making their once-in-a-lifetime visit to the 'old mother country' and who spent in 1974 nearly £200 per visit, twice as much as the Americans. Again, estimates for 1977 indicate an approximate doubling of this expenditure.

All of these visitors naturally demand accommodation, and it is estimated that the licensed hotel/motel accounts for about one third of the demand with friends and relatives accounting for about 40%. The remaining 27% is accounted for by unlicensed hotels, guesthouses, bed and breakfast places, camping sites, caravans, boating holidays and the like. Over the past few years the pattern of overseas tourism has tended to become less seasonal, although the third quarter of the year from July to September still remains the busiest with 39% of the visitors; the first, second and fourth quarters account for 15, 25 and 21% respectively. This seasonal influence can be seen in the pattern of overseas arrivals at hotels in England, although for London the easing of the seasonal flow is considerable. Thus, in the month of November 1972, overseas arrivals in London hotels accounted for 46% of all arrivals, whereas by November 1975 the figure had increased to 54%. For hotels in London the overseas visitor is an important customer, accounting as he does for a yearly average of 59% of all arrivals, whereas that traditional holiday base of the British, the seaside resort, still tends to be the bastion of the

Englishman's holiday at home (and Welshman's, Scotsman's and Irishman's), with only 8% of arrivals at seaside hotels being overseas visitors.

Again, there are slight regional differences. For example, in Yorkshire, with its large seaside resorts of Scarborough and Bridlington, the overseas visitor is a rarity, with only 3% of seaside holiday-makers coming from outside the UK. The great majority of foreign tourists, about 96% of them, tend to go to inland sites.

The overseas visitor tends not only to stay in London with its tendency to higher tariffs, but tends to stay in high-tariff hotels. To quote from a survey by the English Tourist Board, '. . . generally, the higher the tariff of the hotel, the higher the average proportion of arrivals that were overseas visitors and the lower the proportion that were British'. However, in the years since 1972, with the growth of overseas tourists' demand for London hotel-space and the widening range of income groups now able to afford a holiday to the UK, there have been changes, and the lower-tariff hotels in London are now attracting higher proportions of overseas visitors.

The impact of this growth of foreign tourism has been highly significant not only for the hotel industry but also for the British economy. Since 1968 it has generally made an important contribution to the balance of payments as will be seen in Chapter 10. Nor does the contribution of tourism cease there, as it is a source of tax revenue and employment. Consequently both the Government and the hotel industry keep a careful eye on tourist movements, and hence the concern in 1979 when the rise of the pound sterling eroded some of the competitive advantage allied with a weaker dollar and rise in hotel tariffs. In the early part of 1979 the number of overseas tourists fell by 12%, and although the position improved considerably later in the year to give an overall picture similar to 1978, there is grave concern over the current position with the North American trade in particular being less favourable than required.

Thus in 1980, the BTA expect 12.75 million overseas visitors producing foreign exchange earnings of £3850 million as against £12.7 million and £3500 million in 1979.

The British Holiday-maker

In 1965 there were 29.6 million holiday trips made by the British in their own country, and they spent £460 million in enjoying themselves. Twelve years later those figures were made to look puny as 121 million holiday trips were made with an expenditure of £2625 million. In percentage terms the decade 1965–75 saw an increase of about 380% in holiday trips and a 467% increase in expenditure! Well might social observers write of an age of leisure dawning—even against a background of new post-war heights of unemployment. But not everyone shares equally in this age of affluence and leisure, and while 61% of British adults had a holiday of four or more nights there are considerable differences between socioeconomic classes. The categorization used by the British Tourist Board in their 1979 survey is one of AB, C1, C2 and DE grouping, where AB is the professional and managerial groups, C1 is the clerical and supervisory, C2 the skilled manual, and DE is the unskilled, the pensioners, and low-income groups and occupations generally. Thus in 1978 it was estimated on a sample of 2000 adults that 78% of AB classes had at least one holiday of four or more nights, 64% of C1, 59% of C2 and 46% of DE. The differences are further exaggerated when looking at those who took more than one holiday, where the figures are 41%, 19%, 17% and 9% respectively for AB, C1, C2 and DE groupings. The length of the holiday likewise differs from the average 12.1 nights of the DE person to the 16.8 nights of the AB person.

The Tourist Board's figures suggest that the person who is likeliest to take the most holidays away from home is going to be the professional person over the age of 35 and less than 55. This is probably because most people get better off as they grow older and have greater mobility as their children get older and finally leave home. The maturing of the children also relieves the financial burden on the family, thereby allowing the possibility of longer holidays. Thus, the BTA has estimated that about 60% of 16–24 year olds have a holiday of over four nights, and 60%, 68%, 61% and 49% of the age groups 25–34, 35–54, 55–64 and 65 and over, respectively, although there are considerable changes from year to year. However, in looking simply at holidays of over four nights' duration we omit a major part of the total tourism scene, in that 37% of all the trips in Britain involve stays of three or less nights. As to the duration of holidays there is again a regional difference in that holidays taken in Scotland and Wales tend to be longer than those in England. Thus, 42% of all trips in England are of seven nights or more duration compared with 55% in Scotland and 49% in Wales. This is probably due in part to a geographical factor in that for many people (and remember about a third of the UK population lives in the South-east of England) a trip to Wales and Scotland is of some length

THE DEMAND FOR ACCOMMODATION

and consequently many would feel that the journey is not worth it for just a few days or so. This could well be a factor when it is considered that the most popular form of transport for a holiday is, without doubt, the private car. Cars are used for about 77% of all holiday trips in Britain, trains for 10%. The remaining 13% is accounted for by coach tour (2%), scheduled bus and coach services (8%) and 'other' including bicycle, horses and foot (2%), and boat (1%).

Although, almost by definition, there is no Mr Average Holiday-maker it would seem that the average Briton has not only one main holiday of 13 nights away from home, travels to it by car, but also has a secondary holiday, which is often spent with relatives. Thus, while about 20% of main holidays are spent with friends and/or relatives, the percentage doubles for the additional or secondary holiday, although the secondary holiday is of shorter duration.

So, now we know who is likely to go on holiday and for how long, where is the British holiday-maker likely to go, where does he stay, and when does he tend to go on holiday?

Looking at the regions of Tourist Boards in Britain we can see from Table 3.5 that the most popular areas are the South-east of England, probably due to the concentration of population in that area, and the West Country. Indeed, although the South-east attracts about 10% of all tourist trips in Britain, it attracts only 5% of spending, and this probably reflects a proportion of weekend stays by Londoners and those living in the Home Counties. It is to be noted that while England, Scotland and Wales account for 93% of holiday destinations, and 83% of nights spent away from home, the estimated spending at these destinations is only 65%.

While the overseas holiday accounts for only 8% of trips made by British holiday-makers, it none the less accounts for 35% of our holiday-makers' spending; and 8% of all spending is in one country—Spain. It is this figure for expenditure rather than the number of trips made that represents the challenge to the British holiday industry in two senses. First, it is in a sense a loss to the British hotel, catering and tourist industry; also it implies the rewards to be gained from overseas visitors to the UK if other countries' tourists show the same tendencies as the British.

Within Britain there are considerable flows of traffic, particularly in the summer months, to and from popular holiday areas, as anyone who has sweltered in long traffic queues will testify. Of those who holiday

TABLE 3.5 **Tourism in British regions and abroad—1977**

Destination	Trips (% of total)	Nights 100%	Spending 100%
ENGLAND	75	64	49
Cumbria	2	2	2
Northumbria	3	2	1
N.W. England	8	6	5
Yorkshire and Humberside	7	6	4
Heart of England	7	5	3
East Midlands	5	4	3
Thames and Chilterns	4	2	2
East Anglia	8	6	5
London	9	5	5
West Country	10	13	10
S.E. England	8	7	5
WALES	9	9	6
N. Wales	3	4	3
Mid-Wales	2	2	1
S. Wales	4	4	3
SCOTLAND	9	10	9
Highlands and Islands	1	2	2
Grampian	1	1	1
Tayside	1	1	1
Central	—	—	—
Fife	1	1	—
Argyll	1	1	1
Strathclyde	2	2	2
Dumfries and Galloway	1	1	1
Lothian	1	1	1
Borders	—	—	—
ABROAD	8	17	36
Ireland	1	2	2
Channel Islands	1	1	2
Spain and Balearics	2	4	7
Others	5	10	25

N.B. Percentages are rounded.

(Source: *BTA British Home Tourism Survey*, 1978)

in Wales, for example, 80% originate from outside the Principality. Within Scotland, 45% holidaying there are non-Scots. In an area such as Yorkshire there is a significant difference between seaside and inland resorts, in that 52% of those holidaying at the seaside in Yorkshire are Yorkshire lads and lasses, whereas inland 79% of the holiday-makers exploring the dales and other areas are from outside Yorkshire. At the same time, since in Yorkshire the duration of inland holidays is shorter than seaside ones, the result is at times a heavy traffic flow along roads not designed to take peak summer tourists.

Since 1966 there have been changes of popularity between various parts of the country. London has become increasingly popular for the British as well as the overseas visitor, for in 1966 London accounted for 3% of trips against the present 9% of trips. The South-west on the other hand has suffered a relative decline, from 21% in 1966 to the present level of 10% which is a return to the relative levels of 1951. Scotland and Wales have both shared a slight decline in favour, whilst the South-east has had a slight increase in popularity.

These shifts of popularity over the two decades since the 1950s show how difficult it is to plan hotel siting and provision for tourism, especially in a period when the continued economic growth of the post-war period has come to a stop, albeit one hopes a temporary one. One implication of the different pattern of popularity between seaside and inland resorts and between different regions of the country would be a differing degree of occupancy in hotels; and this we will look at in a moment.

Having arrived at their destinations, holiday-makers can find a wide range of accommodation, from the various categories of hotels to camp sites (Table 3.6). The majority of holiday-makers stay with friends and

TABLE 3.6 **Accommodation used on trips in Britain (in %)**

Accommodation	1968	1977
Licensed hotel/motel	14	16
Unlicensed hotel/guest-house	23	7
Holiday camp	5	3
Total hotel and catering industry	42	26
Caravan	16	10
Rented flat/flatlet	9	2
Camping	4	5
Paying guest in private house	4	2
Friends'/relatives' house	25	48
Other	4	10

N.B. Percentages add to more than 100 as some trips use more than one type of accommodation.

(Source: *BTA British Home Tourism Survey*, 1978)

relatives, which coincides with BTA survey findings that 42% of all holiday trips have as their purpose the visiting of friends and relations. Indeed, in comparing the results of the British National Survey with the 1977 BTA survey we find that there has been a significant increase in the proportion staying with friends and relatives, a fact that in part reflects the economic situation and explains the falling occupancy of seaside hotels and particularly seaside guesthouses. At the same time the proportion of people holidaying at seaside resorts has fallen, and more are aiming for inland places.

However, the licensed hotels have maintained their market share of a growing market even if unlicensed hotels and guesthouses have failed so to do. This comparative decline in the guesthouse market may be in part due to its providing a smaller proportion of bed capacity as the trend of holidaying moves away from seaside resorts. Also the need to comply with new fire regulations from 1 January 1978 meant the closure of some guesthouses, the loss of rooms of others, and an increased cost for those wishing to enter the market legally. As noted previously in Chapter 1, there is a comparative decline in the popularity of the holiday camp, in part caused by higher incomes, competition from package holiday companies offering Mediterranean holidays at comparable prices, increased mobility through a wider ownership of cars, and possibly because holiday camps now have an outdated image, although this is something that some companies are seeking to overcome.

One of the problems facing the holiday trade is the seasonal nature of this business, which creates difficulties in employment and maintenance for hotels. The summer months are particularly busy not only because of the weather, but also because of school holidays. July and August are the busiest months, for at that time 38% of all holiday trips take place in Britain, with Wales having an above-average figure of 47%. Indeed, holiday-making in Wales deviates from the British average far more than England and Scotland with a much higher peak in spring and summer, and a lower depth in autumn and winter, with a consequent reflection in hotel occupancy figures, as Fig. 3.1 shows.

Business and Conference Demand

One method for a hotelier to even out the seasonal flow is to attract business and conference demand in the low season, and this has been done in the spring and autumn. Certainly, business and conference

THE DEMAND FOR ACCOMMODATION 59

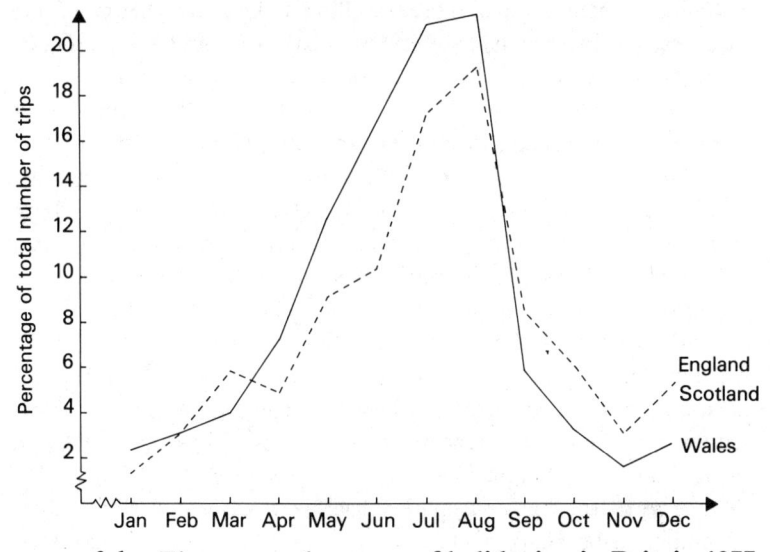

FIG. 3.1 **The seasonal pattern of holidaying in Britain 1977**
(Source: *BTA British Home Tourism Survey*)

custom is worth attracting, for in 1979 it was estimated that £600 million was spent in this category (Table 3.7). *Conferences* or *conventions* consist of people coming together as members of a firm, association, society or commercial organization to discuss some item of common interest, be it medical research, flying saucers or whatever. It is estimated that this accounts for about £65 million of spending. The remaining £535

TABLE 3.7 **Business demand for accommodation in Britain (in %)**

	Trips*	Nights	Spending
Licensed hotel	56	43	70
Unlicensed hotel/guest-house	14	12	9
With friend and relative	10	10	4
Paying guest	2	3	3
Other	23	31	13
Total figures (millions)	19	50	£600

*Percentages add to more than 100 due to more than one type of accommodation being used on a trip.

(Source: *BTA British Home Tourism Survey*, 1977)

million or so is made up of those travelling in the normal course of their business, visiting clients, exhibitions, subsidiary companies, attending job interviews and so on. In the report *Hotels and the Business Traveller*, the Hotel and Catering EDC estimated that, in 1967, the average business traveller made 29 journeys annually, of three day's duration. The same year also saw about 100 000 meetings and conferences, and 20 000 trade shows and exhibitions. In 1977 the BTA estimated that there were 44 000 conferences attracting 5 million delegates who spent £195 million. Certainly the conference market has several advantages for hotels. It can 'top up' occupancy levels in off-peak periods, but it is expensive to provide the required facilities, and the type of hotel which has those facilities is, if in a town site, often the very same hotel that will have high business demand and hence already high occupancy levels. On the other hand, conferences and exhibitions will use space designed for functions and banqueting.

Since 1970 the business market has been reasonably static, about 17 million trips being made each year to 1977 with an increase to about 19 million trips in 1979. The business traveller is three times more likely to use a licensed hotel than the holiday-maker, and is more regular than the holiday-maker, as he or she will be using hotels all the year round. There are, however, some seasonal fluctuations in demand as shown in Fig. 3.2. The relative peaks of April/May and October/November can be in part explained by the incidence of trade fairs and exhibitions, and business conferences, and the relative decline of July

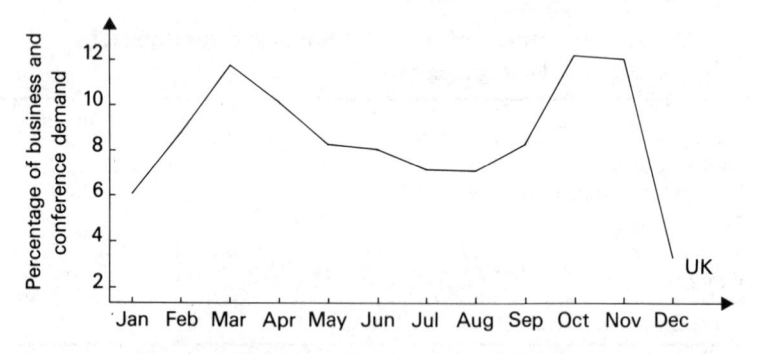

FIG. 3.2 **The seasonal pattern of business and conference demand**

(Source: *BTA British Home Tourism Survey*)

and August in the summer, and December in the winter can be explained by being the holiday period. The Easter date has some significance in that in those years when Easter is early, the April/May peak moves in time as exhibitions and conference organizers take into account the holiday period and its associated demands on existing accommodation.

One reason why the category 'other' appears so large is because of the increased usage of universities as conference centres. Whilst their actual 'bedrooms' may not be to hotel standards, universities provide excellent technical and leisure facilities, often in pleasant surroundings, and active marketing on their part has provided a serious challenge to hotels who have reacted by forming local consortia.

The great majority of business trips are of short duration, and 68% of the total in 1979 were of two nights or less, and the average length of stay was 2.7 nights. London, of course, was a major destination, and accounted for over 20% of all the business trips in England, and 18% of those in Britain. Welsh hoteliers, on the other hand, do not depend very much on the business and convention trade, in that business trips accounted for only 1.4 million trips out of a Welsh total of 13 million, i.e. approximately 10% of the total. This is not simply due to much of Wales being rural in character, but in part to locational factors in firms and organizations choosing central areas for their conventions and exhibitions, and a lack of conference facilities in Wales itself. In Scotland, business demand accounts for 20% of total trips, and in England 16%. Naturally this is not evenly distributed with S. Wales, Central Scotland and London being predominant for business demand for accommodation in each of their respective countries.

The Composite Demand for Hotel Accommodation

In measuring hotel accommodation two criteria are used: bed and room occupancy. A bed-space is space for one sleeping person, and a double bed counts as two bed-spaces. Therefore, if say, ten rooms have ten double beds, the total number of bed-spaces is twenty. If ten separate people book in, one per room, then it would be recorded as 100% room occupancy, but only 50% bed occupancy. Consequently, room occupancy is generally higher than bed occupancy figures, the only general exception being when double-rooms are booked in with adults and their children. It is also more common to use bed occupancy rather than room occupancy statistics when commentating on rates of hotel accommodation, and this section will follow this practice. To calculate the occupancy figures the following formula are used:

$$\text{Bed occupancy} = \frac{\text{The number of people occupying bed-spaces}}{\text{The total number of bed-spaces available}} \times 100$$

$$\text{Room occupancy} = \frac{\text{The number of rooms booked}}{\text{The total number of rooms available}} \times 100$$

To get a complete picture of a hotel situation it is necessary to know both sets of figures. The importance of this can be easily illustrated. Suppose one has two hotels reporting the same room occupancy rate and not the bed occupancy rate. One hotel may have a higher revenue than the other, even though they may charge the same tariff. This is because one may have single beds booked, and the other double bed spaces booked. The hotel with the higher bed occupancy would have the greater revenue. On the other hand, two hotels charging the same tariff and reporting the same bed occupancy would not necessarily have the same revenue. This is because one hotel may be bigger than another, and have a single distribution of single and double rooms; and so one needs also to know the room occupancy figures to make an accurate comparison.

In the USA it is common to use room occupancy percentages with a 'double occupancy' percentage so that '100, 50' would mean that all its rooms were full, and that 50% of those rooms had more than one person. However it is calculated, occupancy figures are important in calculating areas and times of high and low demand.

Hotel accommodation can be looked at from differing viewpoints of location size and tariff structure, and from this analysis it can be said that the larger, more expensive London hotels are likely to have the highest accommodation figures. But before looking at these particulars some general comments can be made. First, since 1971 there has been a decline in home demand for hotel accommodation that has not been entirely replaced by a growth in demand from overseas visitors, but hotel occupancy has remained fairly steady at 47–50%, implying that hotel accommodation has been lost at about the same rate of decline in demand since 1971, a decline estimated at about 7% per year. Most of the loss of hotel space has been in older and smaller hotels and guest houses, although the Hotel Development Incentive Scheme under which hotel construction was aided by the English Tourist Board

THE DEMAND FOR ACCOMMODATION 63

added 97 000 new bed spaces between 1968 and 1974 to about 940 hotels. As indicated in the two previous sections, there is a considerable seasonal variation in occupancy levels for the average English hotel outside of London, and while hotels may be two-thirds full in the peak of summer, from November to February they are more than likely to be less than a third full. Yet there are significant regional differences in hotel occupancy which is heavily influenced by the degree of dependence upon purely British tourist demand. Such areas are Cumbria, the West Country and East Anglia, where 80% of all tourist nights are due to holiday tourism, whereas in the Tourist Board regions of Heart of England (which includes the industrial towns of the Potteries and West Midlands) and London, holiday tourism accounts for just over half the number of tourist nights. As you would expect from the different times in the year which mark the peaks of holiday and business demand, the areas that have a greater proportion of their total demand coming from business also have a less seasonal nature to their activity. The presence of foreign tourists, by and large, does not greatly affect the occupancy levels of hotels, for only in London do they form a large proportion of arrivals, although there is some 'spin-off' for areas within easy reach of London. Consequently, the geographical regions which have the highest annual hotel bed occupancy rates are London (about 65%), Thames and Chiltern (about 53%) and Cumbria (48%—due to very high holiday demand), while Northumbria is below average with a hotel occupancy rate of about 42%. The average number of nights per guest spent in a hotel across all regions and throughout the year is about three.

Of course, location is not only a matter of geographical region, but also of type. A hotel may be situated at a seaside resort, a rural area, a small or large town (Table 3.8). As might be expected with their dependence on holiday tourism, seaside hotels show the greatest fluctuation in levels of activity, and of course it is not an uncommon feature of this trade for smaller hotels to close down in the winter season. This is quite understandable in that for such hotels the cost of staying open to cater for perhaps less than a quarter of their capacity would be greater than the costs involved in closing down, even though closure means no revenue. It only becomes worthwhile staying open if the revenue exceeds the variable costs of operation and makes a contribution towards the fixed costs such as rates. On the other hand, in the summer months seaside hotels do have some advantage in saving

TABLE 3.8 **Bed occupancy by tariff structure 1978**

Tariff	Jan	Feb	Mar	Apr	May	Jun	Jul	Aug	Sep	Oct	Nov	Dec	Year average
Seaside													
Lower	13	17	21	18	37	58	74	74	53	34	17	19	36
Higher	24	26	40	42	54	63	73	76	57	49	34	29	48
Countryside													
Lower	15	19	26	29	40	47	52	57	50	35	20	22	34
Higher	30	36	43	47	53	56	64	60	66	61	44	36	50
Small towns													
Lower	37	34	40	40	53	50	59	61	56	46	39	28	45
Higher	39	43	48	52	56	59	67	66	65	61	49	36	53
Large towns													
Lower	36	38	41	42	41	44	51	48	52	48	42	37	43
Higher	44	50	52	55	54	55	56	57	61	61	52	40	53
London													
Higher	51	54	57	60	75	73	79	74	77	77	66	59	67

The London lower-tariff hotel sample is too small.
(Source: *ETB English Hotels Occupancy Survey*)

administrative costs compared with other hotels in that the length of stay of 5–6 nights tends to be double the average of other hotels located elsewhere. Rural hotels have a lower annual occupancy level of any category of hotel at 43% due to a lower peak of activity in the months June to August. However, they are marginally fuller than seaside hotels in the winter months, and these occupancy levels have been increasing by about two percentage points since the beginning of the 1970s with off-season promotions centred around weekend breaks. London is (one is tempted to say 'of course') a law unto itself, in that it has higher occupancy levels than other parts of the country, including other large towns. Nevertheless, after a scare in the beginning of the

TABLE 3.9 **Bed occupancy levels by hotel size (averages 1974–78)**

Hotel size	Jan	Feb	Mar	Apr	May	Jun	Jul	Aug	Sep	Oct	Nov	Dec	Year average
Small	24	23	28	32	42	53	62	69	59	41	27	23	40
Medium	32	40	43	43	53	58	69	75	70	53	41	34	51
Large	34	39	44	49	57	64	69	69	72	61	45	35	53

(Source: *ETB English Hotels Occupancy Survey*)

decade about the possibility of insufficient hotel room for the summer peak, London saw an increase in hotel building, and thus like other large towns has recorded slightly lower annual occupancy levels in 1976 (55%) than was the case in 1971 (58%) in spite of an increase of tourism in London.

Hotels may also differ in size, and there is evidence to suggest may also be a factor in causing different occupancy levels which favour the larger hotel (Table 3.9). In their surveys of hotel occupancy the English Tourist Board categorized hotels as being small (5–15 rooms), medium (16–50 rooms) and large (51 or more rooms). Small hotels have the lowest bed-space occupancy level at about 40%, with a peak occupancy of 69% in August, and a low occupancy of 23% in December and February. Medium-sized hotels do significantly better with an annual average occupancy level of about 51%, which was an increased rate over the end of the 1960s when medium-sized hotels were operating at 48%. As one would expect, the seasonal factors are still operative, but medium-sized hotels maintain high occupancy levels longer than small hotels, and their August peaks of over 70% have been consistently better in the 1970s than those of large hotels. Minimum occupancy levels are in January when the hotel is two-thirds empty. Large hotels achieve a slightly higher annual occupancy level of 53% in spite of not attaining quite the same high season levels of medium-sized hotels and doing only marginally better in the months of November to February. The difference is due to higher levels of business in the spring and autumn, which reflects the demand from industrial, commercial and other organizations, which obviously tend to favour the larger hotel. The reasons for this are obvious in the case where conference facilities are required, but are not so obvious in other cases except that national organizations tend to build larger hotels in cities where business representatives are likely to go, and such firms may have accounts with the national hotel chains for their employees.

For many people, however, a main consideration in choosing a hotel, assuming there are alternatives in the location, is the price the hotel charges (Table 3.8). Wherever the location of the hotel, one constant factor emerges: that the higher-tariff hotel tends to a higher average annual occupancy level. In seaside resorts the lower-tariff hotels record a lower average annual bed capacity than higher-tariff hotels, but in the peak demand months of July and August they record as high an occupancy level, although the normal state of affairs reasserts itself in September until June.

One possible explanation of this is the school holidays falling mainly in July and August. It may be that childless adult couples have a wider choice of time as to when they can take their holidays and have a higher disposable income per head. Consequently they cannot only afford higher-tariff hotels, but can choose to avoid peak periods. On the other hand, those with children going to a hotel at a seaside resort have to go during the school holidays, i.e. July and August, and since stays at such hotels tend to be for a week, the expense of the exercise means staying at a lower-tariff hotel. In rural areas lower-tariff hotels have lower occupancy levels throughout the whole year than their higher-tariff rural counterparts, whilst in small towns the pattern between high- and low-tariff hotels is akin to those of seaside resorts with the exception that the hotels are operating at higher bed occupancy levels.

In 1971 the higher-tariff London hotels had an overall occupancy level of 69%, whereas four years later it had fallen to 57%, a clear sign of the economic recession. There was a fall in demand of both holiday and business demand, with demand falling through the year except in January and February. London hotels have also suffered a loss of business due to the opening of the National Exhibition Centre at Birmingham which has been attracting exhibitors away from the traditional display areas of Earls Court and Olympia. Even the Motor Show (a big money-spinner) has lost some impetus since the recession following the 1973 oil crisis. As will be seen later, the loss of demand has meant a significant financial impact upon these hotels with, in 1975 and 1976, a subsequent activity in the selling of hotels and amalgamations. Since 1975, however, times have been considerably kinder to the London hotel industry with increasing occupancy levels, from 51% in 1975 to 65% in 1977. This increase has been due to a number of factors, including:

(i) The rapid increase in wages, particularly in 1975, which, until the Healey–TUC wage norms kept far ahead of price increases for considerable sectors of the population.

(ii) The fact that it was not until 1977–78 that hotel prices began to rise rapidly. Until then hotel tariff increases had tended to be below the prevailing inflation rates.

(iii) The fall in the value of the pound sterling until 1978 (from $2.55 in December 1971 to $1.74 in 1977) made Britain an attractive tourist area for overseas visitors.

(iv) Increased promotional activities overseas by the British Tourist Authority, particularly for the 1977 Jubilee Year.

In 1978 the annual occupancy rate for London remained unchanged, but revenues and profits continued to increase due to increased prices, thereby allowing increased investment. However, further price increases in 1979 allied with a stronger pound as the pound rose above $2.20 and also against European currencies, coupled with an increasing inflation rate of 17% in 1979, means that London has become less able to compete with other European capitals, leading to price reductions in the late summer as spare capacity became available. None the less, occupancy rates of about 54% in 1979 were still above those of 1976.

In trying to assess what this demand pattern means for the individual hotelier, the picture is of course incomplete without figures of rates of return and costs of development and building—which items are the subject of concern of Chapter 8. It certainly does seem that events have overtaken even recent reports such as *Hotel Prospects to 1980* by the NEDC which spoke confidently of increasing demand and little change in the regional pattern of that demand. Even as the report appeared in 1973, there was a down-turn of 20 million nights spent away from home compared with 1972. Already it seems its successor *Hotel Prospects to 1985* may be overtaken by events. For while there has been a growth in overseas visitors coming to Britain it is not in line with the expected patterns forecasted by the report. Certainly for any new hotelier considering a location it would seem that the dream of a small seaside hotel could prove a costly one. At the same time, rural hotels are not attracting much development at present, but in spite of their low occupancy levels, there are some trends that operate in their favour—a movement towards inland holidays, and the success of off-season promotions. For the higher-tariff hotel with a good restaurant in a carefully selected site near good access to main trunk roads in an area of good tourist potential, e.g. some of the Yorkshire Dales, the potential could be rewarding. In larger towns occupancy levels are disappointing, due to a probable lack of high tourist demand, although towns with a good festival such as York, Nottingham and Edinburgh can attract tourism. At the same time, competition in the larger towns tends to be high, and it may be a comparative lack of competition that accounts for the higher occupancy levels in small towns. Certainly, any new hotelier would need to look at the number and type of any existing hotels in the area. Finally, in spite of recent downward trends in occupancy levels, London, with its high domestic and foreign tourist demand, and its high business demand must deserve attention, although costs are likewise high. None the less, as will be seen, London hotel profits are comparable with those of other European capitals.

In analysing the demand for hotels the criteria laid down by Chapter 2 have been followed, but it may be objected that the theoretical concepts of the demand curve and elasticity have not been used. However, the statistics are available to construct a statistical demand curve. Fig. 3.3 shows demand curves for lower-tariff countryside and seaside hotels, using annual occupancy figures for a period 1971–75, and the fact that they do not follow the usual pattern of a demand curve falling from left to right implies that factors other than price are important factors in determining the demand for accommodation; and from the previous section it can be argued that income and a change of taste towards inland holidays and day-trips are operative factors; although these considerations may not be independent variables from the question of price.

In attempting to measure the elasticities of demand, which are important from the viewpoint of revenue, the fact that accommodation rates have been maintained at a time of increasing prices implies an inelastic demand. However, it has been stated that the occupancy levels have been maintained in part because of a fall in the number of

THE DEMAND FOR ACCOMMODATION 69

bed-spaces. Obviously, for an elasticity of demand to be meaningful for any one hotel you must use that hotel's data, but a general elasticity can be calculated using figures from the BTA and the Department of Trade and Industry.

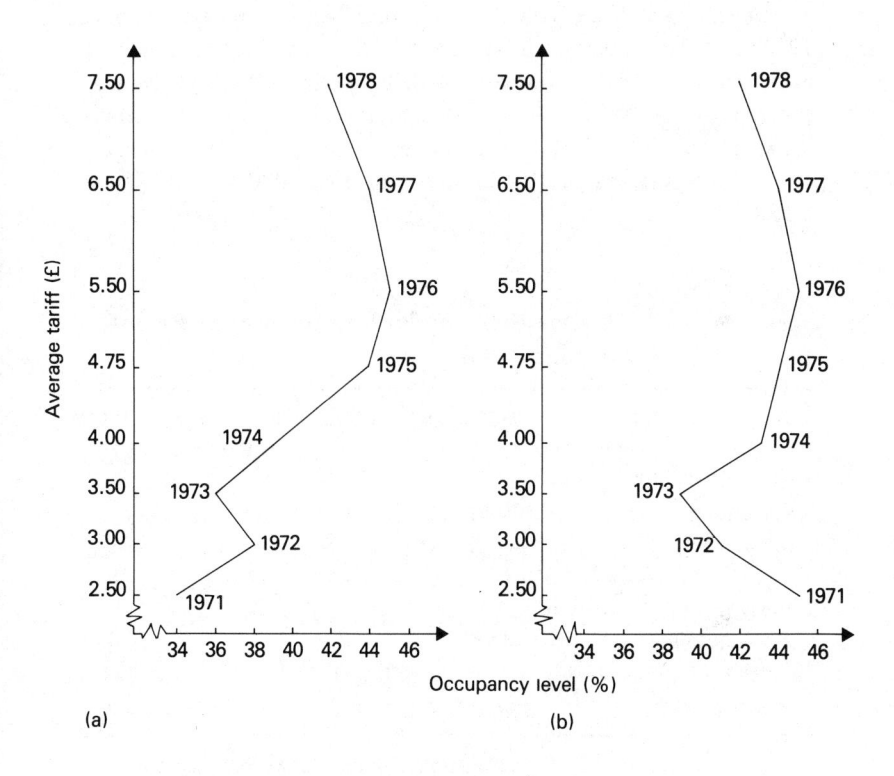

FIG. 3.3 **Statistical demand curves 1971–78.**
(a) **For countryside hotels**
(b) **For seaside hotels**

(Source: *ETB Home Tourism Surveys*)

In 1974–75 the average bed and breakfast price per person, according to the English Tourist Board, rose from £3.50 to £4.00 whilst the number of nights increased by 15 million to 535 million.

This is obviously a case of inelastic demand (0.43), which implies that price is not a major determinant of nights spent away from home, which would be true even if one excludes business demand from the calculations. It has often been argued that a major determinant in the growth of leisure industries has been the growth of income, and generally speaking, holiday expenditure has been about 2.5% of total consumer expenditure, and 2.2% of total personal income, and in 1974–75 when income increased by 18%, holiday expenditure increased by 19%. However, in the period 1972–73 holiday expenditure by the British in England rose by only 0.75% whilst incomes rose by 15.0%, which implies an income inelastic demand as far as holidaying in Britain was concerned at that time (Table 3.10).

TABLE 3.10 **Expenditure on holiday tourism in Britain (in £ million)**

	1972	1973	1974	1975	1976	1977
Holiday expenditure	1 000	1 075	1 300	1 550	2 100	2 600
Total consumer expenditure	39 716	45 044	51 832	63 373	73 538	83 530
Total personal income	44 229	50 954	60 295	73 727	86 155	97 312
Holiday expenditure as % of total expenditure	2.5	2.4	2.5	2.4	2.8	3.11
Holiday expenditure as % of personal income	2.3	2.1	2.2	2.1	2.4	2.7

(Source: *ETB and National Income Statistics*)

Consequently, there are considerable variations in income elasticity, from very inelastic demand in 1972–73 to an elastic demand of 1.04 in 1974–75. It is generally assumed that holiday expenditure is income-elastic—that is, responsive to changes in income—and if this is the case then the period of 1974–75 is a more representative one and we need to look for special circumstances in 1972 and 1973. These are quickly found, however, in two words, *oil crisis*, and with threatened petrol shortages and rationing, and since over 70% of holidays in Britain are by car, the inelasticity of the period is at least in part explained. As we have noted, a third of holiday expenditure by the British is overseas, and thus we would expect this to be very responsive to changes in income, but this does not prove to be the case with an elasticity of 0.81 in 1974-75, but an elasticity of 1.08 in 1973-74. As a generalization it can be argued that the income, elasticity for holiday expenditure, and by implication, tourist accommodation, is about unity tending to elasticity, which means that holiday expenditure will tend to increase that bit faster than incomes, in that as incomes increase people will prefer to use the increase, or at least part of it, for holidaying. This in a sense is supported by the socioeconomic analysis which shows that higher income groups tend to have longer holidays—in short, holiday durations are responsive to income increases.

Problems and Prospects

In 1978 the English Tourist Board forecasted in *Planning for Tourism in England* a doubling of the number of foreigners taking holidays in England from 4 million in 1975, to 7.6 million in 1985, with overseas tourists accounting for about 150 million nights and domestic tourists for about 520 million nights. *Business and Economic Planning* forecasted a 39% increase in domestic tourist trips between 1975 and 1985, with domestic tourist bed nights increasing by 25% in the same period. Overseas tourists were expected to continue to spend more, and by 1985 would increase expenditure by 135% in real terms in the decade, and account for 48% of all tourist spending in Britain; which would total £5380 million at 1975 prices. In July 1977 Melvyn Greene wrote, 'So we see at least two boom years ahead for tourism generally—and stores and hotels in particular.' By the late summer of 1979 the buoyancy of those two years had begun to lose ebb. 1979 opened with hoteliers facing the worst winter for nearly twenty years combined with supplies being held up by the lorry drivers' strike. Inflation was increasing from about 10% to 17%, and tariffs increased to compensate for the previous year's inflation, with the result that by the summer of 1979 prices were 20% higher than twelve months earlier. This was widely reported in North America and, combined with the fall in the value of the dollar, the result was adverse movement in that market. Uncertainty about

VAT regulations over the possibility of levying VAT on only 20% of the accommodation bill for long-term stays (i.e. over 28 days) led to reports in June 1979 of Continental tour operators considering claims for many hundreds of thousands of pounds, alleging they had been overcharged. In the budget of that year VAT was increased to 15%, thereby increasing tariffs, and further tariff increases were forecast due to the Licensed Residential Wages Council awarding a 25% increase in wages in August 1979. The trends were confirmed when the British National Travel Survey showed a fall in the licensed hotel market share from 17% in 1977 to less than 14%. For 1980, tariff increases of 20% and more are expected as, being freed from the need to restrict price movements by the abolition of the Prices Commission in 1979, hotels attempt to protect profitability in the face of increasing costs, and uncertain demand, while trying to maintain standards. None the less, it is becoming increasingly common for breakfast, at least, to involve a degree of self-service as hotels attempt to save labour costs. At the same time a movement to standardization is also discernible for cost saving reasons and there is an increased marketing effort. The expansion of hotels and hotel groups was a carrying out of earlier investment plans as the profits of 1975–78 were ploughed back in modernization programmes or, since construction costs and land costs had spiralled so rapidly, as the larger hotel chains purchased independent or smaller hotel groups. Thus, within the space of three years Ladbroke Hotels grew from four to nearly thirty hotels as the Mercury and Myddleton Hotel groups were purchased as Ladbrokes diversified.

Do the difficulties of 1979 and 1980 mean that the earlier forecasts were over optimistic? In part, they foresaw difficulties in the period up to 1980, and most of the growth is expected in the last part of the period. While the American market is important to the British tourist industry new markets are also growing, notably in the Near East; and the Japanese market has not yet been fully exploited. For many tourists the UK is still a cheap country, and exchange rate movements will help in this respect as the pound sterling, in late 1979 and early 1980, shows signs of slipping back from earlier heights. Much depends on the marketing of the UK and the maintenance of standards. *Hotel Prospects to 1985* shows the importance of the overseas visitor as it forecasts only a 12% growth in domestic demand as against a 175% increase from overseas. That such a growth may be possible can be seen in the extension of the tourist season in that the BTA has been successful in attracting visitors in the second and fourth quarter of the year, and in attracting visitors to areas other than London. However, only by the end of 1980 will it be clearer as to whether or not the forecasts of 1977 will be fulfilled.

4
The Demand for Food and Drink

The demand for food and drink can be divided into a number of different types. Outside the home there is obviously that demand connected with travel, a demand that is as old as travelling itself. Likewise drinking for pleasure has an old and honourable(!) tradition, and although facilities for dining out for pleasure have waxed and waned over the centuries, the restaurateur now offers a high standard of dining. Since the Second World War catering for employees has also become more widespread, and this is but part of a demand which serves as a substitute for eating in the home. In short, it can be said there is an element of the demand for food and drink that is highly correlated with travel, and thus as the demand for tourism increases so too will the demand for food and drink. A second classification is that of eating out for pleasure, or eating out as a substitute for eating at home.

Expenditure on Food

The *National Income 'Blue Book'* gives statistics for expenditure on food by households, and as can be seen in Table 4.1 there has been a marginal increase in expenditure in real terms (that is an increase over and above that due to inflation) since 1970.

The *National Income Statistics* also give a composite table of the total expenditure of household and catering demand for food, excluding food

TABLE 4.1 **Household expenditure on food (£ million)**

	1970	1971	1972	1973	1974	1975	1976	1977
At current prices	6390	7025	7444	8489	9817	12059	14086	16268
At 1975 prices	12072	12117	12025	12210	12099	12059	12172	12051

(Source: *National Income Statistics*, HMSO)

issued to HM Forces but including expenditure by public authorities on hospitals and schools. From the composite table it should be possible to calculate the expenditure of the catering industry on food, but this is at wholesale prices, whereas household expenditure is at retail prices. However, as can be seen from Table 4.2 it would seem that catering expenditure on food has maintained a static share of total consumer expenditure of about 25%, which implies that the main determinant of long-term trends on food is income.

TABLE 4.2 **Total and catering expenditure on food at current wholesale prices (in £ million)**

	1970	1971	1972	1973	1974	1975	1976	1977
Catering	906	1085	1145	1341	1540	1914	2175	2456
Total		8061	8579	9781	11409	14006	16270	18700
Catering as % of total	12.3	13.4	13.3	13.7	13.5	13.6	13.4	13.1

(Source: *National Income Statistics*, HMSO)

Expenditure on Drink

When I speak of drink, you may conjure up images of foaming pints of beer, but in case I wrong you, a steaming cup of tea might also be acceptable. However, it says something about the official collector of statistics that National Income Statistics of drink consumption relate to the alcoholic type and that soft drinks are classified as food. Consequently, this section tends to concentrate on alcoholic matters.

Table 4.3 shows a steady growth of demand since 1960 when over 27 million bulk barrels per annum were consumed to the 1976 total of nearly 41 million barrels.

The consumption per capita in the UK in 1975 was 206 pints per annum, compared with 259 pints of the world's leader, Western Germany. Total expenditure on alcohol in the UK is estimated at about £5000 million.

Since the 1950s there have been a number of changes in demand. In the 1950s there grew a demand for bottled beers, while keg beers became popular in the 1960s. In the early 1970s a demand for brewery-conditioned lagers and draught beers, and canned products for the take-home trade grew under the impetus of heavy advertising by the brewers

TABLE 4.3 **UK Consumption of beer**

Year	Total consumption (million barrels)	Ales, stouts (million barrels)	Lager (million barrels)	Lager as % of total
1960	27.24	27.00	0.24	1.0
1967	31.52	30.57	0.95	3.0
1971	35.78	32.33	3.45	9.9
1972	36.65	32.36	4.29	11.7
1973	38.25	32.55	5.70	14.9
1974	39.09	32.68	6.41	16.4
1975	40.20	32.20	8.00	19.9
1976	40.65	31.06	9.59	23.6

(Source: *Webb Report on Brewing*, 1977)

of lager, the activities of the Campaign for Real Ale, and the granting of liquor licenses to supermarkets, respectively. Consequently Table 4.4 shows there has been a change in market shares with, amongst draught beers, a decline in the demand for mild, and a significant increase in the demand for lager.

Indeed, estimates of a 5% growth rate in the demand for beer between 1976 and 1979 were heavily dependent on a continuance of the increased liking for lager for, since 1960 UK beer consumption has varied in its annual increases between 1 and 5%; and hence a forecast growth of 5% in three years represented little change in this trend, other than the fact that it is not an advance on a broad front for all beers but primarily for one type. To some extent the demand for beers is subject to factors such as, in the short-term, VAT changes and the weather. In

TABLE 4.4 **Market shares (in %)**

	1971	1972	1973	1974	1975	1976
Mild	17.7	15.9	14.2	13.8	13.3	12.5
Premium bitter and stout	17.4	17.8	17.0	16.8	15.9	15.1
Ordinary bitter	31.3	31.1	30.5	30.6	30.9	30.7
Draught lager	7.1	8.6	11.3	12.6	15.6	18.5
Sub-total	73.5	73.4	73.0	73.8	75.7	76.8
Returnable bottles	22.5	21.9	21.3	19.7	16.8	15.4
Non-returnable bottles	4.0	4.7	5.7	6.5	7.5	7.8

(Source: *Webb Report on Brewing*, 1977)

the hot summer of 1976 beer consumption rose by over 2%, whereas in the rainier summer of 1977 consumption fell, according to the Brewers Society, by just under 2%. Yet lager sales have continued to grow, although by 1981 it is thought that growth will have ceased to be as dramatic as in the past due to the increased difficulty of further penetrating the market and the fact that there will also be fewer people in the under-20 age group, who have been an important part of this market. Another factor that may have contributed to the past growth of lager sales has been its acceptance by female drinkers who would not always consider a pint of bitter, and of course pubs themselves have changed their decor and in many city centres are often mainly frequented by younger age groups. Inevitably, the success of lager sales initiated by the Heineken, Harp and Skol brand names has led to increased competition. Originally Harp lager was brewed by a consortium when it was sold nationally in 1961. Bass, an original member of the consortium left in 1968, only to 'rejoin' ten years later, when it took over the Alton brewery in Hampshire which belonged to Courage. However, Bass is only to brew Harp at Alton until 1982; thereafter it will produce its own lagers. At present (1979) the Harp consortium consists of Guinness (70% of shares), Greene King (20%) and Wolverhampton and Dudley (10%), with Courage and Scottish and Newcastle having a franchise to produce Harp. Within the lager market recent trends have shown that the fastest growth is coming from the higher-gravity or stronger beers dominated by Germanic sounding names such as Kronenbourg and Lowenbrau, and the recently introduced low-carbohydrate beers. It is a sign of the competition that in 1978 four of the five most advertised beers were Carling, Heineken, Kronenbourg and Skol, each of which had an advertising budget of over £1 million. Only one other beer was advertised as extensively, and that was Guinness. Certainly, against a background of limit growth the brewing industry has seen considerable change in policies, and has been moving away from its centralization policies (see page 158).

One factor in this has been the Campaign for Real Ale (CAMRA). Its activities have meant that 40 small breweries were set up in the period 1974–79, of which 15 started in the year 1978–79. Medium-sized breweries that existed before the CAMRA campaign such as Fuller's, Young's, Greene King, Marston's and Boddington's have seen turnover double. In 1974 Young's had a turnover of £8 million; by 1979 it topped the £20 million level.

Apart from beers, there has also been an increased consumption and expenditure on both wines and spirits, with the former recording the highest growth rate. At the beginning of the 1960s about 26 million gallons of wine were drunk in the UK; by 1970 the figure was 45 million gallons; and the estimate for 1980 is over 70 million gallons. This increased liking for wine has been due to a loss of the snobbish image of wine and the availability of a wide selection of good, inexpensive wines from Europe by bottlers and wine importers. That they could sell this wine is usually explained by an increased British awareness of the value of inexpensive wines gained through experience on overseas holidays. An important factor already mentioned has been the increased ease of purchasing wine through supermarket outlets, a policy deliberately introduced as wine consumption was seen as a fast-growing trend offering high turnover and reasonable mark-ups in an otherwise fairly static food and drink sector.

It is thought that catering establishments account for approximately 25% of the total sales of table wine, and for the wine trade hotels and restaurants are important as they take a much higher share of fine wines. In hotels and restaurants wine sales can account for as much as 30% of turnover, but because a gross margin of 50% is not uncommon, the sale of wines would account for over 45% of total net profit. In the *HCIMA Review* of 1974 M Howley estimated that wines sold through catering outlets cost about 70% more than comparable wine found in off-licence premises. On the other hand, the demand for spirits has not grown so rapidly as the demand for wine, partly because of the heavy taxation that whisky and other spirits bear tending to make them expensive. In 1960, 15 million gallons of spirits were drunk; in 1970, about 17.5 million; and in 1976, 19 million gallons.

Expenditure on drink is about 7.0% of total consumer expenditure, but has been growing at an uneven rate throughout the seventies. (Table 4.5). Generally speaking the demand for beer has recorded the slowest growth rates, and wines have tended to increase their market share of alcoholic drink at the expense of beers, with spirits retaining a fairly constant market share of 28%. The downturn in the business of spirits and wines in real terms in 1975 can be explained by the counter-inflationary government measures of the time and tax changes, though it is to be noted in money terms expenditure continued to increase. Certainly the fluctuating levels of growth are noteworthy, and the demand for alcohol can be influenced considerably by short-term

TABLE 4.5 **Consumer expenditure on drink (£ million)**

	1965	1969	1970	1971	1972	1973	1974	1975
Total								
Current prices	1499	2029	2299	2593	2910	3415	3926	4902
1970 prices	1849	2149	2299	2454	2641	2989	3085	3091
Beer								
Current prices	882	1201	1355	1526	1662	1807	2071	2679
% of total	59.5	59.5	59.0	58.4	57.2	53.0	52.8	54.6
1970 prices	1122	1309	1355	1419	1464	1549	1551	1609
% change	—	—	3.0	4.1	0.2	4.0	0.1	3.0
Spirits								
Current prices	420	520	611	670	777	1004	1140	1392
% of total	28.1	25.8	26.5	25.8	26.7	29.5	28.9	28.4
1970 prices	485	522	611	650	739	916	991	970
% change	—	—	11.7	6.5	12.8	12.5	7.9	−2.5
Wines, cider perry								
Current prices	197	308	333	397	471	604	715	831
% of total	13.4	15.3	13.9	15.1	16.2	17.7	18.4	18.9
1970 prices	242	318	333	385	438	524	543	512
% change	—	—	4.7	15.5	13.9	17.3	3.6	−5.5

N.B. Percentages do not add up to 100 because of rounding.

(Source: *Business Monitor*)

measures, such as a spell of hot weather and tax changes; but since it tends to maintain a constant share of consumers' expenditure its long-term prospects are seemingly tied to economic conditions and the growth of consumer expenditure generally.

The Patterns of Eating Out

Eating outside the home can take place in any one of three sectors: (i) the purely commercial (meaning restaurants and other places providing meals whose main business and profitability lies in catering); (ii) the partly commercial—that is, catering which has a financial goal to achieve but which is subsidised (by and large represents catering at a place of work); and (iii) the non-commercial (hospital and educational catering) where, although financial controls may operate, the suppliers of the catering service have a responsibility to cater for people who are in their care in one form or another. The first two sections account for most of the business, with the purely commercial accounting for about 76% of annual expenditure and the partly commercial 19%. However, the criteria of expenditure underestimates the size of the task of the non-commercial sector where obviously the clientele are paying little, if anything, for their meals. By the criterion of the number of meals served, then, it is estimated that the purely commercial serve about 48% of the total, the partly commercial 41% and the non-commercial 11%. The sums of money and numbers of people catered for are, of course, quite considerable, with an estimated £35 million spent per week in 1977 and 90 million meals per week being served to well over 23 million people. This is of course, generally the midday meal, although large numbers of people have two meals a day, at their place of work at midday and at about 5.00 pm, while in addition many on some occasions go to a restaurant for pleasure. This raises the question of where people eat, for there is a range of eating places besides restaurants and places of work. In terms of where most people go, the answer is that about 30% eat at their place of work, and 27% regularly use cafés and snack bars. The following table from *Trends in Catering* gives one such indication, but readers should be aware that these figures only serve as a guide, as various issues of the report show quite large changes depending on time of year and possibly methods of sampling.

Of course it is difficult to be precise in this matter, even when the statistics are collected on a survey of eating-out habits in one week, as one person could use all three of these places, and others too, in any one week. Consequently, the answer as to where people go to eat is, quite simply, anywhere. If we are to measure the success of different establishments, better criteria are the market shares in the number of meals served and of expenditure (Table 4.6). In that case, place of work now definitely leads the way in serving 39% of meals consumed per week, with cafés and snack bars, and take-aways as the next most popular eating places. Obviously the popularity of these places is due to their convenience and easy access in terms of, generally, the midday meal, and as an alternative to eating at home during the normal working day. The average cost of a meal in these places tends to be low, less than 50p in 1976, but when it comes to looking at eating places by the criteria of expenditure, hotels and restaurants account for 29% of the trade, with pubs and public-house restaurants accounting for a further 17%. Naturally, in accounting for such a large part of expenditure, and a comparatively low part of the total meals served, expenditure per

TABLE 4.6 **Market share of eating establishments**

	% of expenditure	% of no. of meals served	% of no. of people served
Purely commercial	76	48	78
Partly commercial	19	41	31
Non-commercial	5	11	12
Take-away	13	16	30
Public houses	17	9	21
Store restaurants	1	1	4
Cafés/snack bars	16	14	27
Hotels/restaurants	29	10	16
Place of work	19	39	30
Other places	1	—	1
Educational	4	11	12
Hospital	n/a	n/a	n/a

N.B. Percentages add up to more than 100 as people use more than one place.

(Source: *NEDO Trends in Catering*)

meal is considerably higher at, in 1976, about £1.40 per person. This figure may seem low to those who dine at hotels and restaurants, but it is an average figure and consequently does not simply relate to only evening meals when the chef shows his excellence, but also to simple teas. Indeed, analysis shows that in 1976 over 60% of the bills for hotels and restaurants were over £12; compared with the place of work where the bill is seldom above £1.50. Since hotel restaurants are also included in the category, breakfast would be included.

In interpreting the above statistics it must again be repeated that the percentages serve only as a guide to comparative importance and are estimates of market shares, for looking at any of the quarterly issues of the report *Eating Out* will show variation around these figures, though the magnitudes and orders of the figures and categories remain the same. Many factors cause these variations, including short-term seasonal factors such as holiday periods when the place of work loses some business, and hotels and public houses gain; educational holidays likewise affect business of various outlets. Short-term factors such as unemployment could be considered to have an effect, while long-term factors such as age distribution in the population could equally well have implications in that an ageing population would be one where there was a growing proportion of the population who did not generally eat away from home.

It is estimated that at present just about half of the population do not regularly eat out of the home during the week, and as one would expect, the great majority of these are the young, the old, and housewives. Thus the *Trends in Catering* reports usually indicate about two-thirds of the over-45s have not eaten out in the period of the survey, nor have about a half to two-thirds of housewives and generally at least a third of children of ages 11–15 (though the figure for the children fluctuates considerably).

In terms of the type of meal, the snack meal is eaten away from home about an equal number of times as the main meal, though usually the main meal is just that little more common in a ratio of 52:48. However, in terms of expenditure about twice as much is spent on a main meal as on a snack. While it is generally true that many catering establishments serve twice as many snack meals as main meals, including restaurants at the place of work, there are three areas of catering where this is not true. In educational establishments over 85% of meals are main meals, although increasing costs of food preparation allied with a cutback in real terms of local education authority budgets has led some authorities to consider (and recently implement) the provision of a wide range of snacks rather than the traditional three course meal. Likewise over 70% of hospital meals are main ones. In hotels and restaurants the overwhelming majority of meals (80% plus) are main meals, and of course, for the restaurants it is this type of catering that is the source of revenue, rather than the provision of snacks.

The Socioeconomic Framework of Demand

In looking at the demand for meals outside the home one finds that the AB groups account for about 16% of the meals, C1 for 22–27% of meals, C2 for 35–45% and DE for about 20%, compared with a class distribution throughout the British population where the AB group makes up 16%, C1 21%, C2 35% and DE 28% of the total. This implies that while the higher income groups have a proportional demand for eating out, the skilled manual group is proportionally more dependent on the catering industry, whilst the unskilled, unemployed and pensioned are less so. However, whilst both the doctor and the docker may eat away from home the same number of times in a week, there are differences in the type of meal and the occasion of the meal. For everybody the workday meal is by far the most common, but as expected for the C2 group it is for many the only reason in most weeks that they eat outside the home, and in most cases they eat at the place of work.

The other three social classes are more likely to just have a meal out, which accounts for about a fifth of their total expenditure. Generally speaking the AB group are more likely to go to a hotel, a steak house or a restaurant than other social classes in that 16% of their meals are eaten in these establishments compared with 10% for C1, 3% for C2 and 5% for DE. Moreover, when they visit such establishments, they are likely to spend more than other groups, namely about 40% of their total (or higher) expenditure on eating out as against 28% of C1 and C2, and about 15% of DE. The DE groups when eating out are, apart from the place of work, more likely to eat at a cafeteria, café or pub; these categories accounting for almost a quarter of all their meals outside the home, and a third of the expenditure such eating entails. Pubs are also popular with the C1 category who spend about 18% of their expenditure on eating out in their friendly hostelry. Indeed the pub is probably a common place for the midday workday meal for many, since nearly half of the meals that pubs serve are at this time. For those interested in these statistics one source is the *Household Food and Consumption Surveys*.

Levels of Activity

From the figures published in *Trends in Catering* it is possible to make some generalizations. There is of course, no such thing as the average diner, but certain trends do emerge. The user of a cafeteria is more likely to have a snack meal than a main meal, and to have spent, in 1977, usually under a pound rather than over a pound. He (it is more likely to be male than female) will probably be a skilled manual worker, and will spend about half-an-hour on his snack. It will be of English food, and he will prefer self-service. In contrast, the user of a hotel restaurant is more likely to be aged 25–45; he will probably be of the professional classes, stay much longer, will have company, and in 1977, to have spent over £3 per head on a main meal. In many ways the NEDC statistics perhaps tell us little that we did not already intuitively know about what the clientele of certain categories of eating establishments do, although they do tell us a certain amount about the scale of the operation, the market share held by each type of establishment, and the eating habits of certain groups of people;

which information is obviously of use to those in large-scale catering organisations who are responsible for planning their firm's activities and attempting to find areas of growth or untapped parts of the market. Does this mean that these figures are of little use to the individual caterer? Certainly it does not necessarily help him to find the most profitable form of catering because while it is true that the average price of a meal is more expensive in certain categories of restaurant, revenue depends on volume and rate of turnover and not on revenue per meal served alone. However, the individual caterer can attempt to draw up a profile of the average user of a type of catering establishment, (although the categories are broad in their definition—perhaps too broad in some cases) and compare his clientele with that average. If there are strong deviations from the norm then this may be because of some local conditions in which case it could be potentially profitable to identify these conditions and act accordingly, e.g. by slanting one's advertising and diverting it to the appropriate market. On the other hand, it must be remembered that the provision of certain specialities can attract its own clientele. For example, a vegetarian restaurant can work profitably in a large city, because the city population will be large enough to provide a vegetarian-only market.

Restaurants can be situated anywhere, but not all are equally busy. To give a crude statistic, for example: while in responses to NEDC surveys just over half the population of metropolitan London do not regularly eat out, about 57% of those living in Scotland claim they do not. It is estimated in those same surveys that the place of work accounts for about a quarter of all the meals eaten in a week by the adult population at a cost to them of about £5.5 million. This is, of course, only about a quarter of total expenditure on eating out, and the reason why the figure is not higher is because much of it is subsidized. About 50–60% of the business of hotel and restaurant catering is found in city and town centres with village and country areas accounting for a further 10%. The remaining 30% of their business is accounted for by hotels and restaurants at motorways, airports, on trains, boats and planes, at seaports and seafronts. The proportion of town business is of course heavily influenced by the London hotels. Of course these figures are very approximate and serve only as a rough estimate because of the difficulty of obtaining turnover figures. For example, annual accounts of large firms do not even break down turnover between various catering activities, much less indicate the level of seaside as against town businesses. In the case of store restaurants, then obviously most of their business is in city and shopping centres, though the evidence implies (it is impossible to be sure) that they are proportionately less popular in the West than in other parts of the country. For pubs, between a quarter and a third of their total catering is in country areas, and about another half takes place in town and city centres and shopping areas. Since the British population is mainly an urban one, such figures imply that the liking of the British for a country pub is not insignificant, and they are prepared to travel to such pubs.

As one might expect, for hotels, restaurants and steak houses, the early part of the week tends to be the quiet period. Thus, both restaurants and steak houses will, on average, have about 5–10%, at that time of their total weekly turnover. The levels of activity generally remain low until Thursday, although Wednesday sees a significant increase on the two previous days. Friday and Saturday are obviously the busiest nights, and a restaurant can expect to get about 40–50% of its turnover on those two days, with Sunday yielding a further 5–10%. Naturally these figures will vary from restaurant to restaurant and the capacity that it has, but the implication is that if the restaurant has limited seating capacity and is full most nights of the week, then it is losing business at the latter end of the week. The question then is, assuming there is space for expansion: would the additional revenue from expansion exceed the costs of such expansion and the additional variable costs such as part-time labour to cope with the end of week rush, or the costs of more full-time labour that may be under-used at the start of the week? On the other hand staff-restaurants have a smooth level of activity throughout the week, with the main cause in variations in the year being due to holidays.

However in these cases previous experience would be a good guide to overall demand.

Let us return to the favoured subject of alcoholic drink. Alcohol is rarely drunk with meals eaten at the place of work, if only because it is rarely provided. In hotels it is served in about one meal in two, though people are less likely to have alcohol in restaurants, with only one meal in three being accompanied by alcohol. In steak houses however there is a greater propensity to alcohol, drink being taken with three-quarters of all meals served; and in pubs over 80% of meals are accompanied by drinks. Again, there is of course a significant difference between restaurants. Those that offer a higher-priced menu are much more likely to have customers ordering wine and alcohol generally; although there does, in my experience, seem to be a difference by type of cuisine as much as by price, in that, for example, people often tend not to have wine with Chinese meals though they will with French cuisine, even if the two cost approximately the same. The reason for this may well be that the western palate is accustomed to the one and not the other.

The low figure for hotels is explained in part by the fact that they include breakfast among their meals, and may have a separate bar to which people go after their meal, but none the less, to quote *Trends in Catering* (Jan–March 1975) 'it would seem that for hotels and restaurants there is an untapped potential for increasing sales of alcoholic drinks with meals'.

In recent years one of the fastest growing areas of catering has been that of fast foods, and in view of the 'invasion' of these shores by American companies and the interest shown by companies such as Tesco and Bejam as well as more traditional catering companies a separate section on this area will be found on page 162.

The Elasticities of Demand

Generally speaking it can be stated that of all the meals eaten, about a half are eaten at home, and of those eaten outside the home, about a tenth are eaten for pleasure. In so far as much of the business of eating out is a 'home substitute' meal, it could be argued that the demand for eating out would tend to be inelastic. There have been attempts, direct and indirect, to measure the elasticity of demand for meals, but a failure to distinguish clearly between the two types of demand can only lead at best to very approximate answers. At the same time it must be recognized that whilst meals eaten for pleasure account for only a small proportion of the total meals eaten, they have a more than proportionate share of expenditure. And it can be argued that such dining out is going to be more elastic in demand than is the demand for 'home substitute' meals. It must also be recognized that meals can serve more than one purpose. The businessman, for example, who entertains a client at lunch-time is not only having his midday meal but conducting business, and at the same time he may be enjoying himself.

In the face of these objections, does the elasticity of demand matter? The answer is that it can in any number of situations. Take the example of a city centre restaurant which will have both a lunch-time and evening trade. The lunch-time trade will tend to be inelastic, but it is a trade which spends less on its meals than the evening diners, and it is also a trade which tends to operate at lower profit margins. Also, while the demand for lunch-time business is generally inelastic, a policy of increasing prices may prove ill-founded if there are alternative cafés and snack bars around. In other words, for an individual restaurant there has to be calculated an individual elasticity, the value of which depends on the intensity of competition in that area. As we have seen, with regard to both food and drink, since both maintain a fairly constant share of consumer expenditure it would seem that the main determinant of demand is changes in income. This opinion was also arrived at in the research done by M. Bryn Jones in his work *Food Services in Britain, 1970–1980*.

TABLE 4.7 **Personal income, consumer expenditure £ million at current prices**

	1972	1973	1974	1975	1976	1977
Personal disposable income	44 229	50 954	60 295	73 727	85 979	97 123
% change		15.0	13.0	18.4	22.1	16.6	12.9
Total consumer expenditure	39 716	45 044	51 832	63 373	73 538	83 530
% change		13.7	13.5	14.7	23.1	+16.0	+13.5
Catering expenditure	1 145	1 341	1 540	1 914	2 175	2 456
% change		9.5	13.4	11.5	12.4	13.6	12.9

(Source: *National Income and Expenditure Statistics*)

As table 4.7 shows, since 1971 catering expenditure increased at marginally below increases in consumer expenditure until 1975, when, because of high rates of inflation, the pattern was broken. This can usually be expected to happen when incomes increase more rapidly than food prices. In more recent years food price rises have come to the fore with, in 1976, a potato shortage, followed by spiralling tea and coffee prices. There would, therefore, be a faster rate of expenditure by catering organizations assuming demand for this service was maintained. Because of fluctuation caused by recent inflation any estimate of income-elasticities can only be extremely approximate at best, but estimates in the period concerned range from 0.56 (1971) to 0.98 (1975) which indicates income inelastic demand approaching unity. With an income-elasticity of less than one, yet a pattern of increasing catering expenditure as income increases, one can generalize and say that as incomes increase, so people will tend to eat out more often for leisure purposes—a statement in part supported by the socioeconomic groupings evidence—but, at the same time, with an increase in income the range of leisure alternatives available widens, and thus the link between income and eating out could weaken.

5
The Demands of the Industry

Introduction

As long as there is a demand for the services of the industry, the industry will itself have a series of demands. It will make a demand upon the producers of food, upon the providers of equipment, and upon the staff it employs. As was seen in Chapter 1, the industry is important not only because of its turnover but because of the employment it provides both *directly* and *indirectly*: *directly* in the number of people active in restaurants and hotels, and *indirectly* in the firms that supply the industry with goods and services. In this chapter we will try and assess the industry from the viewpoint of the services and personnel it requires.

On turning to an economics textbook you will be told that in order to produce, a firm requires factors of production, and these are fourfold—namely (in no particular order):

(i) **Land**—In the confusing way economists have of putting things, this means not just the soil upon which we walk, but 'the free gifts of nature all the natural resources'. It is important to remember this wider definition, which incidentally shows the liking of economists for hallowed labels, as this definition can include the sea. Only an economist would include sea as land! You might query how this state of affairs arose. Basically it is because most of the early thinking in economics took place in the late eighteenth and early nineteenth centuries when land was still an important source of wealth, and so economists, being men of their times, accorded land a special place in their thinking.

(ii) **Capital**—This term can be used in different senses—the financial, and the equipment required. In other words, to produce we need money to buy the natural resources, and the machinery to turn those resources into the final desired product. Hence a common definition of capital is that it is a 'resource not wanted for its own sake, but for its ability to produce the final product'.

(iii) **Labour**—Labour is likewise required, and is defined as 'all human effort, whether mental or physical'. In the past it was a subject of economic intellectual debate as to whether there was a distinction between *productive* and *unproductive* labour, and whether someone such as an opera singer was productive and hence 'valuable'. From our materialist viewpoint we can argue that if someone will pay for the service, then it is productive in that it satisfies a want. Consequently the work of a waiter from this viewpoint is both productive and valuable.

(iv) **The Entrepreneur**—You will not be surprised to learn that the term *entrepreneur* is a French word—one which means 'undertaker', in the sense of one who undertakes a task (including the one to place you six feet under). In undertaking a task the entrepreneur must do three things: provide the capital, organize the factors required, and decide what is to be done and how it is to be done. He is a provider of capital, an organizer, and a decision-taker, and those three elements define him. Today, with large-scale business it becomes well-nigh impossible to point a finger at any one person and say 'that is the entrepreneur'. Not even the Managing Director need be an entrepreneur since it can be argued that those on the shop floor also take a risk if business turns downwards—the risk of losing their jobs. However, failure to identify the entrepreneur is not to say that the entrepreneurial functions do not exist. They do, but in large organisations are shared by many: shareholders, managers, employees and, some argue, customers also.

Any firm in the catering industry is going to require all of these factors of production. Sometimes one is asked, which is the most important? The answer is two-fold. First, they are all obviously interdependent, in that to achieve a given task all are required in some ratio or other. So we cannot make an absolute statement which says, for example, that labour is the most important. Labour without the other factors would not be particularly effective. So, in answer to the question, which is the most important, it can be said that the important one is the one that might be lacking in any given situation, or the one that is most expensive. If, for example, the cost of labour is high, then the entrepreneur would try to do two things: (i) ensure that he does not become too dependent on the labour factor, and so move the capital/labour ratio in his form of production to capital rather than labour; (ii) attempt to use labour as productively as possible, and so again supply it with as much capital as possible. In countries such as India and China where labour is plentiful, labour is substituted for capital and building may take place using labour instead of heavy earth-moving equipment. The catering industry, because it is a service industry, tends to be labour-intensive, but with the increasing cost of labour due to higher wages, it is looking to labour-saving devices and means of using labour more effectively.

Thus, it becomes possible to substitute one factor for another, and we attempt to substitute the scarce, and hence expensive, factor with the more plentiful factor. This process will be seen in operation when we look at the factors of production the industry requires. From the above listing of factors it seems logical to look at the industry's demand for land, labour and capital. However, because of the way the information is available the demand for land is reflected by the price paid, and the price reflects also available supply. As such, this factor will be considered when looking at the cost structure of the industry in Chapter 8 and will be touched on in the next section.

The Industry's Demand for Capital—Investment Finance

Financial capital can be divided into working capital and investment capital. The former is the financial provision for the day-to-day working of the firm, covering the payment of food, linen, laundry, wages, etc., whereas investment capital is concerned with the money required for new, large undertakings, such as modernizing existing buildings, creating additional new units, or building totally new hotels or restaurants. The flow of monies associated with working capital will be looked at more closely when the cost structure of hotels and restaurants is examined, and our present concern will be with investment capital.

The industry's demand for capital is considerable whenever new buildings are being considered, with two particularly heavy costs being the cost of land and construction costs. Obviously the figures quoted below are approximations in that the location of the land will in part determine its cost, and the density of accommodation provided and the ratio between accommodation units and service areas will considerably affect the construction costs. Recently land costs have fluctuated, with between 1970 and 1973–74 an almost doubling of costs with property speculation, followed by a period of comparatively stable prices before land and property prices began to move upwards again at about 12% p.a. in 1976–77 and have continued to rise since then at about the same rate. In a 1977 report by the management consultants, Greene, Bertram and Smith, entitled *Should We Start Thinking About Building Hotels Again?*, it is pointed out that from 1975 there was little hotel development due to previous increases in land prices, falling demand for accommodation, and high interest rates that were for many firms higher than the rate of return on an hotel operation. The report calculated that in 1977 the cost of building a city centre hotel would be £25 000–£30 000 per room, though a two-storey building would mean a cost of £12 000–£15 000 per room. Although this makes low-rise hotels appear very attractive from the viewpoint of construction costs, it does mean that to build the same number of rooms as a high-rise development requires considerably more land, and thus higher land costs; assuming the availability of land in the first place—yet another case of 'swings and roundabouts'! These figures mean that a 100-bedroom hotel could require an outlay approaching half a million pounds in total; and in their conclusions, Greene, Bertram and Smith see little new building in the next few years. Indeed, hotel investment tends to be an improvement and extension of existing premises. The costs that can be involved are indicated by the project at Abu Dhabi which is due for completion in 1980, where a 422-room hotel is being built at a cost of £18.5 million at £43 500 per room. In the light of these figures the considerable investment required by the hotel and catering industry at a time of expansion becomes considerable indeed and somewhat risky when interest rates are high (as they have been since 1976 when the Bank of England's Minimum Lending Rate was over 10% on many occasions), and particularly so as rates of return in the industry tend to be low (5% on capital employed was representative in 1976). Naturally there are differences between hotels and areas as we would expect from the different occupancy levels previously discussed, but as the report *Hotel Prospects To 1980* illustrates, even in good years prior to 1973 with the Hotel Development Investment Scheme the most profitable London hotels were only just equalling the average rates of return for manufacturing industry. In the period 1966–73 small rural hotels were only marginally profitable with, on a DCF basis, rates of return consistently below one percentage point. This is no surprise in view of the 1968 report by the Hotel and Catering EDC, *Investment in Hotels and Catering*, which included a survey by the large accountancy firm, Cooper Bros., and which came to the conclusion that 'the majority of projects outside London in the sample revealed rates of return on capital, if inflation was ignored, which made only a marginal contribution, if any, over what appeared to be the current market rate of interest on the capital employed'.

This relatively low rate of return is obviously a drawback in trying to attract investment capital from commercial lenders of money, and to make the problem worse there are additional reasons why commercial providers of investment capital might be wary of making advances. As a security for a loan a hotel suffers from being a purpose-built construction with little immediate alternative use on a viable scale if things unfortunately fail to work out. At the same time, if hoteliers try and raise a mortgage on buildings then, in the case of new construction, there is a period when an expensive bridging loan may be required before the mortgageable asset (i.e. the hotel) actually exists. Not all of these problems are associated with additions to existing establishments, and the rate of return on such investment tends to be good in that it may be possible to build bedroom space without adding to service or communal areas, but by the same token the opportunities to undertake such developments are limited.

In some senses the hotel and catering industry has perhaps not been entirely without blame in planning new projects. In 1968 Cooper Brothers commented to the effect that there were wide degrees of thoroughness involved in planning. They implied, however, that all was not as it should have been with comments such as 'we consider that a greater understanding of the determinants of demand in general . . . would assist . . .' and 'the most commonly used techniques for evaluation are the third year return on original capital . . . we consider . . . that these techniques are not generally sophisticated enough to take proper account of the various factors that characterise hotel investment projects'. In the next paragraph they state 'we consider that the wider use of budgetry control techniques should be encouraged'. Unfortunately this criticism of the industry was to be repeated later, for the September 1971 issue of *Architectural Review* singled out the hotel industry as an example of a client obtaining poor design because of poor selection procedures and cost control. By and large, it is not really possible to see if matters have improved since that time because there have been comparatively few developments in the last few years and many that have taken place have been partly shielded from normal commercial risks by the availability of special loan schemes. However, for those pondering new developments there is now an easier access to general information than there was in the late 1960s and early 1970s since the Tourist Boards and Department of Trade and Industry now regularly report trends in demand, while management consultancies and trade associations are likewise publishing a continuous stream of reports on trends and profitability. Indeed the very stream of literature that is now available implies that the industry has stepped forward to take its rightful place in the blaze of publicity.

The burden of attaining high rates of return on capital employed can be illustrated by the example of a £500 000, 100-room development seeking a rate of return of 15% p.a. If the hotel operates at 50% annual capacity, then this occupancy level will have to raise £75 000 p.a. before contributing to other costs, and this represents a tariff of about £4.30 a night. In the case of a £250 000 project with the same capacity and target rate of return, a £2.15 tariff. These are very approximate figures but serve to show the costs involved before taking into account wages, linen costs, food costs, rates, heating, lighting, etc.

In the period since 1975 with the increase of demand generated largely by foreign tourists, the industry has found itself in a more enviable position which has allowed a significant easing in its profit position. From 1972 to 1974 profits fell, but in 1975, according to management consultants Greene, Belfield Smith and Co., profits returned to their 1975 levels. A combination of increased demand, tariff increases that were below the rate of inflation, and an easing in the rate of increase of rents, led to an approximate 50% increase in sales in 1975–77. The impact of the increased revenue on profits was marked with new hotels achieving a 300% increase in profits in this period, whilst older hotels also saw profits advancing by over 50%. In 1978 and 1979 the level of profits continued to rise as tourist levels remained high; but with an increasing contribution to profits coming from increased tariffs as hotel groups faced with inflationary costs began to increase tariffs at rates higher than the rate of inflation. More recently hotel groups have been maintaining profits as well as they can by a combination of tariff increases keeping in line with inflation and cost saving techniques whilst competing for a more static level of demand.

Compared with hotel investment, catering investment is small, and also tends to be small in comparison with the turnover involved. Consequently the rates of return on capital employed in the catering industry tend to be higher than those found in hotels, though the same factors as choice of site and accurately forecasting and meeting demand are equally vital. If successful in these factors caterers can approach commercial providers of money with a better proposition than hoteliers, for the payback period on investment tends to be short, and so caterers need apply for only short- or medium-term finance with the possibility of being able to repay fairly quickly out of cash flow. Restaurant chains are, generally speaking, in an enviable position, in that while catering is speculative, the risk is spread geographically, which also increases the chances of success. At the same time, should restaurants suffer a comparative failure initially, it is normal to re-design and refurbish the interior decor with the aim of building up turnover by appealing to a different market, and this type of exercise can also be financed by short- and medium-term finance. At the same time, if a restaurant chain is prepared to forego the cost savings of a uniform catering operation, it can further minimize risks by market diversification as well as by geographical diversification.

Over the last ten years the hotel and catering industry has shared British industry's general decline in profitability, although 1976–79 has been a period of recovery. In the mid-1960s hotels were achieving median profits that were in the range of 12–23% of turnover dependent on location, whereas in 1976 companies were reporting much lower rates with a median of about 10–15%. The result has been the buying and selling of hotels and also wide changes in profitability—points that will be discussed in Chapter 8.

The Sources of Finance

Traditionally, British industry is self-financing out of profits, and this has tended to remain the case even in the period 1975–77 when industry suffered problems. Consequently, although one thinks of the Stock Exchange and shares as being very important in the world of finance, it can be argued that the stock exchanges finance only about 5% of all new investment. Indeed, in the period 1976–77 with central government budgetary deficits of over £8 billion, much of the money raised by the Stock Exchange has been for the Government rather than for industry. On turning to the hotel and catering industry this tradition of self-financing is even stronger. This is in part due to the large number of self-employed and family businesses in the catering industry, and the fact that most companies are not public limited liability companies and thus have no access to the Stock Exchange. If a firm is not a limited liability company, then, in the legal jargon, it is unincorporated; and as we will see, the rate of unincorporation in the industry is high. A second reason is that the industry, particularly hotels, have had a poor image as a recipient of investment capital for the reasons discussed above. However, there are advantages in going to external sources of finance in that a dependence on self-generated finance may mean a holding back of growth and development, and possibly the loss of opportunities that might arise. An example of this might be the vacancy of an adjoining property to a restaurant or hotel that has high usage rates. The purchase of the property will allow expansion, but no vendor will wait for the hotelier or caterer to accumulate profits to pay for the property; and thus, recourse to borrowing must be made. In the final resort, of course, all borrowed sums have to be paid back out of profits, and so in that sense it involves a degree of self-financing.

Borrowing may take different forms:

(i) **Debentures**—These are long term debts sold on the Stock Exchange with the firm's assets as security for the debt. It is a means of borrowing that is available only to larger organizations, and is usually comparatively cheap in that the debentures carry a fixed rate of interest over a period of 20–25 years, after which the debentures are redeemed, i.e. the debt is repaid. The actual rates reflect the degree of risk attached to the company. Trusthouse Forte, for example, have debentures issued at 4.8%, 6.25% and 10.5%, reflecting risk and current interest rates.

(ii) **Mortgage loans**—These are loans based on the security of the buildings and land, and the lender will usually advance about 60% of the required money on this basis. Like debentures the loans are usually made for a period of 20–25 years, and the rates of interest are usually one or two points above debenture rates and depend on current interest rates.

(iii) **Bridging finance**—This is a loan generally made for a short-term period of time while new arrangements are being made and an asset being acquired or built. They tend to be quite costly.

(vi) **Sale and leaseback**—Companies sometimes resort to this when experiencing cash flow difficulties. The firm sells an asset to the lender, often a finance company, who then pays for it, and leases it to the original owner at a 'rent' which is usually expressed as a percentage of the sale value. Like many leases these are reviewed at regular periods, usually 5–7 years. In this way a firm can raise cash on an asset and still retain the use of the asset. However, it does mean the loss of an asset and should really only be done if the rate of return on the cash received from the asset's sale is higher than the rental—and such an arrangement tends to make for marginal profitabilty. Sale and leaseback is sometimes used when other methods of borrowing fail.

(v) **Hire-purchase**—This is where a deposit is paid on the purchase of an item, and the balance is paid in regular instalments of set sums over a repayment period of usually three years or so. The balance so borrowed is subject to very high rates of interest and the true rate of interest in 1979 could often be over 25% p.a. Ownership of the asset passes to the borrower after the last instalment and purchase fee (usually £3) is paid. A similar form of purchase is a credit sale, where ownership passes to the borrower at the outset.

(vi) **Bank loans**—These can take various forms. That most commonly used for day-to-day cash flow requirements is the overdraft where the bank allows a current account to be used up to a certain figure 'in the red', and interest is charged on the amount so used. Other loans are available at higher interest rates which are payable on a set figure, even if all the money so borrowed is not used. For a long-term bank loan the company or individual will have to provide collateral or security, which may range from life insurance policies to the assets being acquired.

Hotels and restaurants can borrow from a number of bodies, some of which are orientated to the tourism, hotel and catering industry; most of which, however, are not.

(i) **Joint-stock banks**—These generally provide short-term finance, designed in part to ease daily cash flow and to finance extensions or the purchase of equipment where the repayment can be made in usually three, sometimes up to five years, and where the cash flow generated by the investment is sufficient to pay back the loan and interest. Banks will also provide bridging loans. Recently, for various reasons, the high street banks have increasingly made medium-term loans for capital equipment, but much of this has been directed to manufacturing industry. It is very difficult to assess how much the banks lend to the hotel and catering industry, but in May 1979 the total amount outstanding from the London clearing banks to 'service industries' was £5 894 000 000.

(ii) **Merchant banks**—These are essentially mobilizers of funds rather than providers of capital, and generally speaking only the largest firms in the industry would use their service. They are invaluable when it comes to the flotation of shares on the Stock Exchange and will even take up unsold shares of a new issue.

(iii) **Building societies**—These are primarily concerned with the advancing of money for private house purchase, but under the relevant Acts they are allowed to make loans to business so long as such loans do not exceed 10% of their total lending, and no one loan exceeds £15 000. The Bolton Committee which investigated sources of finance for small firms suggested that building societies should be given a chance to expand their lending to small businesses, but the government has not acted upon this. Certainly they could be a source of finance for owners of restaurants or guest-houses.

(iv) **Insurance and pension companies**—These companies are primarily concerned with long-term investments of security that yield a rate of return that will enable them to meet their obligations to their investors and those making claims. Consequently they will usually make only long-term loans, and these are generally in the form of purchasing shares and debentures. However, they are diversifying their investment activities, but the history of comparatively low rates of return on hotels may make them wary of loans in that sector, and while they are large investors in property the specificity of usage of a hotel might also be seen as a drawback.

(v) **Trade creditors**—Trade credit is usually offered by suppliers to the industry, even if it is only by allowing a fortnight or a month before settlement of the bill, although there would be a cost involved which is the loss of the discount granted for prompt payment. So a loss of a $2\frac{1}{2}\%$ discount for payment within a month would mean borrowing at an interest rate of roughly 30% p.a. (12 × $2\frac{1}{2}\%$). Equipment suppliers will not only offer such discounts, but may also make arrangements for hire purchase, credit sale and leasing. In some cases where an entirely new venture is being undertaken, loans may be made, or purchase terms may be offered on the basis of deferred payment.

(vi) **The Industrial and Commercial Finance Corporation (ICFC)**—This makes loans between £5000 and £500 000 for periods of 10–20 years, and also offers advisory services in accountancy, marketing, etc. In the period of March 1976–March 1977 the ICFC lent £400 000 to the hotel and catering industry, made up of fifty separate loans. The following year the increased profitability of the industry was shown in that as the ability to repay loans increased, so more was lent, and in 1977–78 the ICFC advanced £2.02 million to the hotel and catering sector. The Corporation has now over £6 million outstanding in loans to the industry.

(vii) **The Council for Small Industries in Rural Areas (CoSIRA)**—This is prepared to make loans for tourist projects in specified rural areas, and is orientated towards small firms and business in that their loans are severely limited. The maximum loan that can be made is £35 000, for up to 85% of the total cost of building accommodation, and the repayment periods are up to 20 years on buildings, and seven years for equipment. They are prepared to make loans in conjunction with other bodies, and allow a moratorium on repayments so that the business can become established without being burdened with interest repayments from the very outset.

(viii) **Equity Capital for Industry Limited**—This was set up in 1976 by a city institution in reply to criticism that the city was providing insufficient capital for industrial investment. Many thought the institution was unnecessary, believing that the reason financial bodies were not supplying more investment capital was simply due to a lack of demand by industry due to a lack of confidence. Furthermore, it has been argued that if firms are unable to raise money through the normal channels of finance, then it probably means that the firm is in an uncertain financial situation. Certainly the critics were given ammunition because in 1977 one of the early investments in a carpet manufacturing firm, Bond Worth Holdings, was lost as the firm concerned accumulated debts of over £20 million. Generally speaking, Equity Capital for Industry Ltd. seeks a shareholding in the company it aids, and thus the many unincorporated firms of the hotel and catering industry would not receive any benefit.

(ix) **The Tourist Boards**—In 1969 the present system of Tourist Boards was initiated by the Development of Tourism Act. The government gives an annual grant to the Tourist Boards, and in the financial year 1976–77 it was about £8 million. Of course not all of this money is available for development by individual hoteliers and caterers since the Boards have their own expenditure and have regional and area promotions to finance. However, there is some money available for aid. In 1976–77 the English Tourist Board received about 40 applications per week for development aid and approved about one in three of the requests. Up to the end of 1976 the ETB had assisted 500 projects at £5 million, and in giving aid towards schemes, has stimulated about £15 million of private investment.

(x) **The Government**—Government can be the direct source of grant aid, but has tended to treat the industry as being separate from manufacturing industry with the consequence that the hotel and catering industry has had no automatic right to the grant aid that is made under regional development schemes. In 1966 there was a Hotel Development Incentive Loan and Grant scheme introduced on an experimental basis which produced £300 million with £70 million from public funds when it was in existence, but the scheme had effectively ceased in 1974. The impact of the HDI will be discussed on page 225. This is not to say that Government has ceased to provide money. Under the Fire Precautions (Loans) Act 1975, £121 904 was lent to hotels and guest-houses to enable them to meet the new fire regulations. In June 1977 the Welsh Secretary, John Morris, announced that in the period 1973–77, £354 839 from EEC funds had been spent on promoting tourism in Wales.

The industry has long felt that it is not treated as favourably as it should by government, and it is constantly lobbying

Parliament for parity of tax treatment with EEC partners, and the setting up of 'tourism development areas' for financial assistance, particularly for smaller establishments.

To some extent the industry's case was recognized by the 1978 Budget when hotels of over 10 rooms providing breakfast and an evening meal (in fact the same criteria laid down for aid under the Hotel Development Incentive Scheme) were allowed an allowance against tax of 20% of the cost of new buildings in the first year, and an annual allowance of 4% for the next 20 years. This form of aid has helped the cash flow position of hotels, but with inflation, the 4% allowance will be worth little in real terms in 20 years hence. While the news was welcomed by the industry, the concession still falls short of the capital allowances of 50% that is available on manufacturing industry's construction.

The Government has also chosen to inject capital into selected areas for purposes of tourist development schemes, but the response to these has been disappointing. In 1977 only 36 out of 750 hoteliers in Scarborough applied for a share of a £3 million injection scheme, and in Bude and Wadebridge, in North Cornwall, a lack of local support in 1979 meant that the area was no longer designated a 'tourism growth point'.

(xi) **The National Enterprise Board (NEB)**—This was set up by the Government in 1975 with several aims including the injection of capital into industry. It is, in fact, the NEB which has been the channel through which Government has purchased British Leyland shares, but as this example implies, the NEB is more generally concerned with manufacturing industry.

(xii) **The EEC**—Under the Common Market Regional Aid Fund monies are available for tourism development schemes. In September 1978 the *Caterer and Hotelkeeper* ran a headline *Hotels expected to apply for share of £21 million tourism fund*. Yet again the response has not been overwhelming. Up to 1978 there had only been 12 recipients of UK aid which included the Ambassadors Hotel in Scarborough, yacht marinas in Scotland, an indoor tropical swimming centre in Rhyl, and hotels in Northern Ireland. One of the reasons for the comparatively small take-up of monies may have been due to the fact that British companies have not been able to approach the EEC Regional

Fund directly, but have had to go through the Department of Trade and Industry. It is noteworthy that successful applicants have generally been strongly supported by the Regional Tourist Board who have helped to assess the validity of the claims, costed the schemes and drawn up the applications. Nor must it be thought that the EEC is there to consider solely multi-million pound schemes. In Northern Ireland, schemes have been accepted based on an extension of hotel bedroom space so that grants of £75 000 have been considered for a 10-room extension of £15 000 per room.

It may be that, as with the special schemes sponsored by the UK government mentioned in the previous section, that hoteliers and restaurateurs are not aware of their availability. Already they receive considerable amounts of forms etc., and perhaps, in this case, telephone contacts might yield a higher response.

The Value of Investment

The amount of investment undertaken by the industry has a trend of growth in money terms, but an uneven one. Generally it has tended to follow the activity peaks and declines of consumer demand and general economics as firms seek to remedy lost revenue due to a lack of capacity, and then slow down investment in buildings when consumer demand slows down in its rate of growth. Figures for the industry's investment up to 1969 are easily available, but thereafter, in official statistics, such as input-output analysis issued by the Department of Trade in the Business Monitor (P1004), the industry is included with other services such as hairdressing. However, some estimates are possible based on the knowledge that in the 1960s the industry regularly accounted for about 10% of the estimated fixed capital expenditure of the total distributive and service industries category; and since separate statistics for entertainments, retailing and hairdressing are available, it is possible, by deduction, to make an estimate of the hotel and catering industry's investment. At the same time, the figures can be checked against occasional surveys. The general trend is indicated by the estimates in Table 5.1, which is in current prices. The figures are meant to serve solely as an indication for they are based on an

TABLE 5.1 **Estimated fixed capital expenditure in the hotel and catering industry (£ million)**

	1971	1972	1973	1974	1975	1976
Total	209	225	260	260	210	240
% growth	—	+7.6	+15.5	0	-19.3	+14.2

(Source: *Based on National Income and Expenditure Tables*)

assumption of unchanged relationships between business sectors in the economy from ten years previously, and are thus prone to error.

In the mid-1960s it is known that the hotel and catering industries accounted for about 2% of total fixed capital expenditure, and the above figures are about the same level of present total investment expenditure. This signifies that the industry's demand for investment capital tends to follow the general movements of fixed capital formation by private and public business, and hence hoteliers are at least as heavily influenced by factors such as interest rates, availability of investment funds, and government lending restrictions (and relaxations) as by changing demands for their services.

The rate of investment is important because it determines the individual firm's, and industry's capability to generate future income when its existing assets depreciate to the point where they are no longer attractive to use. Of course a large part of investment is ploughed into existing buildings in order to maintain their effectiveness. A low rate of investment would mean that tourism generally could be adversely affected in the future, for while people perhaps tend to take for granted comfortable accommodation, many would show their complaints by their absence if the accommodation and catering was poor, however beautiful or interesting the surrounding countryside, monuments or whatever else attracted them to an area. Today, when tourism plays an important role in the British balance of payments, the ability of the industry to sustain reasonable investment levels is a matter of importance not only for future industry profits, but for the general pattern of British trade.

The Demand for Capital Equipment and Convenience Foods

The equipment used by the industry has become increasingly sophisticated over time due to a continuous improvement in technology. At the same time firms have been willing to purchase such equipment because of the time-saving involved, the higher productivity it affords to labour, which is important with increasing labour costs, and because the final consumer has been generally prepared to purchase the product. There are many examples of specialized equipment that are purchased by the hotel and catering industry, and the following is only meant to show the savings involved. Not all of technology is directed at cost savings; some enables the caterer to attempt additional dishes, and so avoid menu fatigue, while others contribute to hygiene. For example, a waste disposal unit that is powered by a 3 h.p. motor will process about 900 kg of average food garbage per hour, and can deal with glass. Such an investment is basically for improving hygiene, and although it may make an economic contribution on the grounds of making working conditions more pleasant because the smell of rotting vegetables is avoided, and the place is not littered with packaging, the economic savings are probably small. Although it could be argued that labour is saved the task of carting around some smelly dustbins!

When, however, we look at the alliance of special equipment with food preparation techniques, then savings do become possible (Table 5.2). This is particularly so with convenience foods. Canned foods need only heating; frozen foods, whilst taking longer to prepare, are perhaps the best alternative to fresh foods, and come today in convenient portion packing. It is possible to get raw pre-peeled potatoes, and the market in such is today worth over £7 million. Pies and puddings can be bought which just require reheating, and in 1968 the catering industry purchased about £22 million worth of such, when it was estimated that the demand for them was increasing at about 4.5% p.a. That cost savings from a use of convenience foods with the appropriate equipment is possible is illustrated by the following example from a 1971 *NEDO* report on *Convenience Foods in Catering*, although the actual saving in any one restaurant's case depends on their particular situation.

Indeed, it is possible that a switch from fresh food preparation can involve higher costs. Frozen vegetables cost more than fresh, and although slicers and other preparation equipment can be replaced and labour saved, refrigeration units have to be purchased. In such a case it becomes a question of the value of the room saved. In this respect it is interesting to note that few caterers in 1976 had freezer space of above 10–19.8 cubic feet, which compares with the domestic user's average

TABLE 5.2 **A comparison of food service systems**

Item	Change from conventional to combination system*	Change from conventional to frozen meal system
Capital equipment	15% saving	26% saving
Floor area	25% saving	40% saving
Staff	15% saving (including vending sales)	20% saving (not including vending)
Portion cost	Lower food cost (greater flexibility)	25% increase (would vary with supplier)
Disposable articles	Use only those acceptable to customer	All items disposable even if customer does not like**
Standard of food and variety	No limit	High quality—but only 24 meal variations
Customer acceptibility	High—30% increase recorded	Low—menu fatigue

*Fresh, frozen and dried.
**1.2p per person per day saved on washing up.
(Source: *Convenience Foods in Catering*, 1971, NEDO)

freezer capacity of 10–14 cubic feet. This indicates a possible loss of trade discount on bulk purchase in that caterers are making purchases more often than they need due to limited frozen food storage. In 1976 the catering industry purchased about £150 million of frozen foods (Table 5.3), of which 73% was purchased by hotels, restaurants and take-aways and public houses, 15% by industrial caterers, and 12% by social services' catering establishments. In addition, an estimated further £68 million was spent on other convenience foods.

Sometimes the term *fast foods* is confused with that of *convenience foods*. There is much in common between the two, and the fast-food operation is based on convenience foods, but recently fast foods have come into a category in their own right. Fast-food operations may be defined as a catering outlet offering a limited range of menus based on a few foods that are precooked, quick to prepare, and often served on disposable trays. The operations are capital-intensive and labour-saving, and profitability rests on high turnover. Convenience foods, however, although precooked and purchased as either frozen, tinned,

TABLE 5.3 **UK frozen foods expenditure (£ million at current prices)**

Year	Total	Catering	Catering as % of total	Annual growth of catering consumption as a %
1971	234	69	29	—
1972	277	82	29	18
1973	345	100	29	21
1974	418	125	30	25
1975	500	135	27	8
1976	600	150	25	11
1977	n/a	170	n/a	n/a

N.B. n/a indicates *not applicable*.

(Source: *Birds Eye Annual Review*, 1977)

boil-in-a-bag or dehydrated, and although labour saving, are rarely the sole component of a menu, being used to complement fresh foods in more traditional styles of catering. To summarize the position, the advantages to a 'traditional' caterer of using convenience foods are:

(i) **Labour saving**—The NEDC survey on convenience food found a 50% reduction in the number of employees. Since labour costs can be 40% or more of total costs, this can be a source of significant savings. At the same time, the lower skill element means that younger, less skilled people can be employed, and these are lower-salaried staff. Against this is the fact that such staff tend to have a higher turnover, and hence the costs associated with advertising, training and lack of experience will be more than before.

(ii) **Less waste of food**—Nearly all the convenience foods can be used, whereas there is waste associated with fresh foods. If the caterer is in a position to undertake bulk purchase of such foods and can therefore negotiate favourable discounts with the food manufacturers, the net costs of convenience and fresh foods are comparable.

(iii) **Possible space saving**—Since convenience foods are neatly packaged, stacking and storing is easier than with fresh foods. The space saved may simply make for more spacious a preparation area which may aid staff morale, or it may make possible the keeping of larger stocks. This in turn can mean bigger purchase discounts, while it also means less deliveries and the possible disruption they cause.

(iv) **Extension of the menu**—Convenience foods cover a wide range of dishes, including entreés, sweets, main courses, sauces, etc. They allow the serving of out-of-season foodstuffs and can be used to complement fresh foods. They also allow more advance menu planning.

The major disadvantages to the caterer are:

(i) **The increased cost of equipment**—Although some savings are possible, convenience foods require refrigeration equipment, special ovens and additional storage equipment. The installation of such equipment can lead to redesigning and redecorating kitchens, and high initial investment costs are involved. This is particularly true where one is converting existing premises, whereas if one is building new purpose-built kitchens these costs are much easier to absorb.

(ii) **Increased fuel and power costs**—Although microwave ovens cook convenience foods faster, they use, with the preparation equipment and refrigeration plant, considerable power, which may increase electricity costs. However, continued technical improvement will mean that the increment to fuel costs from converting to a convenience food system will diminish in real terms over time.

One result of this move to convenience foods has been an additional impetus to the demand for additional catering equipment. A somewhat far-out example is the machine for 'instant chip mix' which is needed to create chips out of instant chip mix that contains dehydrated potato powder, sodium alginate and cellulose ethers. On the other hand, a piece of equipment like the microwave oven, which is well adapted to reheating already cooked dishes, or precooked frozen dishes and which works best when portions of a uniform thickness are placed in the oven, creates a whole new range of precooked meals for use with the microwave oven. Whatever the reasons, there has been a striking growth in demand for catering equipment, for the Catering Equipment Manufacturers Association reported that sales increased from £59 million in 1975 to £76.6 million in 1976, an increase of about 30%.

Incidentally, the marketing of microwave ovens for domestic use could increase the market penetration by frozen food manufacturers. In 1977 there were only five frozen food manufacturers with a turnover of over £10 million: namely, Birds' Eye (£109 million), Ross Foods (£41 million), Findus (£41 million), Young's Seafoods (£22 million), and McCain International (£10 million); and it is interesting to note that all five are wholly owned by companies whose names probably produce different images to the public. They are Unilever, Nestlés and the Imperial Group, of which the last are best known for their tobacco and brewing interest.

The Demand for Labour

As was stated in the introduction, the hotel and catering industry is labour-intensive and is in consequence a major employer, employing 3.6% of the total working population. However, not only is it labour-intensive, but it is a major employer of female labour, and the proportion of women within the industry has increased, with the result that the industry employs, according to the 1975 returns, 1.75% of the male working population and 5.55% of the female. Indeed, women outnumber men by 255 000, there being 538 000 women employed as against 283 000 men. Contrary to the trend which has seen a marginal fall in the working population, the numbers employed in the industry have increased from 612 000 in 1965 to about 821 000 in 1975. These figures are based on statistics published by the Department of Employment which are collected on the basis of National Insurance cards, and consequently people are categorized by the Standard Industrial Classification Number to which their firm is allocated. As was seen in Chapter 1, such a system severely underestimates the numbers of people employed in the industry. The size of the problem is indicated by Census of Population returns when people described their own occupation, and by the 1971 studies of the Hotel and Catering Industry Training Board on patterns of labour mobility and personnel records and manpower planning. From 1976 to 1981 the HCITB has made a commitment in its five-year plan to examine the labour position in the industry, and has embarked on a three-stage plan as follows:

> **Stage 1**—A feasibility study concerned with the methods of collecting information, the type of data available, highlighting gaps in our knowledge, the best means of analysing and presenting the data.

Stage 2—This took place in April 1977. It is a monthly collection of statistics from 2000 establishments. Within each establishment the employer is asked to provide information on no more than 20 employees, whether he employs 20 staff or 200 staff. Obviously, for those employing less than 20, the information required is as appropriate.

Stage 3—This began in August 1977 and provides the basic reference point in that it is a major survey of 12 000 establishments covering all sectors of the industry other than take-away shops and catering for the forces.

The purposes of the survey are:

(i) to provide information about the total number of people employed in the industry and the various sectors;

(ii) to provide information about labour movement within the industry—the frequency for movement, reasons for leaving and the sectors of the industry which have the greatest turnover, and movement in and out of the industry;

(iii) to provide information about the qualifications people have, the training they receive, and the nature of the jobs they do.

Part of the information is quantitative, some of it qualitative; in other words it is recording not only actual numbers involved but also what people think.

In this way it is hoped that the HCITB and employers will be able to identify the skills required for various posts, the training that is required, and the areas where manpower is required. Already the HCITB has published figures which will be described later in this section. However, if we wish to trace the pattern of employment in the last decade or so, then obviously the HCITB statistics will not help and hence one has to refer to the Department of Employment.

These figures show an increase in employment in the industry over the last twenty years (Table 5.4). However, it has not been a story of a continual increase in numbers for between 1965 and 1968 the numbers employed fell from 612 000 to 571 000. A number of factors caused this. The main one may well have been the introduction of Selective Employment Tax, which meant that employers in the service industries had to pay a tax levied on the number of employees they had. A second factor was the number of amalgamations within the industry in that period. And a third factor was possibly the slowing down in the level of

TABLE 5.4 **Hotel and catering employment (thousands)**

	1968	1969	1970	1971	1972	1973	1974	1975	1976
Numbers employed	571	596	569	680	722	784	796	816	850
Annual % change	—	+4.2	−7.0	+19.2	+6.0	+8.4	+1.8	+2.1	—

(Source: *Annual Abstract of Statistics*)

general business activity, which did not begin to increase until about 1969–70. However, the industry has sustained a significant increase in employees in the 1970s in a period of greater economic difficulty. While the percentage increase in the number of employees between 1970 and 1971 looks considerable, it is, however, in part, due to the Department of Employment making some changes in the basis of collection of the statistics.

The downturn in employment in 1970 reflected the general increase in unemployment which was then climbing to a, then, postwar height of over half a million before it was to fall in the years following 1972, only to increase again in 1975.

Labour Demand in Different Sectors of the Industry

For the purpose of analysing the distribution of the labour force between different sectors of the industry, the DEP divides the industry into five categories which are based on the sections of the Standard Industrial Classification. This classification has been continued by the HCITB but enlarged upon to give a fuller picture. Table 5.5 is drawn from their survey.

From these figures certain characteristics of the labour force are apparent (Table 5.6). Nearly three-quarters of the labour force is female and over half the labour force work on a part-time basis (i.e. less than 30 hours per week). The largest sectors in employment terms are the hotel sector which employs 26% of the total and the public house sector with 22%. However, public houses as one would expect, are far more reliant on part-time staff. The HCITB survey also surprised some as to the extent that the industry is dependent on female labour. Indeed, the women outnumber the men by about 1.5 million. This could be

TABLE 5.5 **Employment in the hotel and catering industry. Estimates drawn from 1978 HCITB survey (thousands)**

Sector	Male Part-time	Male Full-time	Female Part-time	Female Full-time	Grand total
Hotels	32	153	133	167	485
Guest-houses	3	9	19	17	48
Restaurants	16	66	77	50	209
Cafés	10	25	58	39	132
Industrial canteens	7	34	77	124	242
Pubs	69	86	230	75	460
Clubs	24	23	69	17	133
Local authorities	2	3	243	92	340
					2 049

significant for the industry in that with equal pay legislation an increase in wage costs over and above increased wage settlements has had to be absorbed by the industry, particularly the hotel, restaurant and public house sector. A second significant factor is that in the British economy it has been traditional for a female dominated labour force in an industry to be highly correlated with lower than national average wage levels. If we wish to compare employment changes between sectors of the

TABLE 5.6 **Labour in the hotel and catering industry (thousands)**

	1970 Male	1970 Female	1970 Total	1975 Male	1975 Female	1975 Total
Hotels and other residential establishments	108.7	161.8	270.5	100.7	154.9	255.6
Restaurants, cafés, snack bars	43.0	77.5	120.5	56.2	107.4	163.6
Public houses	24.2	52.0	76.2	71.1	148.9	220.0
Clubs	24.9	27.5	52.4	38.9	58.7	97.6
Catering contractors	11.6	36.9	48.4	16.6	68.8	85.4
	212.4	355.7	568.0	283.5	538.7	822.2

(Source: *Annual Abstract of Statistics*)

industry, we need to refer to the DEP statistics. From these we can see that the growth in employment has not been evenly distributed throughout the industry, and that the hotel sector has in fact reduced its labour force over the half-decade 1970–75 which tallies with the decline in accommodation demand.

The major part of the growth has come from the public house sector which has increased its labour force threefold in the five year period. However, the public house sector has one common feature with the restaurants sector, and that is the heavy dependence on part-time female labour, each having approximately a half to a third of its female workforce part-time. Indeed, as we noticed earlier, the industry has maintained a high attraction for women in that the female component of the industry total has increased by over 150%. These statistics raise a number of questions. The downward turn in the numbers employed by the hotel business can be explained by reference to occupancy figures, yet the demand for drink has not increased so rapidly as to account for the increased need for labour in pubs. The increase in public house labour cannot be explained by an increase in part-time working either, for it is an industry that has a long record of such working. A cumulation of reasons could explain the increase, even if there is no one particularly dominant reason. Pubs have obviously changed their style over the last decade with the introduction of soft lights and soft music. They have also increased the catering side of their activities considerably, and have tended to have several different bars instead of just the public and saloon bars. The brewing industry has been able to absorb much of the cost of extra catering by closing many of the older, less economic pubs. So even though demand has grown slowly in terms of gallons drunk, business has made possible the absorption of the higher labour costs. One might also ask why women have been drawn into the industry. This may simply be because women have been increasingly drawn into the working population anyway. In 1966 women accounted for 34.2% of the total working population in Britain, but this figure had risen to 37.6% by 1976. An increasing financial need allied to changing attitudes towards women at work could account for this change. As far as the hotel and catering industry is concerned, it has been able to attract female labour because it offers part-time work without a great deal of training and many find this attractive. Some writers have also argued that the industry has attracted women because it can, in a sense, be seen as an extension of the domestic skills

THE DEMANDS OF THE INDUSTRY 113

traditionally possessed by women. This may be so, but it is hard to prove. The other reasons just outlined may be more important.

The Geographical Pattern of Labour Demand

The geographical distribution of labour in the hotel and catering industry can be estimated from Census of Population returns (Table 5.7). As can be seen, just over a third of the labour force in the industry actually work in hotels and residential establishments, but there are some interesting deviations.

TABLE 5.7 **Distribution of labour in the hotel and catering industry in percentages by sector in the regions**

	Hotels	Restaurants	Public houses	Clubs	Contract Caterers
North	35	21	22	19	4
Yorkshire and Humberside	38	20	21	18	3
North-west	31	28	24	11	5
East Midlands	28	28	32	10	8
West Midlands	24	22	35	10	9
East Anglia	36	29	24	5	5
South-east	31	29	22	7	12
South-west	47	23	20	4	6
Wales	37	25	20	15	5
Scotland	47	24	18	9	4

(Source: *Census of Population*, 1971)

For example, the East Midlands, which is not an important tourist area, has but only just over a fifth of its share in the hotel sector, whereas those areas that cater for tourism, such as the South-west, Yorkshire, Scotland and Wales, have about 40% or over of the industry's workforce employed in hotels. Indeed, in the more urban regions such as the Midlands, the hotel sector has to give way to the public house sector as the most important employer, and in the East Midlands it takes only third place. Indeed, on looking more closely at the 1971 Census returns for the main conurbations within the regions, this pattern is continually repeated. It can be argued that the South-east is as densely populated as the Midlands, if not more so, but busy holiday trade in the South-east obviously accounts for the overall importance of the hotel sector there—though again conurbations within the South-east have as many and more employed in the public house and restaurant sectors than in hotels. However, there is more of an equality here than in the Midlands due to the 'tourism pull' exerted by London. Indeed, there are no constant features across the regions; in each region the order of importance varies. Even contracted catering, which is usually the least important, moves into fourth position in the South-east instead of its customary fifth, and last, place. The overall picture is one of variety and change.

What is clear is that most people working within the industry are in the South-east, and indeed that area accounts for about a third of the total workforce.

With regard to the sex ratio between the various sectors, it tends to be 2:1 in favour of females in the hotel sector (except in the South-east where it is almost 1:1 ratio). In the restaurant sector there are about three times as many working women as men (except again in the South-east where the men marginally outnumber the women!). Public houses have similar sex ratios to those of the restaurant sector, while in contract catering there are about five times as many women as men, except (of course!) the South-east where this time the women outnumber the men 2:1. Finally, the women also outnumber the men in working in the clubs on a national average of about 5:2, but with considerable regional variations—for example, in the North the ratio is 3:1, in the South-east 1:1, and in Wales 2:1.

The Nature of the Jobs

The Census of population, as far as the hotel and catering industry is concerned, denotes ten categories of jobs. However, the Department of Employment has ten different categories of occupation when collecting its statistics of unemployment. In comparing the 1966 and 1971 censuses, one has to bear in mind that the period covered was one of rising unemployment, and therefore a downward trend will show; but such figures will indicate those jobs that are at greatest risk for various reasons which may help to illustrate long-run trends when we come to look at current unemployment statistics. In analysing the 1971 census returns, one can make some broad observations. While it is true that there are more women than men employed in the industry, there are more men than women in the higher status jobs. For example, in the category *proprietors, managers of hotels and boarding houses* there are 26 000 men as against 25 000 women, and in looking at the managerial status of the posts involved, one would guess that men do even better. It would be interesting to see if the trend has favoured women over the last fifteen years or so, but two technical factors make this difficult. The 1966 census did not separately categorize proprietors and managers in its sample, and there was no 1976 sample census of population as part of the Government cut back in expenditure. Similarly, in 1971 there were more male restaurateurs than female: 39 000 men and 28 000 female. The females make their presence felt in functions such as waiting at table and acting as maids. Indeed, about 45% of all females employed in the hotel and catering industry are employed in the capacity of *maids, valets and related service workers* as the official census category not too glamorously puts it. Even in the kitchens, the traditional domain of the woman at home, the female gives way to the male in the commercial sector, at least in numbers, for men have slight numerical advantage over the 38 000 females. Where women do have a considerable advantage over men, in numerical terms, and where they do have a degree of responsibility and authority to exercise, is in the role of housekeeper.

It can be argued that the use of 1971 Census returns is increasingly invalid as these figures are now 10 years old, but they are useful for comparative purposes when used with the DEP statistics. A more accurate estimate of the situation can be given by the HCITB survey. Table 5.8 indicates the main occupations.

TABLE 5.8 **Occupations of the hotel and catering industry**

	Full-time	*Part-time*
Manager/proprietor	241 900	—
Chefs/kitchen workers	254 000	250 000
Food service	125 900	152 000
Barmen, barmaids	81 000	303 000
Housekeeping	73 600	132 000
Front hall porterage	17 200	9 000
Washers-up	12 900	23 800

(Source: *1966 and 1971 Censuses*)

This shows that managers and proprietors account for about nearly a quarter of the full-time workforce. In assessing the skill levels of the industry the HCITB estimated that 29% make up what they term as *sub-craft level* workers, and 14% of full-time workers are *skilled craftsmen and technicians*. The picture the HCITB surveys paint is one of about half the full-time workforce being unskilled. In hotels and industrial catering the figures of unskilled full-time workers are 54% and 60% respectively, and if part-time workers are included, then 80% of all catering workers fall into the lower levels of skill. This figure is partly a question of definition. For example, not everyone would agree with the Board's allocation of waiters into the category of sub-craft level workers, but even if these are removed from the category of the less skilled, the position is still one of over 60% possessing skills below the craft level.

It has already been noted that the industry once suffered a decline of employment on account of a payroll tax levied on the basis of the number of people employed (SET), and therefore a fall in demand in that period. Most of this unemployment was felt by the relatively unskilled such as kitchen hands and chambermaids.

The abolition of SET would probably have meant a rise in the numbers of unskilled employed, but by the time of its abolition after the 3–4 years life of the tax, employers had learnt how to get by without the same level of employees. Consequently, faced with a possible declining holiday demand, it is unlikely that so many jobs will become available again in these areas. It is also noteworthy that the number of cooks employed fell significantly.

However, we do know that in the period since 1971 the industry's demand for labour has increased and now exceeds the 1966 figure. Consequently, it would appear that the industry does possess in its unskilled jobs an 'organizational slack' that it can manipulate when times improve or get worse. Although the growth for eating and drinking out of the home has been slow in real terms, the industry's revenue has significantly increased in money terms. It may be that management is, to a degree, taken in by their growth in money income, and with increases in income, is prepared to take on unskilled labour in order to ease the burden on the skilled staff and give a better service to customers. That this may be the case is supported by other indirect evidence. First, since about a third of the women employed in the industry are part-time, this gives management a degree of flexibility as to working hours. Secondly, the seasonal fluctuations in employment indicate an industry that has a traditional flexibility to changes in business activity. Incidentally, because of the seasonal nature of employment, it may be thought that the employment figures of the Census could be influenced by the date when the Census was taken. This is indeed true, but the 1966 and 1971 Censuses were both surveyed at the same time of each respective year, namely in the third week of April. A third element of indirect evidence comes from work study surveys which indicate that some jobs, such as being a hotel porter, have considerable slack times. Consequently, job duties are being amalgamated, but such events imply the existence of slack time which can be used when the need arises. A fourth factor, which has added to the growth of employment, is one that has already been mentioned: namely the development of the public house and the number of bar staff it now employs.

A further picture that emerges from the HCITB surveys shows just how much of the labour force is still concerned with the preparation and sale of food and drink. As we will be seeing, the most profitable sector of the hotel industry is the accommodation side, yet most of its staff is involved in food and drink. This is likely to remain the case in as much as the selling and reservation of accommodation and the keeping of records associated with it lend themselves to automation more easily than food preparation, unless there is a still greater public acceptance of convenience foods and cook-freeze and cook-chill methods. None the less, there has been increased automation in a number of areas, and certainly the introduction of washing-up equipment has influenced the number of washers-up employed, and in the past the number of kitchen hands was reduced rapidly when the industry contracted the labour force after the introduction of SET. According to the 1966 and 1971 Censuses, the number of kitchen hands fell from over 100 000 to about 31 000, indicating again a high degree of flexibility on the part of the industry.

The Self-employed

It was previously noted that the industry is one where the self-employed are a considerable proportion of the total, being about 20% of the whole. For these figures we are again dependent on census returns, and these show that in catering the self-employed are losing ground just as they are in other fields. In 1961 the self-employed accounted for 21% of the total workforce in the hotel and catering industry, by 1966 the proportion was 19%, and in the last census of 1971 the figure had fallen to 16%.

More recent estimates indicate that the self-employed now account for about 12% of the workforce. In terms of actual numbers there were about 130 000 self-employed in both 1961 and 1966, and 126 000 in 1971. This is one field of catering where men do outnumber women—the number of males has remained stable since 1966 with about 75 000 employed, whereas the females have declined from 55 000 in 1966 to just over 50 000 in 1971. (I would not feel, however, that this is evidence that women have been less successful than men, for over half the women do head organizations where others are employed!) The public house is the form of catering that is most favoured by the self-employed and obviously for many the dream of having one's own pub is a reality, even though it may not necessarily be set in the country with ivy or rambling roses climbing alongside doors and windows. For many women, particularly if they do not want to employ people, the small boarding-house appears to have great attraction, and the decline of the boarding-house since the middle 1960s accounts in part for the decline in numbers of the female self-employed.

Unemployment

Generally, total unemployment in the hotel and catering industry has reflected the levels in the national economy, falling when the national level falls, and rising as total unemployment rises. And this has been true of all sectors (Table 5.9).

It is also interesting to note that while the hotel sector accounts for about 35–40% of total employment in the industry, it accounted for over 50% of the unemployment in the trade in each of the years under consideration. However, the industry, although it has in some ways a reputation of a 'hire and fire' business, does marginally cling to its labour more than the national average, as can be shown by comparing an hotel and catering unemployment rate with the national average unemployment level in Table 5.10. This can be accounted for by the growth in business achieved by a number of regions, but the picture changed in 1976 as income restraint and increased unemployment hit British demand for holidays and hotel accommodation with the consequent radical fall in demand experienced by seaside resorts, and a consequent increase in unemployment in the industry.

TABLE 5.9 Unemployment in the hotel and catering industry (June)

	1970	1971	1972	1973	1974	1975	1976*	1977*
Hotels and licensed establishments	11 197	12 680	14 965	11 330	10 798	19 139	29 985	47 672
Restaurants/cafés/snack bars	2 969	3 776	4 855	3 434	3 122	5 612	9 462	13 342
Public houses	1 612	2 273	3 094	2 313	2 083	4 016	7 140	9 530
Clubs	2 231	2 147	2 201	1 515	1 437	2 243	3 800	4 405
Catering contractors	756	970	1 225	819	784	1 446	2 479	2 889
GB, all unemployed	523 638	687 219	774 716	551 898	522 720	841 157	1 277 884	1 421 800
Hotel and catering, unemployed	18 765	21 846	26 340	19 411	18 224	32 456	52 866	77 848

(Source: *DEP Gazette*)

*February levels.

TABLE 5.10 **Unemployment rates**

	1970	1971	1972	1973	1974	1975	1976
Hotel and catering unemployment	3.1	3.2	3.6	2.5	2.3	4.0	5.9
National unemployment average	2.6	3.6	3.7	2.6	2.6	4.1	5.7

(Source: *DEP Gazette*)

Generally speaking, the increase in unemployment has been evenly distributed between all the sectors.

There has, for a long time, been a seasonal pattern to the industry's demand for labour reflecting the seasonal patterns of holiday demand (Table 5.11). Thus unemployment falls in the summer months, only to increase in the off-season period of winter. If anything, however, the number of unemployed in the winter months is now higher than it was in the 1960s, but this is probably a reflection of the higher levels of unemployment that exist today, and which increasingly seem to be accepted as a permanent feature of our society. Indeed the increase in unemployment in 1975 was so fast as to almost obliterate the seasonal pattern (although it is marginally discernable because unemployment in the industry declined until June and then really climbed from October, which usually marks the end of the holiday season).

The same seasonal pattern of employment can also be discerned from figures of vacancies unfilled (not given here), where the number of vacancies increases in the summer months but declines in the winter. This pattern of seasonal employment varies from region to region and location to location. As was seen from the hotel occupancy figures, the

TABLE 5.11 **Unemployment in the catering industry on a seasonal basis (excluding school leavers)**

Year	Jan	Feb	Mar	Apr	May	Jun	Jul	Aug	Sep	Oct	Nov	Dec
1973	37	34	32	28	22	19	19	20	20	24	26	24
1974	29	28	27	24	20	18	19	22	23	30	34	n/a
1975	n/a	37	36	35	34	32	37	41	43	55	65	

N.B. n/a indicates *not available*.

(Source: *Monthly Digest of Statistics*)

big London hotels hardly feel it in terms of rooms and beds taken, whereas it is very significant for seaside hotels. This fluctuation in the demand for accommodation, and hence in the hotels' derived demand for labour, has some specific results. It means that the hotel industry is often in a situation of having to cope with peak demand when it has its greatest proportion of unskilled, inexperienced labour. Naturally, not all the labour taken on during the summer months is inexperienced; many in fact have a pattern of summer working and winter rest; but it is traditional for the industry to take on student help and similar inexperienced labour in the summer. This is not without a hidden cost in that mistakes are almost inevitably made, while at the same time the element of casual labour that does not work all the summer period also tends to increase costs of obtaining labour because of repeated advertising, retraining, etc.

In the previous section it was argued that certain categories of jobs were more prone to unemployment than others—and that generally it was the unskilled that were most at risk. Certainly this is true in terms of numbers. Over 7000 kitchen porters and 5000 waiters and waitresses were unemployed in March 1977, and although the number of unfilled vacancies has increased there is simply an insufficient number of jobs available to afford employment to all. This makes it more likely that people will change jobs less frequently, whereas in the past the industry has had a tradition of high labour turnover with workers broadening their experience by working in different establishments. Certainly the situation is extremely difficult for hotel managers where the number of vacancies is usually below 60 with over 600 managers unemployed; competition for jobs is very stiff. However, the absolute figures do not really show whether the hypothesis that the less skilled are in the position of most risk as far as unemployment is concerned. And really it is difficult to say. The increase in unemployment of hotel managers between March of 1976 and 1977 was about 7%, and that of counter hands and assistants 30%. Unemployment amongst publicans rose by 25%, and in the same period by about the same amount for barmaids and barmen. However, as a generalization it can be shown that unemployment has increased more quickly for cooks, waiters, counter hands and kitchen porters than for hotel and catering managers, and catering and housekeeping supervisors. One factor that must play a role in this has been the increase of wage costs and the possibility of switching to labour-saving devices.

Labour Turnover

It has been repeatedly stated that wage costs are increasing, and certainly in 1969 staff costs were about 31% of sales, whereas in 1973 they were 35%. Perhaps today they are an even higher percentage, although government income policies have held them back. Certainly, personnel policies are important for the reason that employees are an asset in which a considerable amount of money is involved—quite apart from any moral reason of why one should be nice to people! Generally speaking, the industry has much to put right in this field. The 1974 Hotels and Catering EDC report *Manpower Policy in the Hotels and Restaurant Industry* concluded that 'personnel policies in the establishments studied were not adequate . . .' and that 'these shortcomings were largely responsible for the difficulty in recruitment and retention

TABLE 5.12 **Length of stay of entrants in different job categories**

	% leaving in quarterly periods of service				% remaining after 1 year
	1	2	3	4	
Kitchen					
Chefs, cooks	38	20	7	11	24
Coldroom, larder	76	8	—	—	16
Porter	75	11	7	1	6
Washers-up—male	60	20	8	2	10
—female	24	24	24	4	24
Service					
Waiter	56	17	9	8	10
Waitress	55	17	12	3	13
Housekeeping					
Housekeepers	27	18	18	—	37
Chambermaids	43	19	13	5	20
Secretaries, book-keeping	29	11	15	6	39
Reception					
Receptionists	41	22	9	—	28
Canteen workers					
Total	47	14	8	2	29
Waitress	—	6	11	6	77

(Source: *NEDO 'Labour Turnover'*, 1969)

of staff referred to in the opening . . . of this report'. Likewise a 1969 NEDO report on the industry found that the high rates of labour turnover created a low morale and tarnished the image of the industry as a whole. In 1973 the Industrial Society published a report on absenteeism which tended to destroy some of the myths that are held to cause absenteeism, and by extension, high degrees of labour turnover. It is known that the hotel and catering industry uses shift work, that people work unsocial hours, and that working conditions in hot kitchens are unpleasant. The Industrial Society found that absenteeism was less, not higher, with shift workers, and stated there was little evidence to support the allegation that poor working conditions made for absenteeism, unless the environment was so bad as to be definitely hazardous. The major factor they found was the quality of managerial and supervisory staff, and in this respect their report confirms the NEDO statements.

The NEDO report on labour turnover in the hotel and catering industry looked at 33 establishments, and used various criteria of turnover. The turnover rate is usually given as the ratio of total number of leavers in a given period with the average number employed by the organization in that period (Table 5.12). Within the 33 work-places, turnover rates varied from 34% to 216% p.a. with an average of 70% p.a. This is both extremely high and extremely expensive. The costs of re-advertising, re-interviewing and retraining at today's costs are unlikely to be less than £20 and could, in a reasonable size organization, well exceed £300. There are also many hidden costs: of revenue lost through inexperienced staff, and of the unsettling effect on other staff. Yet few managers try to cost the consequence of high labour turnover which is seemingly a feature of the industry. Obviously, a hotel or restaurant which is able to keep its staff will avoid these costs, and thus a means of analysing staff patterns is to look at the length of service of those currently employed. The NEDO report showed that in the 33 establishments as a whole, only 17% of the entrants had remained with the one employer for over a year, and only 10.7% for two years or more. Canteens were by far the best at keeping staff since over 51% of those working in canteens had been with the same employer for over a year, compared with 4% for one hotel. A factor that may explain the canteens' success in retaining staff is that the canteen tends to have a regular pattern of work with the same hours as the institution it serves, whereas hotels and restaurants have what has been termed 'unsocial hours' which many people simply do not like. Certainly, the short stay with an employer is characteristic of all types of hotel and catering outlet other than canteens, and hotels are no worse than restaurants or snack bars in this respect. Labour turnover is much higher in the hotel and catering industry than in manufacturing industry. It also differs from manufacturing industry in another respect, namely that its male turnover is faster than its female labour turnover. Thus 58% of the males in a sample of 1260 men left their employer within three months compared with 46% of the women. Men appear to have the greater difficulty in settling down than women, and a common reason given for leaving is customer rudeness and the stress of the job. This may also indicate why canteen staff tend to stay longer, for in serving a regular clientele they have a chance to build up relationships with customers. Also cooks, who are removed from the public in the commercial trade, tend to stay longer at their job than other occupations.

The fact that so few staff stay beyond a year makes it very difficult to build up a stable core of employees who can help newcomers in the period of induction and who can answer most queries quickly. It is perhaps an indictment of selection procedures, low pay (particularly for male workers) and of post-employment help given by management that this is the position; and indeed the hotel and catering EDC found that many managers believed that the industry attracted far too many unsatisfactory employees who were misfits. In addition, the NEDC found too many cases of 'managerial abdication' which meant that management was isolated from its staff. Indeed, a vicious circle would be set up where, as one interviewee put it, 'wages are low in the industry because managers expect the staff to fiddle'. Part of the blame for the turnover rate is laid at the door of the tipping system, especially when tipping forms a significant part of the wage combined with a situation of 'management abdication'. In this case, the chain of authority is both unclear and weak, and the excuse of 'the customer is boss' tends to throw stress on staff who do not have the authority over others to ensure that customer wishes are always fully met, even assuming that they are reasonable. The size of establishment does not affect the rate of turnover, though location does, with the London hotels having the highest turnover rates of over 130% p.a. and seasonal hotels having the lowest turnover rates of, on average, 70% p.a.

A 1973 Department of Employment enquiry yielded the same results as the earlier 1969 survey, and also found that management changed its jobs with a high rate of frequency. Thus, in its survey, 40% of the managers interviewed had held their current jobs for less than one year, although 75% of them had been with their current company for periods of 3–15 years. It could be argued that the common industrial practice of having managers change location within a high degree of frequency unsettles the staff and so contributes to the high labour turnover.

As a consequence it was estimated that labour turnover cost the industry £22 million in 1973.

It would appear that where labour turnover is low a major cause is the ability of management to identify with the labour force and help as best it can in solving the problems that arise. There is some evidence implying that the smaller establishments have a lower turnover than larger ones, but the hotel and catering chains will not necessarily gain from this unless individual hotel and restaurant managers have a high degree of autonomy and are allowed to settle in that particular branch of the national organization.

Nor can the blame be entirely that of management. As has been indicated, many managers feel that the industry attracts 'misfits'. Certainly, it would appear that the industry is a large employer of unqualified and unskilled labour for whom comparative rates of pay between unskilled jobs would be important. Therefore, there will be a tendency for such people to move between employers as in any other industry. Unfortunately, this sector of the workforce also includes many who do not accept the discipline of regular hours. On earning sufficient money for their needs there appears little need to attend work the next day. Consequently, managers will find themselves short-staffed. There is a difficulty in identifying a common interest between management and labour when, for some, the job is simply a means of attaining short-term aims and there is no further commitment beyond self-interest. On the other hand, it can be argued that low self-concept is in part formed, and in part reinforced, by low pay. This whole area of ascertaining directions of casuality between labour turnover, low pay, unsatisfactory management and labour, is a complex one as the studies of the Open University into the low-paid show. Ideally, a situation of economic growth would help in allowing the creation of a high-wage, highly efficient labour force, but this too is a chicken-and-egg argument. At present the situation is far from satisfactory and perhaps an initial onus does rest on management to create congenial work places as a first step.

Levels of Pay

It has been noted that 'tipping' has been accused as being in part, at least, a cause of the high rates of labour turnover, and indeed a heavy dependence on tipping for a reasonable wage does nothing to lessen anxiety and uncertainty amongst staff; although, on the other hand, under favourable circumstances it can be a most remunerative method of income. Certainly, it is an issue which in time becomes quite contentious. But first let us try and establish the context of pay within which tipping is a part. To some extent the industry has a reputation of being a low paid one, and it is true that the Department of Employment's *New Earnings Surveys*, published annually in its *Gazette*, show that adult male workers in the industry are in the lowest 13% for 'all industries and services' average wage levels, and that females are in the lowest 27%. The industry does, however, make several payments 'in kind' such as accommodation and free meals in addition to tips, yet there is evidence to show that even when these are taken into consideration the industry pays less than average for 'all industries'. In 1973 the Hotel and Catering EDC carried out a postal survey of wage levels and

TABLE 5.13 **Fringe benefits and weekly earnings**

	% with accommodation	% with 9 or more free meals per week	Earnings as % of average for all industrial earnings with allowance for meals of £2.50 per week at 1973 prices
Men			
Chef/cook	25	76.7	85.4
Kitchen hand	27	70.5	62.3
Waiter	26	91.1	74.2
Barman	38	73.6	74.5
Women			
Chef/cook	5	28.8	111.7
Washer up	9	35.8	89.2
Waitress	21	56.3	89.8
Room maid	49	75.3	94.1
Barmaid	29	67.0	98.8

(Source: *EDC Postal Survey*, 1973)

found considerable variation as to the incidence of free meals and accommodation (Table 5.13). Thus, while nearly half of the room maids had accommodation supplied, only 5% of female cooks and 25% of male cooks were in the same position. Perversely, while women do not receive anything like the fringe benefits that the men do, they are paid much nearer the average wage than the menfolk.

While these figures are for full-time female employees, it may be possible that with the industry reliant on such a large number of part-time female employees, they have to pay a competitive wage for that part-time labour, and consequently, since full-time labour has to be paid accordingly, the wage levels are correspondingly better (Table 5.14). At the same time, the fact that the industry offers a combination of reasonable, if not high, wages for women with the type of work with so many are familiar which, then it succeeds in attracting female labour with the result that its labour force is predominantly female. It is an interesting observation that a significant proportion of the women in

TABLE 5.14 **Wage levels**

	Total (£)	Overtime (£)	PBR* etc. (£)	Shift etc. (£)	£40	£50	£70	Average weekly hours (including overtime)
Women								
Catering supervisor**	43.0	1.4	0.3	0.5	6.8	47.9	80.8	38.3
Chef/cook	46.4	1.8	0.4	1.4	34.4	71.7	94.3	37.8
All manual occupations	49.4	1.7	4.8	0.9	26.0	57.2	92.5	39.6
Men								
All male manual catering (incl. other services)	66.4	9.2	2.5	2.6	22.8	72.2	91.9	46.2
All manual occupations	80.7	11.6	7.2	2.4	6.4	46.7	82.0	46.0

(Columns under "Average gross weekly earning" are Total, Overtime, PBR* etc., Shift etc.; columns under "% earning under" are £40, £50, £70.)

*Payments by results and incentive payments.
**1977 figures.

(Source: *NES Department of Employment Gazette*, 1978)

the industry come from large families, for in such families the traditional domestic roles of women are reinforced, the skills are learnt, and the hotel and catering industry provides an outlet for the use of these skills as a means of earning a living.

With regard to the number of hours worked, the industry tends to the norm for the 'all-industry' average with a working week of about 46 hours. But, as is well known, the pattern of working is distinctly unconventional, with less than a third in hotels and restaurants working conventional day shifts. About half of the waiters and chefs are on split shifts with a break of over two hours, while room maids start shifts before 7.30 a.m. Receptionists, on the other hand, can be at their desks until the early hours of the morning.

Since the industry is both one that pays below-average wages and demands unsocial hours, it can be argued that additional income is necessary to bring the employees' pay up to average and beyond to compensate for the unconventional hours. But to argue this is not to imply that tipping is a satisfactory method of payment, even while recognizing that many customers like to show their appreciation of personal service. Part of the unsatisfactory nature of tipping as an element of income is that not all establishments use tipping. Larger firms and hotels tend to prefer the levy of a service charge, though practice varies in restaurants. There is also doubt as to whether tips are allowed in addition to the service charge, or are entirely replaced by service charges. It would also seem that there is considerable variation in practice as to how service charges are distributed. *Trends in Catering* reports indicate that a service charge or a tip is only involved in about 2–5% of all occasions when people eat out, and the great majority of such tips come to less than 50p per head. The tip is of importance only for eating in the commercial sector, since the take-away, partly commercial and non-commercial sectors account for an insignificant proportion of the total number of tips. Yet, even within the commercial sector, a tip is left on only about 8–12% of occasions. In 1975 it was reported by the March 1975 *Trends in Catering* that in the commercial sector it was usually about 2.5% of the total bill; and in total, tipping and service charges accounted for about 5% of total expenditure on meals—about £66 million in 1975. With the increasing use of the service charge that is now levied on restaurant meals in the commercial sector at rates significantly above 5%, one is tempted to the conclusion that management is passing part of the wage bill direct to the public while continuing to pay below-average wages. In as much as wages are paid out of revenue and thus out of the consumer's purse, this is only a difference of method rather than principle, but it does make all the more important the question of how the service charge is distributed, particularly to the kitchen staff who do not come in contact with the customer but whose services obviously are important.

6

The Supply of Services in the Hotel and Catering Industry

Theoretical Concepts

In looking at the demand for the services of the hotel and catering industry, various aspects of the supply of those services have been implied. But just as a theoretical concept of demand was found to be useful, so too a summary of economic theory of supply might aid in asking pertinent questions about the industry. In many ways the basic theories of supply and demand share common facets. Thus, when we looked at demand we noted that demand was only measurable in the sense that there was a quantity, price and time element. And so it is with supply. So to write of the supply of services within the industry we mean, when asked to be specific, the supply of a service at a given price within a given time period. From the supplier's viewpoint, he is much more prepared to supply more when the price is high than when the price is low, for the possibility of higher revenue and greater profits when prices are high will induce him to greater effort. So argued the nineteenth-century economists. This means that we can draw a *supply curve* just as we drew a demand curve. But this time, acting on the assumption that higher prices will induce greater supply, we have a situation where the supply curve slopes upward from left to right, as in Fig. 6.1.

A supply curve may be defined as *a series of points joined together, each showing the amount supplied at a given price within a given time period by a particular supplier or group of suppliers, assuming that everything else remains the same.*

Thus, in Fig. 6.1, when the price is OP_1, the supplier supplies OQ_1, but on the price increasing to OP_2, the quantity supplied rises to OQ_2. Of course, since the supply curve is but a series of points joined together representing supply within a given time period, it *need* not have that shape and may even slope in the opposite direction. Indeed,

THE SUPPLY OF SERVICES

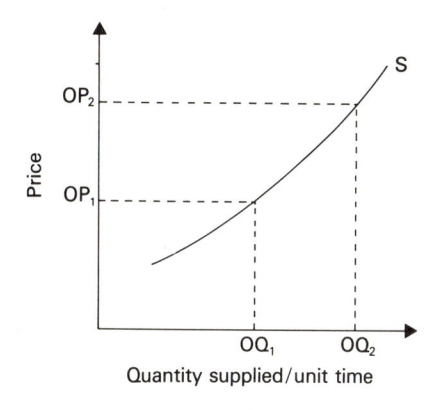

FIG. 6.1 **A supply curve**

we can probably think of some perfectly good reasons to cause such a phenomenon. A firm may anticipate a fall in sales at high prices and its costs of production may increase faster as sales increase (faster indeed than the increase in revenue), and consequently profits would fall even whilst sales increase. In short, the actual supply curve can depend on a number of factors. Incidentally, just as we spoke of a statistical demand curve, so too it is possible to have a statistical supply curve which is a record of actual past supply/price relationships instead of the theoretical supply curve which represents a series of possible alternatives. If you ask which alternative to choose, the classical economist's answer is that you choose the point where profits will be at their greatest. This is an answer to which we must return, for first we must ask ourselves what determines the shape of the supply curve.

Determinants of Supply

Supply can depend on many factors, and it can be argued that it is not necessarily a totally independent variable from demand in that few will supply an item for which there is no demand at any price. On the other hand, it may be contended that it is not until you supply something that you will find out whether or not a demand exists; and, as some cynics have stated, it is not until a supply is established that people find that they have that need. So, while accepting the interdependence of supply and demand, let us first describe the determinants of supply before trying to unravel the forms of interconnection between demand and supply. It is usually stated that the determinants of supply include:

(i) **The price of the item supplied**—As previously noted, the supplier may be tempted to produce more or less depending on whether the price is high or low.

(ii) **The price of other items**—In the case of supply a producer will look at the price of similar goods being charged by others and so estimate how many he can sell of his own product or service.

(iii) **The costs of production**—This is probably an important factor in that costs may react differently to changes in output, and it may not always be profitable to expand output when prices rise if costs rise faster than revenue. Factors influencing costs include:

   (a) **Expectations**—These may be as important as the costs of production in that a firm will have to anticipate demand, the levels of prices and the actions of competitors before starting production, since the period of time between starting and completion dates can be quite long. Every restaurant owner, for example, will have an expectation of demand for a given dish, even whilst he begins ordering a week in advance.

   (b) **Staff relations**—In these days of influential trade unions, when strikes can interrupt supply, good personnel relations are a must. Sometimes even having good relationships with one's own staff does not guarantee supply if you are dependent on parts coming from another manufacturer. Indeed, in manufacturing industry it is now not unknown for firms, when calculating their costs, to make an allowance for interrupted supply due to strikes elsewhere.

   (c) **The state of technology**—Obviously this affects the productivity and output per person; and it affects cost structures. It could also be important to know the flexibility of one's equipment so as to be able to work effectively at low levels of output or be able to produce more than one product. An automatic potato peeler has few alternative uses, and therefore might have represented the tying up of money when potato substitutes were used at the time of high potato prices in 1976.

   (d) **Taxation**—This can also affect the supply of items. In the UK marginal taxation rates tend to be high; that is, an increasing proportion of additional revenue gained is lost as personal income tax. Consequently, in an industry such as hotel and catering where many people work for themselves and are therefore subject to income tax rather than corporation tax, they may simply decide that expansion beyond a given profit level is simply not worthwhile; and so supply is held back. The small hotelier often limits his supply, rather than take bigger risks by expanding, only to pay more tax. Also, reductions in a tax like VAT reduce the price of an item and so might stimulate demand.

The above is not a full and complete list of the factors that can influence supply, but they do illustrate some of the considerations that can apply, and already indicate some of the factors that will have to be looked at when considering the supply of services of the industry.

Changes in Supply

Changes in supply can come about as a response to a change in price, or to other factors without a change in the price of the item supplied. In the first case, it may be a move along the supply curve. Thus in Fig. 6.2(a) the result of the price rising from Oa to Ob is an increase in the quantity supplied, from Oc to Od.

Figure 6.2(b) represents a case where, if the price remains unchanged but more is supplied, we have moved off the original supply curve

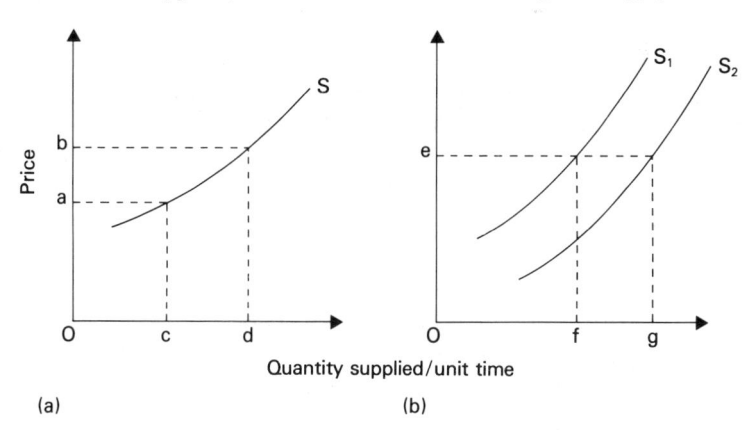

FIG. 6.2 **Changes in supply. (a) A move along the supply curve, (b) an increase in supply**

at the point with price Oe and quantity Of to a new point with price Of and quantity Og: which is on a new supply curve (S_2). So increases in supply are represented by drawing a new supply curve to the right of the original; whereas a fall in supply is shown by a curve to the left of the original. (Why?)

Elasticities of Supply

Just as we read earlier of elasticity of demand, so there is an elasticity of supply, by which we mean the responsiveness of supply to changes in the price of the item supplied. It is not only defined in a similar way to elasticity of demand, but is also measured in a similar way—thus:

$$\frac{\text{Elasticity}}{\text{of supply}} = \frac{\text{Proportionate change in the quantity supplied}}{\text{Proportionate change in the price of the item supplied}}$$

and can be calculated from the formula:

$$E_s = \frac{\Delta Q}{\Delta P} \times \frac{OP}{OQ}$$

The Supply of Accommodation

In as much as it is known that the higher-tariff hotel has the highest occupancy rates, and that most new hotel building has been in the above median tariff range, then it can be said that the supply of hotel accommodation tends to follow a traditional supply curve. However, this is to argue that all hotels are the same, since the classical economist's supply curve is about the supply of one product; and this is obviously not the case with the hotel industry, not to mention the other forms of accommodation that exist.

There are approximately 34 000 hotels, 109 holiday camps, 50 universities and 5400 caravan sites, which together provide about 2.5 million bed-spaces. There is considerable regional variation between the distribution of types of bed-space. In Wales, for example, caravans and holiday camps outnumber hotel bed-space in a ratio of 5:1; in England, it is 2:1. Three areas in England account for nearly 60% of all hotels: namely the South-west, the South-east and the North-west (Table 6.1); in short, the regions that we have previously seen to be the most popular holiday areas. London has a further 5% of the total hotels. However, many of the UK hotels are old (about 75% of them were

THE SUPPLY OF SERVICES

TABLE 6.1 **Number of UK hotels (by region and type of location)**

	\multicolumn{5}{c}{Type of location}
Region	Coastal	Rural	Urban (under 100 000)	Urban (100 000+)	Total
London	—	—	—	1 309	1 309
Other South-east	5 173	526	1 456	214	7 369
South-west	5 275	1 192	1 359	290	8 116
East Anglia	1 020	134	281	96	1 531
Midlands	—	275	753	339	1 367
North-east	924	311	359	398	1 992
North-west	3 843	376	744	290	5 253
England	16 235	2 814	4 952	2 936	26 937
Wales	1 769	665	669	143	3 246
Scotland	1 882	1 241	1 365	588	5 076
Northern Ireland	149	51	69	57	326
Total UK	20 035	4 771	7 055	3 724	35 585

(Source: *Digest of Statistics*, British Tourist Authority, 1975)

built before 1920 and only 8% of our hotel stock is less than 20 years old); only about a third of them are licensed, and the standards of service vary considerably. The great majority of British hotels are small and the 'average' hotel is likely to contain 13 rooms and be at the seaside. Indeed, about 90% of British hotels have fewer than 25 rooms, and 75% have less than ten rooms. Generally in such hotels only one or two rooms will have private bathrooms, and in fact, in unlicensed hotels less than 1% of the bedrooms have private bathrooms. For licensed hotels the comparable figure is 24%. There are again regional differences as to the availability of private bathrooms for, as befits the country's capital, London hotels offer private bathroom facilities with about 50% of their rooms, although the higher-tariff London hotels offer about 95% of the rooms with private bathrooms. On the other hand, Welsh seaside resort hotels come bottom of the list with only about 5% of rooms having this amenity.

The habit of closing for part of the year is still very strong, although the larger the hotel, the less likely it is to close. Thus, only 8% of hotels with over one hundred bedrooms close during the off-peak season, and the great majority of these larger hotels that do close are seaside resort hotels (though some in Cumbria likewise close). On the other hand, 55% of hotels that have less than 25 rooms close for at least some time in the year. Within this size category it is again the seaside hotel that is the most likely to close. Rural hotels are more likely to remain open, although in the off-season the greatest part of their revenue comes from their restaurant business, and indeed, over the whole year, on average, the restaurant side of such hotels provides about a third of total revenue. The period of closure varies, and it is perhaps astonishing to learn that about 70% of all hotels close for at least a month. Small coastal resort hotels, particularly those away from the South-east, are apt to close for considerably longer and make up the greater part of the 16 000 or so hotels that remain closed for about five months of the year.

Because catering covers such a large range (from fish and chips to the Savoy Grill) it is difficult to be sure just how many establishments exist. The last full enquiry into the catering industry by the Government was in 1969, and although there are regular quarterly statistics on the turnover of the catering industry, they are based on the 1969 returns. We can guess that in the meantime there have almost certainly been a number of changes since then. One of the changes has been in the increased range and sophistication of take-aways. There have been an increased number of Chinese take-aways, and there has been a growing American influence with the franchising of shops such as Kentucky Fried Chicken (KFC). There are now 260 KFC shops which are run by 215 franchises, which is a considerable change from the early days of the KFC in Britain when giants such as General Foods were heavily involved with over 100 shops. The KFC 1976 turnover was about £20 million in Britain, a figure which has grown from almost nothing in 1970. Because of the possibility of such comparatively fast changes, changes that are made all the more complex because not all new establishments are in addition to existing ones but may be replacements, estimates vary as to the actual number of outlets. For example, there have been various estimates of the numbers of public houses, ranging from 62 000 to over 70 000. Public houses are an example of an establishment that has been changing, in that, as previously noted, the provision of food has become increasingly important, and so the distinction between pub and restaurant has become blurred. Possibly the best known example of this is the Berni Inn chain. At the same time, in calculating the number of public houses, the statistician is faced with the problem of whether or not to include such items as 'beer cellars' which may be similar to pubs, but differ in the terms of their licence.

Indeed, the whole question of counting the suppliers of food and drink is in part bedevilled by definition. We have aleady noted in Chapter 1 some of the different definitions for a hotel. Similar confusion reigns in other areas. The Wages Councils, for example, feel that their influence applies only to those fish and chip shops that sell most or all of their produce for consumption on the premises, and thus its statistics omit take-away fish and chip shops, although such shops were included in the Department of Trade and Industry's 1969 enquiry. Categorizing various types of restaurant is also difficult, and generally many of the published statistics simply group together restaurants, cafés and snack-bars, regardless of style of service or price range of food.

S. Medlik has defined the catering establishment as one where:

(i) The goods purchased are consumed on the premises.
(ii) The seller determines the size of portions and so the unit of sale is determined not by the purchaser, as in ordinary retailing, but by the vendor.
(iii) The caterer, and not the customer, decides the quality, since a meal is ordered without it being previously seen. The exceptions are cold buffet and self-service sales.
(iv) The caterer is both a producer and a retailer.
(v) The caterer keeps relatively small stocks and has a short cycle of purchase of raw material to final consumption.

In assessing the number of catering establishments that now exist, up-to-date statistics are difficult to obtain because the Census of Distribution no longer covers hotels and restaurants, although it does cover other service industries such as laundries and hairdressing—although hairdressing is probably as susceptible to easy entry and leaving of establishments as catering. Consequently, bearing in mind this ease of entry, and the lack of settled criteria, the figures in Table 6.2 give but a guide to the services provided by the catering industry, and although the turnover figures published quarterly by the Department of Industry in *Business Monitor SDS* are a consistent series of statistics, they are, none the less, based on a 1969 enquiry as to number of catering outlets.

Within the grouped totals in Table 6.2 are about 22 500 unlicensed hotels and 13 000 licensed; and today there are about 200 motels. In addition there are about 26 000 registered clubs.

TABLE 6.2 **Numbers and indices of turnover of catering outlets (1969 = 100)**

Outlets	1974	1976	1978	Estimated 1976 turnover £ million	Estimated number of establishments
Licensed hotels and holiday camps	186	257	365	1 048	35 600
Restaurants, cafés, fish and chip shops	157	199	248	1 239	40 000
Public houses	174	240	288	3 237	62 000
Canteens and catering contractors	143	191	236	292	5 000*
All caterers	170	230	287	5 826	

*Excludes many canteens run by firms doing own catering as statistics are based on the main activity of a business.

(Source: *Department of Trade and Industry*)

Yet, as we know from Chapter 4, we have not exhausted the list of places where prepared food is served for consumption on the premises, for, as we then noted, the place where food was most likely to be eaten outside of the home was at the place of work (Table 6.3). In terms of where food is served, there is some variation due to seasonal factors. Thus, as expected, the proportion of total meals served at educational establishments declines in the third quarter of the year. Conversely, the proportion of the total meals served by the hotel sector in that period increases to 10% from the average of 3% during the remainder of the year. On the whole, however, many establishments, particularly in urban settings, have a consistent pattern of service throughout the year. What the figures do show is just how important the take-away purveyor of food is, with fish and chip shops, and other similar outlets accounting for 12% of the total number of meals served. If American experience is a guide, there may be some growth in this field, but generally speaking it is unlikely to increase its market share to any significant degree.

There are more likely to be changes within the sectors than between market sectors, although the increased range of food styles offered by the take-away sector could make a little advance against the restaurant sector if price differentials are important. It probably remains true

TABLE 6.3 **The seasonal provision of meals—outlet type**

	\multicolumn{4}{c}{Percentage of total meals served}
	\multicolumn{4}{c}{Year's quarters}
Outlets	1	2	3	4
Take-away, stall	16	13	12	12
Club	2	2	1	2
Hotel, motel	3	3	10	3
Hamburger establishment	2	1	1	1
Store restaurant	1	1	2	1
Cafeteria, café, snack bar	12	10	12	9
Steak house	1	1	*	*
Other restaurant	4	4	4	3
Place of work	39	38	42	49
Other	*	2	1	*
Educational establishment	11	17	5	10
Hospital	*	2	*	*
Pub, pub restaurant	7	6	7	5

*Less than 1%.

(Source: *NEDO Trends in Catering*, 1975)

however, that a main determinant of success for the take-away is its location, with perhaps 'bed-sitter' areas representing one of the best locations for the take-away. Finally, in looking at the supply of food, it is perhaps worthwhile emphasizing again the point that the catering industry is in a situation where about half the meals eaten are within the home. It is of course difficult for caterers to penetrate this market, and to make inroads upon it depends in part on the continued themes of providing convenience on the one hand, and 'atmosphere' on the other. However, for those firms that supply caterers with both equipment and prepared food stuffs, the home market is a susceptible area of sales, and it is no coincidence that the main sellers of convenience foods are large in both the home and professional catering fields. The same could be true of many equipment manufacturers.

Industrial and Welfare Catering

If the hotel and catering industry has been regarded as a Cinderella industry, then this is the Cinderella section. There has been an inadequate recognition of the importance of this sector in part due to the working of the Standard Industrial Classification referred to on pages 5–7. Yet this section employs over 340 000 in local authority sector catering of which an important sector is the school meals service, and about 242 000 in industrial catering. The 1978 HCITB survey estimated that 13 000 industrial catering units, 38 000 educational units (both advanced and non-advanced education, public and private education), 3000 residential homes and hostels, were operated by this sector; and these are not the complete figures. Probably well over 8 million people eat at least one meal a day in units served by these catering concerns. It is a sector that is heavily subsidized to produce meals at low cost (or, in some cases, like hospitals, at no cost) to the final consumer and M. Koudra in the *MCIMA Review* of 1974 estimated that £800 million expenditure a year was involved of which £440 million were subsidies in one form or another. However, as he admits, these are only estimates, and it is probable that since then total expenditure and subsidies will have increased, with the subsidy figure having increased the faster. One reason for supposing this is that in the industrial sector, works canteen prices have become increasingly an area of negotiation between management and trades unions. In the periods of wage restraint under successive Conservative and Labour Governments in the period of 1971–78, trades unions realized that one way of increasing the real income of employees was at least to peg the prices of their meals. Simultaneously, the contract caterers have moved away from operating units as principals, i.e. as a body setting their own prices and making their own profits from the provision of catering facilities in a firm. It is now more common for them to aid the client firm in calculating budgets, but they provide the service for a set fee (plus, in many cases, a percentage of the turnover as a motivational factor). Koudra estimated, in 1974, that by 1980 the respective market shares of the 'Industrial and Welfare catering sector' would be: industrial catering, 22%; school meals, 38%; residential homes and meals for the elderly, 13%; hospitals, 14%; and Further and Higher Education, 6%. Until 1979 there was little reason to suppose that these forecasts would be far from the truth, but in 1979 the policy of the Government in reducing public expenditure to reduce the Public Sector Borrowing Requirement to hold back money supply as part of its anti-inflationary policy meant that the educational sector found that past growth was no longer being sustained. By the end of 1979 there was emerging a body of opinion that the school meals service should be reassessed and money saved, either by changing the dietary regulations by which meals of a given protein value need to be served and switching more to the provision of snacks, or (as a last resort) by changing the school hours to a continental pattern so that schools would close at 2.00 p.m. and children be sent home (somewhat hopefully?!) for their midday meal. Opposition to these proposals, particularly the latter, is strong and at the time of writing (September 1979) the position is not yet clear. Considering the amount of past investment in the school meals services, and the hardship that its withdrawal would cause, it is probable that government may decide on changing the regulations controlling types of meals and further increase school meal charges, but the reader must realize this is but a tentative forecast. Certainly, the school meals service has undergone a change in the last decade towards centralization. The provision of already cooked meals to schools has meant that kitchen staff are now often more concerned with warming-up and food service that food preparation, and different authorities have proceeded at differing rates in their investment in microwave ovens, chill-freeze techniques, etc.

Contract catering has also undergone a change. It is generally recognized that the potential for further growth is limited after the rapid growth of the post-war period. The resulting competition has lead to increased standards and increased use of technology and carefully planned kitchen and restaurant design aimed at minimizing the amount of labour required consistent with the desired service. Today, contract catering has lost the image of the kitchen hag with a cigarette butt sticking from the corner of her mouth, ladling out ash-strewn soup, and now at least one major contract caterer has a policy of having a differing nationality's cuisine in its units once a month, with staff dressed in the appropriate national costume. The limited growth potential has also led the caterers to amalgamate and to diversify their activities. The amalgamations will be described in Chapter 7, but among companies' the diversifications have been the setting up of restaurant and kitchen design activities, the selling of 'own label' convenience foods, overseas expansion, the take-away food business, acting as agents in equipping overseas hospitals and similar institutions, cleaning of kitchens, and the provision of relief management for hotels and restaurants. In addition, the major contract caterers are withdrawing from the smaller units and are increasingly concerned solely with units that serve a given minimum number of meals per day. The advantages to a firm in using contract caterers rather than providing their own meals are basically three-fold:

(i) **The gaining of catering expertise**—These companies are not only experts in catering but, particularly in the case of the major companies, are subsidiaries of larger firms involved in the hotel and catering industry and are therefore able to draw upon considerable resources.

(ii) **Cost savings**—Among the resources of these companies is the ability to purchase equipment and food on a large enough scale to earn discounts from suppliers. This reduces the average cost per item and such savings can be passed to the client firms.

(iii) **Competition**—If the client does not feel he has received a satisfactory service, he can approach any one of the number of competitors. Competition can serve to maintain the quality of the service and avoid excessive prices to the advantage of the customer.

7
The Market Structure

Simply to state the number of hotels and catering outlets is not to give a full statement of the supply conditions that exist in the industry. If we remember, the definition of supply is one of a quantity and price relationships within a given time period. So, by looking at the numbers of hotels and restaurants we have, in a sense, looked at only the quantitative aspects of supply. And while there is some evidence as to the numbers of hotels that exist within various tariff ranges, which will be looked at later, this too will present an incomplete picture. What we need to do is look at what the economist calls the *market structure*, for this will influence the supply, and the price at which the service is supplied. We can illustrate this by giving two simple and extreme examples. Let us suppose that all the hotels were owned by one firm. Then we could envisage a situation where the monopolist could have a national tariff structure, but if he was totally deaf to complaints, his uniform standard of service and hotel might not appeal to anyone. At the other extreme we could have a fully competitive situation where tariffs reflected the supply and demand of a particular service, where hotels and caterers were keenly aware of the prices charged by their competitors, and where the public had offered to them a choice of service. In short, the market structures of monopoly and competition have an influence on the nature of supply. Now this is easy to see in our example, but how do we define the terms *monopoly* and *competition*, and what is the effect on prices and service? One way of answering these questions is again to take heed of the economist's approach to see whether this is applicable to the hotel and catering industry, and to see whether the answers (if any) have implications for the industry or its consumers.

The economist offers a number of market structures, which can be outlined as follows.

Perfect Competition

This is a situation where there are a large number of independent buyers and sellers. The competing small firms offer a homogeneous product, and none of them are large enough to dominate the market. Because of this they have to sell their goods and services at the market price, which is determined by the forces of supply and demand. By this, the economist means that there is one price which will equate both supply and demand, known as the *equilibrium price level*. This is illustrated in Fig. 7.1, where OP is the equilibrium price. DD represents the demand for the industry's product, and SS represents the alternative supplies the firms in that industry are prepared to make at each price.

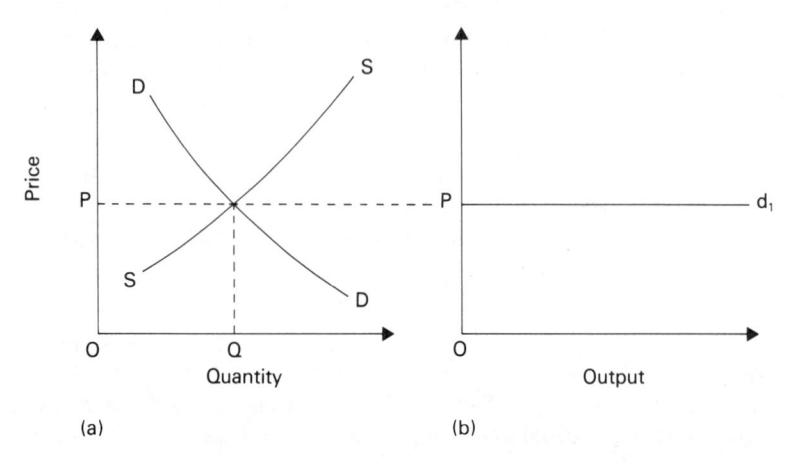

FIG. 7.1 **The equilibrium price level.**
(a) The industry in perfect competition,
(b) the firm in perfect competition.

Only at OP will the supply equal the demand. If the industry supplied more than OQ, then supply would exceed demand, stocks would build up, and the only way of reducing stocks would be for firms to reduce the price to the point where they would be purchased. The price OP prevents such surplus production. If the firms supplied less than OQ then they would find that demand exceeded supply, and the unsatisfied demand would make itself felt by the wealthier bidding up the price to secure the goods. The higher price would attract more supply, and so output would expand to the point OQ. Since it is assumed that no one firm, or purchaser for that matter, can affect the market price for the product or service, the producers must accept the price OP. So, in a sense, d_1 is the demand curve facing the individual firm since he can sell any amount he wants at that price subject to his productive capacity, which is assumed to be small compared with the total industry productive capacity. If the firm sought to sell above that price, no one would purchase it. If it sought to sell below that price it would probably succeed, but at the cost of reduced profits. And how does the firm determine its output? It looks at its cost structure and its likely revenue, and produces at the point where profits are at their maximum.

Allied to the assumptions already made are a number of others not yet mentioned. The above obviously implies a full state of knowledge as to market conditions and costs. Often in the theory of perfect competition it is assumed there is only price competition; that is, no advertising is catered for, transport costs are excluded, the factors of production are in perfect supply, and all firms are seeking to maximize profits. This is obviously an ideal situation, ideal in the sense that it describes an idea as to how demand, supply and the resultant price allocate products and resources—and it is not a practical description of any particular industry. It can be argued by the economist that it is not for a theory to describe, rather to abstract key factors in a situation, so that by manipulating them, he may attempt to explain what does happen. The purpose of theory is to *simplify* the complexity of real life by identifying what are thought to be the key factors, and see how they interact, and what causes what reaction. How then do we know if we have a good theory if theory is not a description of real life? One criterion is whether or not the theory provides a good predictor of behaviour and whether we can quantify these predictions. So if prices increase, the theory of perfect competition will predict an increase in the firm's output by the amount needed to maintain maximum possible profits. At the same time, a useful theory will provide a criterion by which events can be judged. If, in our example, a firm does not reach maximum profits, then we have a measure of its competence or otherwise. The theory certainly points out some answers which we need to know about the hotel and catering industry. While we know that there are literally tens of thousands of hotel and catering outlets, are they necessarily independent? And what are their cost structures? The industry does differ from the concept of perfect competition in a number of ways. As has already been made clear, it is not a homogeneous industry, its parts offer differing degrees of service and standards. And it is an industry that competes, not only in price, but by service and advertising.

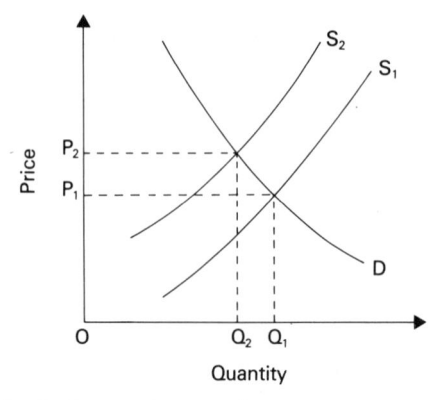

FIG. 7.2 **A change in supply**

Yet, before we leave the theory of perfect competition, it can offer some useful hints. It may be stated that we know prices vary in practice, so if the equilibrium price equates demand and supply, how does any price change? The answer is through a change in either supply or demand. As we know, some products have recently been the subject of diminished supply through poor harvests, such as potatoes in 1976 and coffee in 1977. The result is that the supply curve has shifted to the left, and, as Fig. 7.2 illustrates, the result is an increase in price. The theory of perfect competition is not unique in arguing that prices are determined by demand and supply. It is, for example, possible for a hotel that alone provides accommodation in a beauty spot, to increase prices in the peak period due to an increase in demand (Fig. 7.3). Where

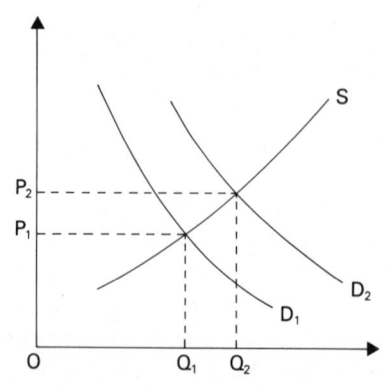

FIG. 7.3 **An increase in price due to an increase in demand**

the theory of perfect competition is unique in its use of demand and supply is in the assumption that there are a large number of independent competing suppliers seeking to maximize profit and a large number of independent consumers who seek to maximize their satisfaction with no one controlling total demand or total supply.

Imperfect Competition

In the theory of *imperfect competition* there is an attempt to control supply by the supplying firms, and indeed they also seek to manipulate demand. Each supplier does this by differentiating its product from that of all other suppliers—a differentiation that may be more apparent than real in that the only difference may be in the way the goods or services are advertised. At the same time, advertising is an attempt to manipulate demand in that the firm hopes to increase the demand for its product and create a brand image which will create a more inelastic demand. In this sense, therefore, each firm has a separate demand curve facing it that slopes downward from left to right. If the price charged is too high, the supplier will lose business to a competitor. Each business can set its own price. In setting up the parameter of the theory, the economist still assumes that there are a large number of independent buyers, and consequently the final price must still take into account the demand for the service. A change in demand will affect a business's revenue, and as the firm, it is assumed, still wishes to maximize profits, the resultant change in revenues combined with the changed costs that occupy a different output level could create a different price.

In as much as the hotel and catering industry does face a large number of independent purchases and that each hotel or restaurant offers some differences from other establishments in terms of service, decor and atmosphere, it would appear that the economist's concept of imperfect competition might be worthwhile considering in greater depth. However, although each firm attempts to create a market of its own, it may be that some are considerably larger than others and so influence an entire industry.

Oligopoly, Duopoly and Monopoly

Oligopoly exists where there are a handful of firms who supply the market, all operating independently, differentiating their products from each other's, and competing by means of service and advertising. In the simplest models it is assumed that there are a large number of independent purchasers. This is a simplifying assumption in that it obviates the need to calculate the effect of large consumer groups on a firm's behaviour, but this is not to say that the economist is blind to such pressure groups. Rather, in order to establish the effectiveness of such groups he must have some idea as to what would happen if they did not exist. It is the not-too-uncommon situation that if you try and gauge the effect of something happening, you can only do so by hypothesizing what might have been the outcome if the scrutinized event did not take place. In more sophisticated models the economist can make use of a computer and analyse possible outcomes by assessing the probability of certain lines of action. In fact this has become a major concern of contemporary business economists who look at the reaction of big firms to other firms and other groups, and they have a series of computer aided theories, some of which betray their origin in such names as the *Monte Carlo Theory*. In the original theories it was again assumed that firms are motivated by the desire to maximize profits, and so output levels would be at the point where the difference between total costs and total revenue is at its greatest. Figure 7.4 illustrates, however, that this is *not* the same thing as saying where total revenue is at its greatest, or indeed where physical sales are at their maximum, for OQ_1 is the output of greatest profit, OQ_2 the point of greatest revenue (and in this example, no profit), and OQ_3 the point of maximum physical volume of sales, achieved by give-away prices!

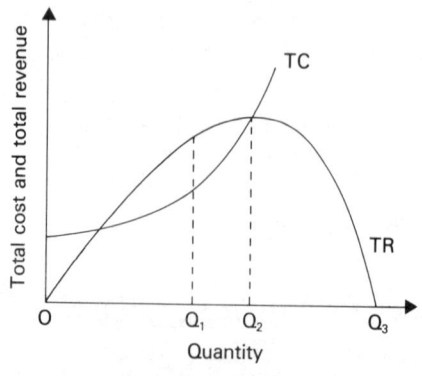

FIG. 7.4 **Alternative outputs**

The sort of service and price structure that exists in an oligopolistic market structure can be different to those of imperfect competition because the firms are generally larger and have more assets, have a greater share of the market, and may be less willing to indulge in price competition, if only because they have more to lose and probably little to gain. This is because the other companies can match their moves comparatively easily, there is little gain in market shares, and a probable loss of profits. We stated earlier in Chapter 1 that the industry was fairly competitive, but on the other hand, particularly in the hotel sector, there are a few companies who, in terms of size, dominate the market. Trusthouse Forte and Grand Metropolitan are two such companies, and thus it may be worth asking if the industry has any other aspects of an oligopoly.

Finally, to complete the categorization we can add: a *duopoly*, where two firms supply the market, and a *monopoly*, where one firm is the industry. Some nationalized industries are monopolies. In practice, though, there are few such examples, and economists when writing of monopoly often use the legal definition, which, under the Fair Trading Act of 1973, describes a monopolist as a firm that supplies 25% of its market. This definition sometimes causes difficulties. For example, suppose there is one hotel at a Cumbrian lakeside. We could say it is a monopoly supplier of hotel accommodation in that area. But is that area its market? Presumably not, as local inhabitants are unlikely to stay at that hotel, and the hotel guests can be drawn from any part of the world. Such guests could of course have stayed in any other region or country, including the next lake due south! So we can argue that hotels are in a competitive situation; but what of a restaurant? The market served by a restaurant consists of the people wanting to eat out who are in that area. If there is no other restaurant, then the existing one has a monopoly. But we can ask: how large is 'an area'? And the answer to that is probably the same as the answer to the question about the length of the proverbial piece of string. In short, while on a national basis a monopoly does not exist, it might do in a smaller geographical basis. And so the economist's theory of monopoly may be of some use. And in that theory the economist again assumes that the basic motivation of the business is to maximize profits. Again then, for profits to be at their maximum, two things must be equal: namely marginal cost, and marginal revenue (Fig. 7.5). To repeat the previous statement: if the producer sells one more unit, and the additional revenue from that sale

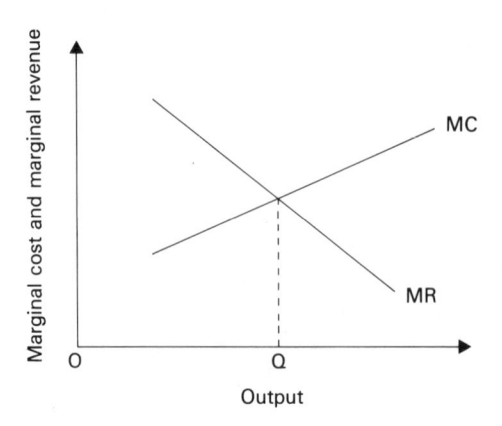

[Figure: graph with vertical axis "Marginal cost and marginal revenue" and horizontal axis "Output"; MC curve rising, MR curve falling, intersecting at point Q on the output axis.]

FIG. 7.5 **Q defines the point of maximum profit, when the marginal cost and marginal revenue are equal**

(i.e. the marginal revenue) is greater than the additional cost of producing that item (i.e. the marginal cost), there is a further addition to total profit, and the monopolist will increase output. If, however, marginal revenue is less than marginal cost, there is a reduction in total profit, and so the supplier will reduce output to the point where total profit ceases to fall. Obviously, where marginal revenue equals marginal cost is a 'tip over' point, from where there is no further addition to profit from increasing sales, to where deductions from total profit begin. At that point, the monopolist will produce.

The Theories and the Hotel and Catering Industry

It can be argued, as far as the hotel sector is concerned, that there is an immediate difficulty in applying the theory in that hotels are not like normal production units as found in manufacturing industry. Once built, their total output is decided by the number of rooms, and empty rooms produce costs in rates, etc., while revenue lost from an empty room is forever gone. The same is also true, to a lesser extent, of restaurants in that, given a layout, the maximum number of customers that can be served is fixed. Yet it can be argued that in manufacturing industry capacity is fixed by available equipment, and one produces at 100% capacity or less. Certainly, in both hotels and restaurant there are variable costs, and consequently, in theory, a pricing policy based on marginal costing can be calculated. The main problem of applying the theories is that certain assumptions of the theories are dubious, and this refers to their application to many forms of business, not simply the hotel and catering industry. Can we assume that hotels and restaurants are out to maximize profits? And anyway, maximize profits in what: the immediate short-term or long-term? Overcharge a customer and you will make a big profit out of him—once! But in due time you may have an empty restaurant. Nor is it always possible to plan a profit-maximizing output level. Costs in particular can change quite quickly, as anyone with knowledge of fresh food prices can testify. In addition, a hotel or restaurant cannot plan its revenue—it does not know how many guests or customers it will have. In short, the carefully drawn cost and revenue curves of the economic theory are difficult to duplicate in practice. And, at the same time, they are supposed to be a theory of the firm but completely ignore the social organism formed by any group of people. Decisions are not just made on the basis of marginal costs and revenue, but also on the basis of compromise and argument between people.

But this is not to say the theories are without worth. The economist's theories of the firm do make some generalizations: that, for example, prices will be higher under monopolistic conditions than under competition where there are no economies of sale; and that increases in demand create higher prices where supply is fixed (and have not London hotel prices increased by about 23% in 1977?). It is also argued that where there is a monopoly supplier, there is a danger that service to the consumer may suffer through complacency. Because of these implications, it is worth seeing how competitive the industry is.

Concentration Curves

One method of measuring competitiveness is by using the concepts of *concentration curves* and *concentration ratio*.

A concentration curve is quite simply a cumulative frequency curve. This means that you take, in the case of hotels, the percentage of the total number of hotels or rooms owned by the largest firm, and add to that the percentages owned by the second, third and fourth largest firms, etc. It is usual practice to draw a diagram with capacity on the vertical axis, and the descending order of firms on the horizontal axis (Fig. 7.6). So, if the largest firm owned 50% of the industry capacity, the coordinates are 50% and 1; and if the second largest firm

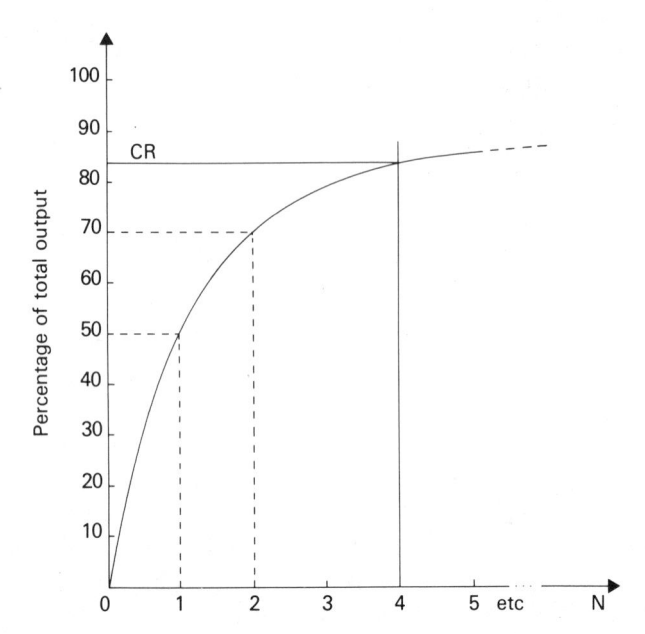

152   AN INTRODUCTION TO HOTEL AND CATERING ECONOMICS

FIG. 7.6 **A concentration curve which could apply to any 'output' in the industry (e.g. capacity, employment, turnover). CR is the value of the concentration ratio and N represents the number of firms in the industry.**

owns 20% of the industry total capacity, the coordinates are 70% (50% + 20%) and 2, etc., until 100% capacity is achieved.

The concentration ratio is the percentage of the total capacity that is owned by a given number of the largest firms: usually three, four or ten. If the concentration ratio is over 66%, then it is said to be high and this is indicative of monopoly. If it is below 33%, then it is low and this tends to mean that the industry is highly competitive. In the hotel industry concentration ratios can be used with different sets of criteria, e.g.:

(i) the percentage of total number of hotels that are owned by a given number of hotel groups;

(ii) the percentage of the total number of rooms available in the industry that are owned by a given number of hotel groups;

(iii) the percentage of the total number of bed-spaces in the industry earned by a given number of hotel groups;

(iv) the percentage of total turnover of the industry for which a given number of companies account.

Other criteria such as labour may also be used. In practice it is usually the first three criteria that are used, but it must be made clear that the use of concentration ratios are not customary in the industry—partly because each of the three criteria used yields a different group of four leading companies. Therefore, in the following section, care must be taken to ascertain which of the criteria are being used.

Hotels

The four largest companies in the hotel sector in terms of the number of hotels owned in 1977 were Trusthouse Forte, with over 180 hotels, and Bass Charrington, Whitbread and Scottish and Newcastle Breweries, each with just over 80 hotels. This gives a total of about 420 hotels, which, compared with an industry total of about 35 500, is a very small percentage. Indeed, the concentration ratio, on the basis of the four largest firms, is 1.1%. Indeed, if the number of hotels owned by the largest 25 operators in the country is taken as a percentage of the total, the result is still a very low concentration ratio, namely 2.4%. In other words, the industry would appear to be very competitive, although we are in a situation where the four largest firms account for nearly half the number of hotels owned by the largest 25 firms in the industry. If we look at the capacity in terms of bed-space, then the figures change, but the position is broadly the same. However, this time there is a change of the four leading companies, which are now Trusthouse Forte (23 000 beds), Grand Metropolitan (12 500 beds), The Rank Organisation (7500–8000 beds) and British Transport (about 6000 beds). The approximate total of the beds owned by these four largest companies is 49 500, and this represents a concentration ratio of 10.3%. Adding the total number of beds of the largest 25 hotel companies yields a figure of about 95 900, which is about 20% of the total. Again we find that the four largest organizations account for about half of the bed-space owned by the largest 25 firms. In other words, we can conclude that from the viewpoint of concentration ratios the industry is a competitive one. However, we are in a situation where there are a comparatively small number of large hotel operators, and these could be seen as the pace-setters. If this is true, they could have an influence that is that much proportionately greater than is their ownership of hotels and bed-space.

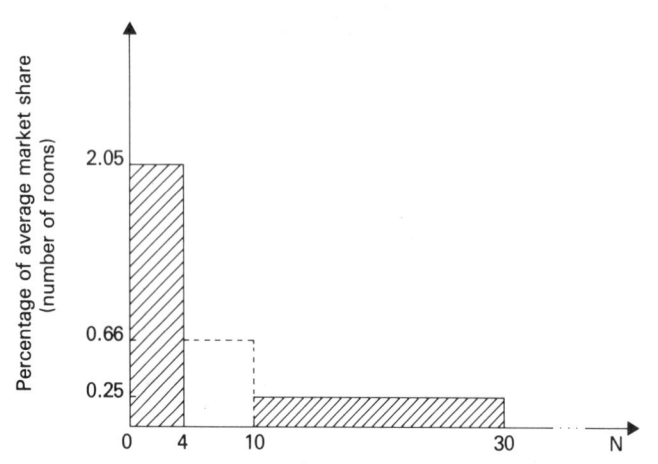

FIG. 7.7 **The relative importance of the four largest hotel companies**

The importance of the largest companies can be seen in Fig 7.7, which is based on the number of rooms of the largest 4, 10 and 30 operators in the hotel industry. The concentration ratios, by the criterion of available rooms, are 8.2%, 12.2% and 17.3%, respectively. This means that the four largest groups* each have, on average, 2.05% of the total number of rooms made available by the industry. The 5th–10th largest hotel groups each have, on average, 0.66% of the industry's total room capacity. This figure is estimated by subtracting the concentration ratio for four firms from that of ten firms (i.e. 12.2% − 8.2% = 4%) and dividing this answer by six. A similar process for the concentration ratio of the thirty largest groups gives us the figure of 0.25% of total market room capability, being owned by the 11th–30th largest firms. This is shown in Fig. 7.7. This shows that whereas the concentration ratio indicates a very competitive industry, in practice the four largest companies are over three times larger than their nearest competitors and over eight times larger than the average size of the 11th–30th company. In this sense they dominate the industry.

A further method of indicating the importance of the largest companies in the industry is to assess the size of their turnover. This is very difficult because companies often present consolidated accounts

---

*By this criterion the four largest companies are Trusthouse Forte, Grand Metropolitan, J. Lyons and Co, and Bass Charrington.

which do not break down the turnover between various activities. However, using information contained in the *EXTEL* cards, which is a listing of company accounts it would appear that the largest four companies account for 48.9% of the turnover of the hotel sector as indicated by Business Monitor SD5 (see Table 7.1). These figures overestimate the importance of the largest firms but may give a more accurate picture of how the large firms in the hotel industry dominate than do the figures for hotel capacity.

TABLE 1.3 **Concentration ratio by turnover**

Group	Hotel turnover (£m)	% of industry total
Trusthouse Forte	190.0	12.7
Grand Metropolitan	90.6 (est.)	6.0
Rank Organisation	34.8	2.3
Centre Hotels	29.8	2.0
Total	345.2	23.0
Industry total (licensed hotels)	1489.0	100.0

(Sources: *EXTEL: Business Monitor,* 1978)

But how then is that influence measured? Do, for example, hoteliers in (say) London, when considering their tariffs, take into account the tariffs that are being charged by the largest groups? Or do they take into account the tariffs of individual hotels, regardless of ownership, but consider rather the star rating and the standard of amenity offered? In as much as it appears that the industry is one of a competitive structure, then the increase in hotel tariffs of about 20% that have taken place in 1979 can be traced to increased demand. If we argue that licensed hotels are a separate category from unlicensed, and certainly the licensed tend to be larger than the unlicensed, then there might be some significance in the fact that the concentration ratio for the four largest operators, in terms of number of hotels, increases to 3.2% and, in terms of bedspaces, to about 8% for licensed hotel capacity. However, these are still extremely low, especially when compared with many manufacturing industries.

For the catering industry it is more difficult to calculate concentration ratios, and with some of the franchises in Wimpys and Kentucky Fried Chicken having been sold in the period since 1972, the concentration ratio would have fallen. One estimate, based on the restaurants owned by Grand Metropolitan, Trusthouse Forte, Associated British Foods and EMI (who, from *Who Owns Whom* 1975, appear to be the largest restaurant operators) is a concentration ratio of under 3%.

Certainly, one is left with the impression that the industry is an extremely competitive one in terms of structure, and certainly, when one bears in mind the high degree of autonomy that managers appear to have, this appearance would seem to be confirmed. The most common unit in both the hotel and restaurant trade is still the proprietor-establishment, and the number of chains who own a substantial number of hotels or restaurants appear to be few. Indeed, so far as the hotel sector is concerned, the number has been reduced since 1970 due to take-over and amalgamations (Table 7.2), a process that still continues with individual hotels being frequently bought and sold as can be gauged from the pages of the *Caterer and Hotel-keeper*.

TABLE 7.2 **Number of acquisitions and mergers in the 'miscellaneous services'* sector of UK**

1973		1974		1975		1976	
No.	£m	No.	£m	No.	£m	No.	£m
133	142.9	53	16.7	21	5.4	32	36.4

*These cover hotel and catering, hairdressing and laundries.

(Source: *Annual Abstract of Statistics*)

In part, a cause of the recent buyings and sellings has been due to factors outside the hotel sector. Many of the leading hoteliers have interests besides hotels, and fluctuating fortunes in these interests have made them look at all their assets, and sometimes a number have been sold to raise cash to meet other problems. For example, J. Lyons and Company Ltd. is a leading hotelier, yet, because of Government price controls on foodstuffs allied with a perhaps overambitious hotel expansion programme, both at home and overseas, at a time of a world trade recession, the company experienced some financial difficulties. The result was that they sold a number of assets, including some overseas hotels and parts of their Strand Hotels group, which often trades under the Albany name, in the period 1975–77. Certainly, the period of 1976 was a very difficult one for a number of hoteliers, with companies such as Mount Charlotte and the Savoy Group making losses, while Norfolk Capital made a 117% increase in profits in the financial year 1976-77. These varying fortunes as to profitability were almost certainly one factor that caused companies to acquire others or their subsidiaries. In addition, increased land and building costs have made acquisition more attractive than building new hotels under certain circumstances. At the same time, many of the larger companies have developed in all manner of directions. For example, some may have started in food, then acquired restaurant and hotel outlets. This in turn has led to property interests, and thus property development companies have been set up or acquired. Likewise, diversification into all sorts of other catering interests will have followed. For example, EMI owns its own hotel and catering interests, The Golden Egg Restaurants Ltd. and The Tennessee Pancake Houses Ltd., as part of a presence in the leisure industry generally. The results of diversification include the diversification of risk, and thus the Rank Organisation which had a poor year in its hotel interests in 1976-77 was none the less able to record a 49% increase in profits, mainly due to success in its office equipment field.

Contract Caterers

In the area of contract catering the sector is dominated by four companies, Gardner Merchant, Sutcliffe, Bateman's, and Midland Catering, who together account for over half of the contracts. Amongst the four, Gardner Merchant are by far the largest, and this company would appear to possess 25% of the total sector business in terms of the number of contracts. As with hotel concentration ratios, so various criteria exist for assessing the market share of the largest contract caterers. One can measure their importance in terms of the number of contracts issued, the number of units involved, their share of total turnover, or the number of people employed. However, unlike hotels, whatever the criteria, the same four companies dominate. One estimate* is that the four major companies account for 60% of all contracts, 50% of employees, 60% of turnover and 61% of units that serve over a hundred meals a day. The largest nine companies account for about 75% of the sector's business. The companies date from the 1930s, when industrial concerns like Ford and Fairey Aviation opened their works' canteens and employed outside caterers, but the main growth occurred in the post-war period. By the late

---

*By M. Koudra in an article *Catering Contractors* in *HCIMA Review*, Spring 1975.

1950s and early 1960s most large companies had set up their canteens and the potential of growth, while still present, had undergone a change. No longer could the mere provision of a service be sufficient. Expectations were greater, and as market penetration increased so competition intensified. The result was an increasing professional service, for which it became necessary to have access to additional resources. At the same time, the past growth of these companies made them attractive to the major hotel and catering companies who saw contract catering as a means of diversifying into an allied activity. Thus, the 1960s saw Trusthouse Forte acquire Peter Merchant Ltd. in 1962 and John Gardner Catering in 1964 to form Gardner Merchant Caterers in 1965, to which was added, in 1970, Trusthouse Forte's own hospital and schools division.

On the other hand, Grand Metropolitan purchased Midland Counties and Bateman's, but have decided to keep them fairly independent. By the same token, Trusthouse Forte have kept Ring and Brymer Ltd. reasonably independent from Gardner Merchant. The reasons for this are possibly two-fold. The first is that the companies' activities still portray their original regional basis. Bateman's are at their strongest in the Southeast, Midland Catering in the Midlands, while Sutcliffe's have over 50% of the market in the South-west. The second reason is the area of business in which the contract caterer operates. The large contractors are primarily concerned with industrial catering, Ring and Brymer provide catering at race-courses and private functions, while the numerous small caterers live primarily by catering for private functions such as weddings. The major companies find the one-off special affair by and large uneconomic and hence there will, in the foreseeable future, remain a part of the market which family firms can still serve. Koudra (see footnote on page 157) argues that there is a tendency for the major companies to opt for catering for small units, but against this one can argue the possibility of minimizing delivery charges by making bulk deliveries and using modern equipment to minimize the workforce. The use of vending equipment to meet demand outside normal times has also meant a continuing reassessment of the position, and at least one of the major companies is happy to provide facilities for units involving less than 60 dinners at competitive prices.

Brewing

Another sector of the industry that has seen considerable change is the

THE MARKET STRUCTURE

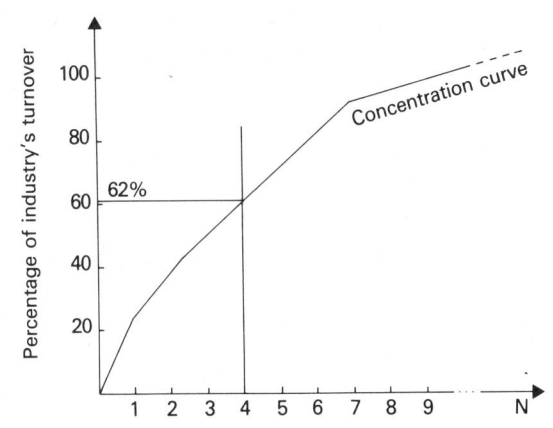

FIG. 7.8 **Concentration curve for brewers, 1978 (N being the total number)**

brewing industry, and here concentration ratios have increased rapidly in the last decade or so (Fig. 7.8). In terms of volume of beer sales, it has been estimated* that the largest four companies account for 62% of market, with the leaders being Bass Charrington (20%), Allied Breweries (16%), Watney-Truman (14%) and Whitbread (12%). Three other companies, Scottish and Newcastle, Courage, and Guinness, account for a further 28% of the market, leaving a multitude of companies sharing the remaining 10% of the market. However, as previously mentioned, (page 77) these companies include the CAMRA-backed brewers and their market share has been a growing one. The growth of these large companies needs to be placed in the context that about 30 years ago (i.e. in the early 1950s) there were no national brewery chains. That the current situation has arisen is due to keg beer—simplistic this may be, but it contains the grain of the situation. Traditional beers continue to ferment in the cask, whereas keg beer is chilled, filtered and pasteurized in the brewery, a process which stops the fermentation. Consequently, keg beer can be kept longer than traditional beer, and more importantly, it is easily transported, whereas fermenting beer is not. Upon reaching its destination, the 'frothy head' of keg beer is induced by carbon dioxide used in the pumping process. Although today's CAMRA supporters bemoan the introduction of keg beer, in the late 1950s and early 1960s

*By Jordan Surveys in *The British Brewing Industry* (London: Jordan's 1978).

keg beer seemed a good idea. Not all of the traditional beers were good beers because publicans did not keep them properly. There were some good pints, but there were some cloudy, badly kept ones as well. Keg beer did mean a consistent (and often acceptable) alternative. Further, the introduction of keg beer opened prospects of expansion, a factor in sympathy with the expansive atmosphere of the 1960s. As Roger Protz* pointed out, there was an alternative policy to the introduction of keg beers, and that was the training of staff and concentrating on improving the quality of the beers that were brewed. However, in the balance sheets training does not appear as an asset, whereas new brewing equipment does. The decision to introduce keg beers had two implications: a need for capital investment and, as a result, the need for a bigger market. The finance for the necessary investment came from the issue of shares and persuading shareholders to invest. Higher rates of return on investment were to come from increased sales, and increased sales were to result from owning more public houses. The transportability of keg meant that the previous problems of conveying fermenting beers over long distances was averted.

It was Watneys that set the barrel rolling (sorry!) when in 1958 Watney Combe Reid merged with Mann Crossman and Paulin and, having fought off an attempted take-over bid in 1959 by Sir Charles Clore, took over other breweries with the twin purposes of being able to support the investment in keg and making themselves too big for being the subject of other take-over bids.

At the same time, lager was introduced to begin the growth recorded in Chapter 4. Carling Black Label was introduced by Eddie Taylor, a Canadian who in 1960 purchased twelve breweries in the North of England and Scotland. Three years later he merged with Charringtons, and in 1967 Bass Charrington was formed. They are now Europe's largest brewer and have moved into mainland Europe by taking over some Belgium breweries. In due course, all the major brewing groups were formed through amalgamation and takeover in the 1960s, and subsequently, some themselves have been taken over. Watney Mann was eventually taken over by Grand Metropolitan Hotels and Courage's by the Imperial Group, who also own John Smith's, the Taunton Cider Company, and Bampton Brewery.

As the brewers grew in size and acquired public houses, so they rationalized the breweries and pubs and reduced the number of beers on

---

*See *Pulling a Fast One* (London: Pluto Press, 1978).

offer. Double Diamond, Worthington E and Red Barrel were heavily promoted. In addition, to exercise closer control, the companies preferred putting in a manager rather than have a tenant licensee, and in this way they also gained the retail profit from the pubs. The profits were ploughed back into the pubs with the ushering in of the era of soft lighting and seating and (as part of a deliberate policy of widening the appeal of the pubs to a younger group of people) juke boxes and, subsequently, fruit machines. This was a market growing in numbers and income.

The very success of the brewers, however, caused a consumer revolt. The Campaign for Real Ale was started in 1971 and quickly showed that it had real popular support as membership grew to 20 000 with many more sympathetic to its aims. Partly because of the success of CAMRA's agitation, some of the brewers have responded to the demand for 'real' ales. Watney Mann, the leaders of the keg revolution, have now centralized their operations and introduced twelve 'real' ales, Whitbread's have resurrected Fremlin's with a 'real' ale called Tusha; and Allied Breweries have been selling 'real' beers from their subsidiaries Ansell's, Tetley Walker and Joshua Tetley. However, the 'real' ale market is estimated at £600 million a year and whilst growing, this is (sorry once again!) small beer compared with the £3400 million on 'unreal' beer. The attraction of 'real' ale to the major breweries is not solely the taste of bitter. The movement to centralization has also gone sour. The Price Commission has shown that although the companies have been able to buy their raw products more cheaply, the savings so gained are taken up in increased production, administrative, distribution and advertising costs. And, the position continued to get worse. Inflation has increased building costs of giant breweries, and the cost of transport in the post-oil embargo age has increased far beyond what was envisaged when the breweries laid their plans in the early 1960s. As a result, there is now economic sense in having smaller breweries supplying pubs in their immediate vicinity and, as some companies have discovered, real economic savings in using horses for short-journey deliveries. Faced with a poor record on both prices and profitability in recent years, the large brewers are keen to explore any avenue. The brewers with the lowest prices and the biggest profit margins are the smaller ones. The Manchester brewers Joseph Holt and Oldham Brewery achieved, in 1978, profit margins of 29.7% and 19.6% respectively, which is better than the 9.99% of Bass Charrington, the most successful of the large brewers. Courage achieved a profit margin of 6.2% and has not significantly increased profits since its takeover by the Imperial Group. Indeed, in 1976 and 1977 Courage sold 150 pubs because they were not meeting target rates of return on investment.

The response of the major brewers to declining profits has been to adopt differing strategies. Some of the brewers have decentralized and revived smaller breweries. Some, however, are putting their trust in greater size still. Greenhall Whitely, the biggest of the brewers outside of the majors, took over Shipstone's in 1978, Courage in 1979, and completed a £60 million new brewery near Reading. Nearly all the major brewers have accepted that the demand for beer has not grown, as expected, but all are still promoting lager. Lager is the fastest growing drink, and in 1977, £20 million was spent advertising it. The success of the advertising has made possible the charging of a comparatively high price, though duty on it is lower than on beers. Another strategy has been to sell and close pubs that do not reach target quotas. In these ways the brewers hope to maintain future profitability.

Fast-Food Catering

At present one sector of the catering industry that is attracting considerable attention is the growth of *fast-food catering*. This has been defined as *the preparation and service of a limited range of dishes produced to a predetermined standard for consumption on and off the premises in such a way that the process and presentation become an integral part of a marketing concept.* * The recent stir in the British fast-food market was initiated by the arrival of McDonald's in 1978 with its massive advertising campaign of £3 million in the London area, and the comparative success of McDonald's has led to the adoption of similar methods by UK companies such as Wimpy, Tesco and Bejam, and the later arrival of other American companies such as Wendy's, Pizzahut and Burger King. The reasons for the growth of fast food are broadly categorized into two groups. The first, socio-economic, explains the acceptance of fast food, and the second, the commercial, explains the provision of this style of catering.

The first factor has been demographic. Until 1983 the teenage group will continue to grow in numbers and as a proportion of the total population. Other industries have been quick to exploit this market group as, unburdened by mortgages, children and the other concerns of

---

*Harry Guest quoted in *The Catering Times,* page 9, 8 Sept., 1978.

adult life, it has a high disposable income. It is thought that the informal, bright surroundings and the speed of service will appeal to this generation which has already become used to convenience foods. With an increase in the number of working women in the UK, who now form nearly 40% of the total labour force, and of whom over half are mothers, a consequence has been a growth in the domestic demand for convenience foods as mothers arrive home from work and prepare a meal for the family or as children arrive home from school and want something simple to prepare for themselves.

The acceptance of such products by women also means that the appeal of fast-food outlets is not confined to the teenage market. It can also appeal to the busy housewife who is out shopping, particularly where that shopping is under one roof in a hypermarket or shopping centre in the country or just out of town. It is this factor that has interested Tesco, who, by the end of 1979, had 25 Bake 'n' Bite outlets serving hamburgers, chicken, chips and a range of bakery items. Nor must one discount the considerable advertising which has not only aided acceptance of fast foods but has made the public aware of the basic concepts of consistency and quick service, and, some sociologists would argue, has helped create a demand for immediate gratification. In passing we may note that fast food has so far made little progress in some European countries such as France, where, it is argued, there is a strong culinary tradition and public taste rejects the 'bland' products of the fast-food retailers. None the less, fast foods are now making an appearance and are achieving some success in shopping centres. Another factor that may have helped establish the fast-food retailers has been their price competitiveness. From 1974 to 1978 the increase in the price of foods eaten out was 84%, while purchased food for consumption at home rose by 94% in the same period according to the retail price index on a group of 10 food items.

The second factor explaining the increased interest in fast foods is commercial. Caterers have seen rapid rises in rents and wage costs in the past decade. In the late 1960s it was possible to get a reasonable site for £200–£300 annual rent plus £150 rates, so that, given a weekly gross take of £90–£100, the caterer could make some 40% gross profit. This is no longer possible. First-floor London rentals are about £12 000 for a 1000 square feet premises, whilst ground-floor rentals are twice as high for smaller premises near main shopping streets. Nor are high rentals restricted to London. In addition, caught by rapid inflation with a static rent income in the period 1974–79, property owners are increasingly turning to a rent system which is expressed, not as a flat sum, but as a percentage of turnover. Labour costs have likewise increased, partly due to Wages Councils directives and partly due to the need to compete for labour on the open labour market. With labour costs rising 15–20% in 1978 and such costs representing as much as 40% of total costs in a traditional restaurant business, the need to use labour effectively becomes that much more pressing. To many catering operations the answer is to increase turnover through an increase in volume, which in turn necessitates larger premises. Although rentals have increased, a successful promotion can increase turnover to a position where, as in the case of McDonald's London operations, the property costs may be held at 4% of turnover. By the late 1970s the major fast-food operators were seeking sites of 4000–5000 square feet on main shopping areas. In their search they were aided by the fact that many national retailing organizations were moving away from such sites. The average size of supermarket in the mid-1960s was about this size, and the supermarket chains such as Tesco and Sainsbury were finding, by 1980, that 50 000 square feet was a desirable size. Likewise, chain stores such as Halfords, Mothercare, Curry, and W. H. Smith were wanting to move away from premises of 5000 square feet where expansion was impossible to shops of twice the size. Accordingly, where traditional shopping areas had not been replaced by new shopping centres, the fast-food concerns could find suitable premises, assuming the maintenance of high pedestrian flow by their sites. Nearly three-quarters of the sites operated by McDonald's in the London area were previously in non-catering use. The large operators are also concerned that wherever possible they purchase such sites complete with freehold, or, at the worst, with long leaseholds (at least 25 years) so as to avoid the problem of increased rentals, even though the initial purchase costs are considerably higher.

A more recent factor explaining the interest in fast food in the UK has been the slowing down of growth in the American market. Throughout most of the 1970s there appeared no sign of saturation of the US fast-food market. While the Hamburger was king in that McDonald's had over 4800 outlets and, Burger King over 2000 units, there were a number of varieties on a theme. Kentucky Fried Chicken has over 6000 outlets based on the colonel's speciality, while Pepsico had Pizza Hut with over 3000 units. None the less, the ingenuity of the American salesman and the public liking for a hamburger were such that in the

THE MARKET STRUCTURE

mid-1970s success based on a hamburger was possible. Wendy's had just over 100 units in 1974, and by 1978 they had over 900 serving hamburgers with a variety of salads and sauces so that every customer had an individual hamburger made to his own specification. Success bred an imitation in the expansion of Judy's. With a highly mobile society that is used to eating outside of the home to a greater degree than the British population, fast foods was a growth industry in the USA. But by 1979 the first signs of a possible saturation of the American market began to be evident, for although the market was still growing, the rate of growth slowed dramatically. As a signal of this, McDonald's 12% sales growth in 1978 was primarily due to increasing prices and new retail units rather than an increased volume of business in existing units. To revive sales, McDonald's cut the prices of its smaller hamburgers by 10%, though it should be noted that these account for only 15% of its total trade.

Whilst McDonald's was beginning to cope with an unexpected lower rate of growth, other companies with sites in less favoured locations have been taking drastic action. The Ralston Purina subsidiary, Jack in the Box considered selling 270 units in the northern states where turnover was slow, and the Pepsico fast-food chains of Pizza Hut and Taco Bell faced a sharp fall in profits. The reasons for the slower growth was a resistance to higher prices in a period of a rapid increase in the American inflation rate. Beef prices rose by 30% in the USA in 1978, and the minimum wage levels were also increased. The oil crisis in the early part of 1979 tended to reduce some motoring, which influenced the trade of units by motorways. Increasingly, success in the American market will be harder to find, and there will be a renewed emphasis on choosing sites carefully, presentation, competitive pricing, cost control and marketing. The sixth largest American hotel company, Howard Johnson (with 1000 restaurants and 550 motels) was subject to a £208 million take-over by the British Imperial Group. Hojos had been faced with a fall in profits to £12 million in 1978 partly, it is argued, because of an ill-coordinated marketing strategy which the Imperial Group (with its Golden Wonder snacks, Ross Foods, Young's Seafood, J. Player, W. D. & H. O. Wills, and Courage brewing interests) might be in a position to correct.

For many American fast-food companies the hope is that sagging profits can be revived by a move into the European market which is still relatively open. This has been attempted in the past by companies such as Pronto, Dunkin Donuts, and Gingham Kitchens; all of whom have failed. However, the new invasion of American Companies shows every sign of being a more carefully conceived campaign. Firstly, McDonald's and Burger King have placed their sites in London and the South-east. With a population of 8 million in the Greater London Area, and about 30% of the UK population living in the South-east, this policy means there is a wide market to draw upon, and, arguably, it is, at least in London, one that is more prepared to experiment. In addition, it is a market swelled by foreign tourists in the tourist season, of whom Americans are a large part, and consequently business could be expected from them. Further, it is a market that can sustain the long hours that the retail units are open; for example, some of the London units are open until 2 a.m. The longer opening hours mean a more intensive use of the equipment, more turnover, and a higher rate of return on investment. In a business where a change of decor may be considered necessary every three or four years to stimulate interest, the depreciation charges are not substantially greater for having longer hours of operation. And, as has been previously noted, attention has been paid to the size, location and rentals of premises. All of this has been complemented by an advertising effort concentrated on the London area. None the less, the American giants have not been without difficulties. Burger King's site in Coventry Street, London, between Piccadilly Circus and Leicester Square, was redesigned in the light of operating experience and advertising was increased. McDonald's off-centre units in Catford and Lewisham were slow to take off until the city centre units were established and the TV advertising campaign was under way. Hence the view of many British operators that American firms will find very different conditions in the provinces which may force them towards smaller units and possibly lower profits. A more recent American arrival is Pizza Hut which is also concentrating on the South-east of the country. Pizza Hut arrived in the UK in 1978 and by the end of 1979 had 14 units in London and three franchised units outside of the city centre. The company plans to have 30–40 units by 1983.

In 1979 a new company was announced, owned equally by Berni Inns and Wendy's International Inc. This £1 million company, known as Wendy Restaurants (UK) Ltd., trades under the name of Wendy Old-Fashioned Hamburger Restaurants and is a joint venture between the British and American companies. For the American company

THE MARKET STRUCTURE

this is part of their European expansion programme for they have a franchising agreement with another American firm J. C. Penney, a merchandising retailer, to sell in Belgium, Luxembourg, Holland and France. Again, the operators have started with a London market with at least 10 units by the end of 1980, with a possible expansion to 20 units by the spring of 1981. Unlike some of the other organizations, Wendy's operates with smaller restaurants of about 2500 square feet, seating approximately 120. For Berni Inns, already a specialist in limited menu catering with their Berni Inns and Schooner Inns based on the steak, it means a third direction of expansion (the second being the Levy and Franks pubs). It means also for them the gaining of American fast-food techniques, experience and knowledge (the managers are trained in Columbus, Ohio), while the American company gains the experience and marketing knowledge of the British market from the British partner. Another Anglo–American venture, but on a different basis, is the Huckleberry fast-food units owned by Chef and Brewer, the first of which opened in October 1979 opposite Turnpike Lane Underground Station in North London. This, too, is based on the hamburger—but in a seeded bun that comes in five ranges with a variety of pickles, etc. In addition, though, Huckleberry's will offer fried chicken, fish, French fries, and apple pie. The restaurant seats 95 and has a restaurant space of 1115 square feet, but a total space of over 2600 square feet. The Huckleberry chain also indicates the complicated company structure that is adopted in the industry for an assortment of management—and tax reasons. Huckleberry is a new company, totally owned by Chef and Brewer, which is a subsidiary of Grand Metropolitan, while the concept is that promoted by Burger Queen Enterprises Incorporated of Kentucky and the franchise was granted by a Canadian company, A. B. Burger Queen of Edmonton! Likewise, United Biscuits, through its subsidiary D. S. Crawford, has a similar arrangement with Denny's Incorporated to operate restaurants based on the American Denny's Restaurants and Winchell Donut Houses.

Thus, British response to the American invasion has not simply been to enter into partnership. It has been to copy American methods and to utilize knowledge of the British market and their own standing in that market to expand fast-food retailing in areas outside the London area. One of the most publicized responses to beat the American companies at their own game was the decision of United Biscuits to redesign their

Notting Hill Gate, London, branch of Wimpy. This 128-seater restaurant closely follows American practice with a move away from table service to counter service, disposable utensils, and payment at the time of ordering the meal. The initial cost of the Notting Hill operation was £400 000 plus an advertising campaign of approximately £500 000. This design is to be repeated at other large Wimpy outlets owned by United Biscuits. A similar move had also been taken by the former Wimpy franchise holder, Da Costas, in the London area, although that company argued that a major motivation was the taking of the money at the time of placing the order as in certain areas there appeared to be a higher than average temptation for customers to try and walk away without payment! For United Biscuits the move towards a new form of fast foods is not only a means of reviving interest in Wimpy's, but also a policy consistent with an expansionist viewpoint. After the 1976 purchase of the Lyons interest in Wimpy's, the company gave grants of 20% and loans of up to a further 35% to Wimpy franchise holders to update and improve their outlets. Nor are their fast-food operations limited to hamburgers. In 1978 they acquired the Pizzaland chain, having previously purchased a firm of frozen pizza manufacturers, King Harry Foods, in 1977. United Biscuits, through their subsidiary Crawfords, have also been prepared to operate fast-food outlets outside of the London area, namely the Beefeater restaurants in Edinburgh and Glasgow. The company's expansionist policy was further shown by its October 1979 take-over of Da Costa's Empire International Restaurants, which not only has Wimpy's but other hamburger interests such as its Chuck Wagon restaurants and West End restaurants. At the time of the take-over, Wimpy's stated that their main interests were the 23 Wimpy outlets the company owned, a statement which implies possible future up-grading of Wimpy's by United Biscuits, who may find that franchisees cannot undertake the investment capital required to compete with the American firms. United Biscuits is not the only UK company being drawn to fast-food outlets. Tesco, likewise, have entered the restaurant business, based upon their stores and hypermarkets. Bake 'n' Bite also serves hamburgers, but the menu is extended by chicken and baking items which are freshly prepared by the bakery department that is already operating in the hypermarket. By the beginning of 1980, 25 such outlets were operating, some of which were operating from former supermarket sites, namely those of about 5000 square feet which are too small for today's retailing needs, and which are near to other Tesco outlets to gain the bakery items. Another company, Bejam, which was originally a frozen food company, is likewise using its access to food supplies to advantage in its fast-food operations, and by 1980 it had nine units operating. Both Trusthouse Forte and Granada are also changing some of their motorway restaurants to a fast-food operation based on their experience of motorway travellers needs; operations such as Little Chef are learning from past errors. Thus, Trusthouse Forte has its Julie's Pantry outlets, and Granada its Burger Express. Research has shown that 48% of motorway travellers are travelling in pairs, and some 30–35% are travelling singly. Consequently, a traditional restaurant design with tables for four will, outside peak moments, lead to much wasted room as most of the tables will simply be used by one or two people, and facts such as these have been taken into account. British and American companies are very aware of the importance of layout and decor in this form of catering operation as in any other. Since fast-food styles have a higher proportion of C1 and C2 customers than many other restaurant types, there tends to be a predominance of bright, primary colours which such customers find appealing, Where, however, an outlet is appealing to a higher socioeconomic class, tertiary colours such as browns and creams are used. Thus, one can compare the bright reds of a Wimpy with the warmer, subdued reds of a self-service operation at the Guildford Army and Navy department store. The counter-service operation also places an onus on the visual appearance of food, and this is perhaps the more so in the supplementary parts of the menu offered, e.g. desserts.

By the beginning of 1980 the whole of the fast-food industry in the UK was in transition as companies broke with previous practice. For example, the previous success of Kentucky Fried Chicken was based on small units selling chicken as a take-away food item. By 1980 Kentucky Fried Chicken had moved into the sit-down outlet business, a move the company had tentatively taken two years earlier. However, by 1980, the seated areas had become a more dominant sector of its newer and updated premises and over 75% of future Kentucky Fried Chicken units will have seated areas. In addition, Kentucky Fried Chicken was also experimenting with a different menu range including, perhaps inevitably, the ever-present hamburger. The arrival of McDonald's and the accompanying publicity have acted as a catalyst as companies examine again their techniques. However, it would not be fair to lay the blame or praise for the counter-service, disposable utensils and hamburger menu at the door of McDonald's alone. Even before their arrival, the increasing costs, earlier listed, had forced the large organizations to a reassessment, and certainly several were looking at American methods, and undoubtedly would have adopted them. In addition, as one popular television series stated, 'we have the technology'. Six-feet-long griddles are used in the Grand Metropolitan Burger Queen outlets, as are pressure frying machines. High-speed griddles will cook 36 quarter-pound hamburger steaks to a guaranteed uniformity in five minutes. With the cooking process visible to the public, hygiene and appearance are as important to the caterer as speed. Chip frying is moving away from shallow chip pans, which present a large surface area which allows the oil to get cooler, to deeper friers. As with every part of the industry, a rapid pace of change is in the air as the challenge of increasing costs is being met.

Franchising

Many of the fast-food caterers are also in the business of franchise catering. A franchise is a system whereby a franchisor grants the right to a franchisee to sell a product under a national brand name and in a particular way, in return for which the franchisee pays for the right. Often, the relationship is a closer one than this because the franchisor is usually intimately concerned with the choice of site and design of the retail unit, and is the provider of the equipment and raw materials. For example, a Kentucky Fried Chicken franchisee will have to find the money for the premises, and purchase the equipment from Kentucky Fried Chicken and buy his chickens from Kentucky Fried Chicken. In some cases, larger Kentucky Fried Chicken franchisees may buy their chickens from alternative sources, but they have to adhere to Kentucky Fried Chicken specifications. In return, Kentucky Fried Chicken will help plan the operation. The advantages for the franchisee are primarily marketing ones. From the moment he begins operations, he is selling a well-known brand name item that is often supported by a national advertising campaign that, as an individual, he could never hope to finance. He can also draw upon considerable experience and technical skills. In return, the franchisor gains additional revenue, extends national coverage of the market and has the benefit of strongly motivated people furthering the appeal of its products. It is also a system of responsibilities. The franchisor will not want the quality of its product prejudiced by a poor franchisee and, consequently, will maintain a check upon the standards of service. He also has a responsibility to his other franchisees to do this, as the appeal of the product rests on his popularity and everyone gains from the maintenance of standards. Likewise, he must give support, but just as the franchisee expects the profits from his hard work, so the franchisor will not expect to absorb the losses if a particular outlet is not successful. There are many instances where franchisors have entered joint schemes with franchisees in order to promote a new variation on a theme or to market in a geographical area not previously covered. For example, the 1979 Wimpy's venture in Manchester is similar to the Notting Hill Gate operation in London with its counter-service system, and involved almost as high an expenditure with an investment of £300 000. However, in this case, the operation is funded jointly by United Biscuits and National Milk Bars, with the former providing 55% of the capital and the latter 45%. In due course, National Milk Bars expect to purchase United Biscuits' share to establish the more traditional franchisee/franchisor system. Not that franchise licences need be so expensive in every case. Many Kentucky Fried Chicken take-away units were started with approximately £20 000. The more usual sit-down Wimpy normally requires, at 1979 prices, £25 000 to set up and £6 000 to equip in order to attain a turnover of about £70 000 a year. The franchise catering business covers not only hamburgers but also ice-creams (Dayvilles), sea-foods (Seafarer) and chickens (Kentucky Fried Chicken). A list of the major franchise chains is shown below in Table 7.3.

TABLE 7.3 **Main franchise chains**

Name of chain	Operator	1978 Number of units	Of which franchised
Wimpy	United Biscuits	2	610
Kentucky Fried Chicken	KFC (GB)	45	200
Little Chef	Trusthouse Forte	167	17
Golden Egg	United Biscuits	—	100
Dayvilles	City Hotels	12	70
Kardomah	Trusthouse Forte	22	17
Seafarer	Associated Fisheries	—	22
Pizza Hut	Pizzahut	12	3*
Bake 'n' Take	Bake 'n' Take franchises	—	30

*1979 figure from *Catering Times*, 27 September 1979.

(Source: *Fast Food*, November 1978)

Summary

The list of leading hoteliers, breweries and caterers contains some very large companies with many business interests and others that are primarily hoteliers or brewers and little else. For example, both Allied Hotels Scotland and Scottish Highland Hotels are essentially Scottish Hotel operators. On the other hand, Grand Metropolitan has 498 UK companies and 36 overseas companies, among which are many well known catering and restaurant names. These include the contract caterers, the Bateman Catering Organisation, the chain of Berni Inns Ltd, a number of dairies, including the Express Dairy Company, the Mecca organisation, including Miss World Ltd, the brewers, Watney Mann and Truman Holdings, motorway caterers such as Trowell Motorway Limited, and the wine distributors, Gilbey Vintners Ltd and Peter Dominic. The group also owns bookmakers, insurance, finance and property companies. Some of the hotel chains are part of investment groups. The Mount Charlotte hotels belong to Mount Charlotte Investments, who also have a share in the Workington Town Rugby League Football Club Ltd. More than one of the leading groups has shares in Luncheon Vouchers Limited. Many of the chain restaurants belong to these big companies, such as Jolyon Restaurants Limited, which belongs to J. Lyons & Co. Ltd. The breweries are also very much to the fore in hotel operations, and the largest of these in this respect is Bass Charrington, which is another large company having about 108 UK subsidiary companies and 35 overseas companies.

Amongst the acquisitions that have taken place in the last decade has been The Rank Organisation take-over of Butlins and Oddeninos, which last named was, in 1970, the twelfth largest hotelier in the UK. Watney Mann has been absorbed by Grand Metropolitan, as have Berni Inns and the brewers, Truman, Hanbury, Buxton. Many of the hotel groups which trade under their own name are, in fact, subsidiary companies of larger groups. Thus, for example, Thistle Hotels is part of Scottish and Newcastle Breweries. The same is true of catering. The largest contract caterers are subsidiaries—both Batemans and Midland Catering belong to Grand Metropolitan, while Gardner Merchant Food Services Limited belong to Trusthouse Forte. Large restaurant chains such as London Steak Houses Limited belong to J. Lyons & Co. Ltd.

Yet, in spite of this impressive list of interlocking company structures, it can still be argued that the hotel industry is fairly competitive. The concentration ratios that were estimated earlier took into account the subsidiary companies within a given sector. At the same time, it has been argued that there appears to be a high degree of devolved responsibility. Nor must we forget the large number of proprietor-owned businesses; some 35 340 hotels and boarding houses, 43 710 restaurants, and 47 150 public houses are owned or leased by their managers according to the 1971 Census of Population. But there are some obvious inconsistencies between these census figures and other reports, and this is particularly true of licensed premises. In 1967 the Monopolies Commission found that over 80% of all on-licensed premises in Britain, including hotels and restaurants, were owned by the breweries and a greater proportion of public houses were likewise owned by them. Yet ownership does not automatically imply management because of the tenancy system where someone, who is self-employed in other respects, takes on premises and agrees to purchase alcohol from the brewer at a set price, but is otherwise free to run the pub, restaurant or hotel as he sees fit. About 75% of the licensed premises are so tenanted, but the trend to management is apparently growing. Some estimates show that about 60% of restaurants are 'independents', with about a quarter to a third of the licensed ones owned by 'multiples'. Likewise, estimates imply that about two-thirds of hotels are independently owned, but these are smaller than the groups' hotels and have lower turnovers. The detailed figures can be found in the Department of Trade and Industry's 1964 and 1969 enquiries. This implies that the industry has about 20–30 large hotel and restaurant chains which operate against a background of very large numbers of small businesses. Of these, there are a handful of very large businesses comprised of the brewing interests and a few others such as Trusthouse Forte, Grand Metropolitan, J. Lyons & Co. Ltd. and British Transport, who tend to be in the 'big league' of the leading British companies and undertakings. To that extent they probably have a significant influence as 'trend-setters' but cannot really be said to dominate the total market. On the other hand, they must surely be influential in the market for higher tariff-hotel accommodation and in attracting business demand. Yet, they face increasingly severe competition—in, for example, the market for conference business from institutions such as universities who have recently taken to advertising their facilities and who have a not inconsiderable prestige. Certainly, the hotel and catering industry has never had any suspicion of monopoly prejudicial to the public interest attached to it, and has not been investigated by the Monopolies Commission. Like the models of competition, it has presented a great diversity of services to the public, thus ensuring them a choice and an amenity that caters for every income. Nor is the element of competition limited purely to hotel and catering companies. In assessing the competition that exists, one must also take into account the not inconsiderable numbers who stay at caravan sites, camping sites, youth hostels, friends and relatives, etc. If the hotel industry ever did begin to increase its prices as a whole, it would find that it increasingly turned to these alternatives. Indicators of income-elasticity also imply that the industry exists within a generally competitive situation. That the industry is a competitive one would, in part, explain the fluctuations in profit that exist—fluctuations over time and between companies. One of the implications of a competitive industry is not only that prices tend to be lower than in a monopoly, but that the industry structure is less stable, and this has proved to be the case. The industry is susceptible to changes in demand, and thus, in this respect, hotel and catering can be said to be a dynamic industry in that it is constantly subject to a change of ownership and numbers. Likewise, the brewing industry is in a time of change as public houses are closed and the smaller companies grow. In this case, however, the industry has been investigated by the Prices' Commission, and it was found that the major companies had higher prices and lower profitability rates than the smaller brewers. But the existence of these smaller brewers has meant that, although the concentration ratio is high, the level of competition is also high, and within a given area, local brewing concerns provide real competition in an industry where, as with restaurants, service, decor and atmosphere are all part of the product. The restaurant sector is perhaps the most competitive of all. Although franchise operators will not permit the setting up of outlets too near to each other (so that, for example, one Kentucky Fried Chicken outlet poaches trade from another Kentucky Fried Chicken outlet) there is still intense competition in city areas between differing restaurants offering similar services for the same sector of the market.

8
Operating Costs and Profitability

There are a number of costs involved in a hotel and catering operation, some of which were touched upon in Chapter 5 on the demand for finance. The costs fall into two main categories: the capital cost of building and equipping premises, and then the operating costs which include some fixed costs such as rates, interest charges on borrowed money, and the like, and variable costs that depend on the numbers of people served. It will be obvious that the actual costs involved in any one operation are peculiar to that situation, but there are cost surveys and these are interesting in that they illustrate the susceptibility of profits to changes in demand. At the same time, if a hotelier or restaurant owner finds that his costs vary considerably from the average, then obviously factors special to him must be operating and it could be beneficial to identify them.

Capital Costs

To an extent, the original costs of construction will depend on land costs, and these vary with the location of the site. In addition, total construction costs will differ with the size of hotel, and whether or not it is a high-rise operation. And, as we also know, in these present inflationary times, costs can rapidly rise between the time of conception and the final date of completion. Consequently, it is dangerous to state fixed costs of construction, but the distribution of costs can be indicated, and various NEDC reports do this. Generally speaking, if land costs are excluded, the building costs vary between 87 and 92% of the total cost of building and fitting a room. (Table 8.1). Generally speaking, construction and fitting costs per room are lower for the larger low-rise development, but such developments do, of course, incur higher land prices, especially if car parking is around the hotel and not incorporated into a multi-storey construction.

The construction costs themselves fall into various categories, and the

TABLE 8.1 **Distribution of fitting and building costs per room (%)**

	Low-rise hotel 100 bedroom	Low-rise hotel 200 bedroom	High-rise hotel 99 bedroom	High-rise hotel 108 bedroom
Construction	88	87	92	91
Carpets	1	3	2	2
Light fittings	1	2	1	1
Bedroom furniture	3	3	2	2
Public area furniture	1	1	1	1
External works and site drainage	6	4	2	3

(Source: *NEDC Accommodation for the lower-priced market*, 1975)

usual type of breakdown for a low-rise development would include 7% of total cost on substructure, 40% on superstructure, 8% on internal finishes such as plastering and painting, and 28% on plumbing and electrical work, the remainder being concerned with drainage. Again, the distribution of these costs can vary with the type of building involved, as obviously the foundation requirements of the high-rise are greater than those of a low-rise development. The costs of construction in 1977 were estimated at £25 000–£30 000 per room for a city centre hotel, and £12 000–£15 000 per room for a low-rise, two-storey development. These high initial costs mean that even moderate size developments can cost well over a quarter of a million pounds, and whilst the hotel structure will have a long life, the burden of such costs raises a significant question mark against the profitability of new operations, and hotels certainly require a long pay-back period of at least 10 years. At the same time, the main asset of a hotelier is the hotel, and indeed, with the practice of leasing interior assets such as some furniture and equipment being practised, it is quite possible that the hotel building could represent over 90% of the hotelier's total assets. The very specificity of a hotel building also means that it can seldom be used for anything else, and this may be a drawback when seeking to raise money on the security of a hotel building because of reputed poor profitability. The high costs of building hotels have led to two new developments. The first is the attempt to expand existing hotels by motel units whenever land space permits, as these are cheaper per room to build and can utilise existing common service facilities; while the second is to convert existing buildings to hotel usage whenever possible. It is now not uncommon for the hotel to be actually owned by a property development company which leases the hotel to the hotel operator, who then has a fixed cost to pay in terms of a rental which is subject to periodic renewal every five years or so. Some property developers that have experienced financial difficulty over the inflationary period since 1974, due to increasing costs at a time of static rental income, have begun to introduce proportionate rentals where the leasee pays a lease that is a proportion of his turnover, but this is not yet a widespread practice.

In the catering industry the total expenditure on capital costs is considerably smaller, and the ratio of the building to other assets is lower. It is indeed possible for a caterer to operate with little in the way of fixed assets, as the premises may be rented and the equipment leased, and thus the caterer has a fixed cost to cover, but does not necessarily require too large an initial outlay of capital.

Operating costs: 1. Hotels

Hotel operating costs tend to centre around two basic operations, the letting of rooms and the provision of meals and drinks, although it may provide additional services. Consequently, the major cost items will be on the food and alcohol served, and the cost of staff associated with the catering and room services, and together it was found that these absorb about half of a hotel's total revenue in a 1973 survey, which is a reduction from the almost two-thirds figure found by the Inter-Hotel Comparison Survey of 1969. The distribution of costs expressed as a percentage of net sales varies with the type of hotel. The following table is taken from the 1973 NEDO report on hotel prospects and is based on an assumption that about half the revenue of the hotel comes from the letting of rooms, and the rest from the sale of food, alcohol and other services. Generally speaking, there is a significant improvement in profitability in an increase of hotel occupancy from 50–60%, with the improvement most marked in the city hotel, which improves its profitability by about 7% of turnover. The reason for this increased profitability is that labour and service department costs fall as a percentage of turnover, indicating the fairly fixed nature of these costs compared to the variable costs of food and alcohol. Generally speaking, the greatest saving is from an increased productivity of labour in both the operating departments of catering and room service, and administration, in that the fall in sales and advertising costs and, as it happens, in heat, light and power costs, as a proportion of turnover, are marginal. The increased profitability of the hotels in Table 8.2 is proportionately greater in two cases, than the change in occupancy levels.

TABLE 8.2 **Distribution of operating costs as a percentage of turnover**

	100 bedroom low-rise (resort) occupancy 50% 60%	200 bedroom low-rise (urban) occupancy 50% 60%	108 bedroom high-rise (city) occupancy 50% 60%
Operated departments			
Materials	20.0 20.0	21.7 20.7	20.2 20.2
Labour	28.2 26.5	24.3 22.0	29.4 25.8
Other	8.1 7.7	7.8 7.5	8.3 7.9
Service departments			
Administration	12.9 11.4	10.7 9.4	13.7 12.1
Sales and promotion	1.4 1.3	1.3 1.2	1.9 1.8
Heat, light, power	3.5 3.4	3.1 3.0	4.0 3.9
Repairs and maintenance	5.7 5.0	5.3 4.8	6.0 5.3
Hotel net operating profit	20.2 24.7	26.8 31.4	16.5 23.0

(Source: *NEDC Hotel Prospects to 1980*)

The changed occupancy level is one of 20% of the original, and yet this creates a change of 22%, 17% and 39% in profits of the resort, urban and city hotels, respectively. This implies, in the case of the resort and city hotels, a great sensitivity of profits to changes in occupancy level. However, the example is based on unchanged costs, and the profitability of the operation will depend on the change of revenue *and* of costs. In addition, different levels of profitability can be obtained with the same levels of revenue. Table 8.2 shows that labour costs do not rise radically as bed occupancy rises, and consequently, those hotels that concentrate on accommodation and are not so dependent upon their restaurants for revenue, will be more profitable than hotels that depend more on their restaurants. This is confirmed by a study by the University of Surrey in 1969 which showed a 14.9% of turnover profit for hotels concentrating on accommodation as against 10% and 6.8% for those emphasizing food and drink sales respectively. The same was also shown by the 1973 and 1976 NEDO studies on hotel prospects in that a 1% increase in bed occupancy created, on average, a 1.7% increase in profitability, whereas a 1% increase in the demand for food created a 0.5% profit increase. The University of Strathclyde study for the period 1971–73 quoted in *Hotel Prospects to 1985* also indicates the same trend in that the average profit per room in 1973 for hotels with a sales bias towards accommodation was £774, as against £440 per room for hotels with a sales bias towards food. These profit figures were quoted before interest, rent, amortization and other charges, the implication of which will be discussed in the next chapter. As would be expected, motels stood to benefit most from any increase in demand for beds as the lack of services compared to traditional hotels means no consequent rise in many costs when room occupancy increases. The same reports also show that the demand for accommodation tends to be price inelastic in that a 1% increase in the price of a room brings about a more than 1% rise in profitability, with the same also being true of the demand for food, drink and tobacco. However, the effect is, interestingly enough, not uniform across the types of hotels. Those that stand to gain most are resort hotels, and this is understandable in that once the decision has been made for a holiday, then demand will tend to price inelasticity. It is the London hotels that receive least benefit from any increase in prices, and indeed in their case a 1% increase in the price of food, drink and tobacco brings about a less than 1% increase in profitability, reflecting perhaps the range of alternative places in London where these can be purchased.

The effects of any increases in costs likewise vary between hotels with coastal resort hotels bearing the greatest loss as a result of increased costs, according to the NEDO surveys. However, the interpretation of these statistics must be tinged with caution because, in practice, we cannot readily assume a position of variables remaining the same. For example, *Hotel Prospects to 1985* indicate that London hotels absorb a 1% increase in labour costs, the most successfully with only a 0.84% loss of profitability, whilst resort hotels suffer a loss of 1.77% in profits as a result. But can we assume that London hotels are that more efficient? Perhaps they increased prices more quickly than seaside hotels. Certainly, we know that London hotels have had increases in occupancy levels which have been denied to many of the coastal resorts. So other variables have not remained the same, and, in order to make meaningful comparisons, these changes have to be taken into account. This creates several problems for statisticians in that the various changes have to be weighted for their importance, and not all factors are equally important for all the hotel locations. Thus, the final statistic, with its tempting certainty of the second decimal place, flatters to deceive as to its finality. All that legitimately can be said is that London hotels tend to absorb increased labour costs more effectively than other hotels, and, assuming that tariffs did not change, this is probably due to the London hotels operating at higher occupancy levels than hotels in other parts of the country.

The surveys undertaken by the Hotels and Catering NEDC show that profits vary on a locational basis, though these differences may also be a reflection of different occupancy levels. Thus, the London hotels were the most profitable with profits before tax, interest and financial charges, being over 30% of revenue, whilst the coastal resort hotels are the least profitable with 17%. The difference may be partly explained by an emphasis on accommodation in that estimates show that accommodation accounts for 80% of the profits of London hotels compared with a similar figure of 60% for coastal resorts. As a result, material costs, i.e. food and drink, form a much smaller part of the whole cost structure for London hotels than for hotels in any other part of the country. Further, some London hotels have begun simply to offer beds without the accompanying breakfast. Indeed, analysis of Table 8.3 shows support for the contention that the differences in profits is caused by the different sales mix between accommodation, food and drink.

Those hotels that depend most on drink sales, namely small town and coastal resort hotels, are the least profitable in terms of operating costs and revenues. However, London hotels may face higher financial charges than others in terms of rates and other similar expenses. The implication is that hotels in these locations feel they have to offer these different emphases in response to the different patterns of demand that exist in these locations. It is interesting to note that motels have a relatively high dependence on food and drink sales, which seems to confirm the tendency for the old distinctions between hotel and motel to blur. At the same time, hotels having the lowest occupancy rates need to turn to other sources of revenue of which the most obvious is catering, even though the rate of return on these operations is correspondingly

TABLE 8.3 **Costs and profitability by location (% of revenue)**

	London	Urban over 100 000	Urban under 100 000	Rural resort	Coastal resort	Motel
Sales						
Room	54.2	34.7	18.0	25.7	27.3	34.2
Food	23.4	31.3	32.7	35.8	31.3	32.5
Bar	10.9	24.1	43.8	30.6	35.0	26.0
Other	11.5	9.9	5.5	7.9	6.4	7.3
Costs						
Material	13.0	25.6	41.4	33.4	34.8	29.2
Labour	28.1	28.5	26.4	27.8	25.5	28.8
Other	25.6	21.9	13.5	17.9	22.7	20.0
Profit before tax, interest and charges	33.3	24.0	18.7	20.9	17.0	23.0

(Source: *NEDC Hotel Prospects to 1980*)

lower. Consequently, rural hotels that have the lowest occupancy levels have the highest dependence for profits on food sales.

With regard to tax, many businesses either gain or lose by having an unincorporated status—the determinant of loss or gain being the differences between income tax rates and corporation tax. Those hotels that are not operated by limited companies and are run by the self-employed, are taxed at personal levels of taxation, for in assessing income, the Inland Revenue makes no distinction between personal and business income in their case. Normally, the basic rate of income tax is below corporation tax with generally the basic rate of income tax being about 30–35% compared with 40–42.5% of corporation tax. This obviously benefits the self-employed but it depends on the size of profits because there is one rate of corporation tax, whilst income tax rates have climbed to 85% and beyond. So the self-employed person has to calculate whether it is more profitable to be taxed as an individual, or turn himself into a limited company, take a wage as a manager which will be taxed on PAYE and leave the remainder of the revenue in the business, to be taxed as corporation tax. Tax returns for the 'other services' category of business, which includes the hotel and catering section, indicate that, while the self-employed own 80% of the assets (an average which is higher than the hotel and catering sector due to the inclusion of hairdressing and launderettes), they pay about 30% of the total tax revenue. Generally speaking, in the past, the hotel and catering sector has paid less tax than many other industry sectors due to lower profitability and higher degrees of unincorporated businesses; though the industry does not have the same tax allowances and grants that have been, and still are, granted to many manufacturing firms.

With regard to international levels of profitability, some comparison is possible for capital cities (Table 8.4). In 1975 hotels in the Middle East and South Asia had the highest occupancy figures of 78.2% and 74.7% respectively, while both were also the most profitable with profits being 37.1% and 50.6% of total income. European hotels achieved an average of occupancy levels of 64.3% and profitability of 20.7%. Indeed, within Europe, the English hotels are, according to the management consultants Pannell, Kerr, Forster and Company Ltd., the most profitable with the most rapid growth of profits in 1975; a reflection in part of the highest occupancy levels and some of the lowest costs for food and labour. However, the survey is of the largest hotels in capital cities, as indicated by the average number of rooms of the hotels in the sample, and this, as we know, tends to mean the most

TABLE 8.4 **European levels of profitability.**
(Profits as % of sales revenue in 1975)

	Overall average	Belgium	England	France	Germany	Italy	Holland	Others
Average no. of rooms	352	292	376	417	352	358	259	310
Income								
Rooms	52.6	48.0	54.5	57.3	48.6	55.5	48.4	50.7
Food	27.0	30.6	26.9	26.8	26.0	25.1	31.6	26.7
Gross operating income	46.7	40.6	51.4	43.7	46.3	33.8	41.9	46.2
Gross operating profit	20.7	9.3	28.3	16.4	19.2	7.1	16.1	19.1

(Source: *Trends in Catering*, Pannell, Kerr, Forster and Co., 1976)

profitable. Yet, taking this into account, the statistics are of some interest. Thus, across Europe there is little difference in the percentage of income that is spent on administrating, advertising and repairs, and such expenditure, with the range being 23.5% (England) to 34.2% (Belgium), with an average of 26.8%. The Italians' comparative lack of profitability is due to the very high proportion of income that is spent on labour (49.8%), while Belgium records the highest administrative costs. English profitability is due, as already remarked, to lower food and labour costs; yet, on the other hand, the tariffs were also lower in this country, being about US $3 below the European average at $25.98 daily rate per occupied room, though this has increased considerably since 1975. The international comparisons also yield one or two differences in the behaviour of hotel guests. German hotel guests are twice as likely to buy drinks in their hotels as the French. The Dutch are the most likely to eat meals in their hotels, and the French the least likely. English hotels spend proportionately less on linen than their European counterparts but the most on china and glass.

A major cost that British hotels have had to meet in the period from 1974 to the beginning of 1977 was one shared by many British firms, and that was high interest rates on loans. The 1977 accounts of Mount Charlotte, for example, show that 5% of their turnover went on interest payments on loans before any payment of the principal. For Butlins a similar figure in 1975 was 3%, and for Trusthouse Forte 4%. Falling interest rates since the beginning of 1977–78 began to reduce this burden upon companies, but those that were late in arranging loans suffered as interest rates increased in late 1978, indicating the importance of timing.

One cost that hotel companies may be able to reduce is their laundry bills if they have sufficient linen. Estimates indicate that an on-premises laundry can offer a 30% cost saving as the transport costs and laundry's profit are absorbed by the hotel, while it increases the available stock of linen for use in the hotel and avoids loss. On the other hand, it is for hotels to decide whether that 30% saving is worth the trouble of organizing the operation, finding the room, and involving staff. By and large, however, there is little that hotels can do to reduce costs without reducing the quality of the service offered. Catering probably presents the main areas where possible savings may be made, but such changes will often involve a switch away from fresh foods, a switch which may not be acceptable to many, particularly those who seek to attract custom by the very nature of their cuisine. The best way of absorbing costs is by distributing them over a greater usage of accommodation; and this depends very much on general trends of demand which any single hotel can only influence marginally. Yet this would seem to imply that the largest hotels are the most profitable, and, to some extent, this is the conventional wisdom in the trade. This feeling is not without some foundation for the largest hotels tend to have the highest occupancy rates. London hotels are often the largest and most profitable hotels within hotel groups, and, arguably, may attract the most professional management. However, there is some evidence to suggest that one cannot simply equate large size with large profits when concerned with provincial hotels. In a study covering the years 1971–73 a research team at Strathclyde University concluded that the highest rates of return on capital employed were found in hotels of less than 50 rooms. In part, it depends on what is considered as 'profitable'. The 30-room hotel may achieve greater profitability in terms of profits expressed as a percentage of capital or turnover, but the larger hotel can still make more profits. For example, a small hotel may achieve a 15% rate of return on £200 000 turnover, i.e. £30 000, but a larger hotel might achieve 10% return on £500 000 turnover, i.e. £50 000, and so record more profit, but at a lower level of profitability.

Until the middle of the 1970s there was continuous concern over the low levels of profitability in the hotel industry. *Hotel Prospects to 1985* stated (p. 34) that '. . . calculations . . . for groups of hotels indicate average 1973 returns of between 4% and 15%, with the majority of groupings showing a figure of between 6% and 10%. As indicated in *Hotel Prospects to 1980*, even allowing for any weakness in the underlying data and bases of revaluation, the overall impression that these figures provide is not encouraging . . . . Many hotels continue to operate at a level of profitability which is low by any comparison'. The report goes on to comment that for many their continuation depends on the appreciation of their property and land as a hedge against inflation. Yet, even while the report was being written, the hotel industry was moving into a period of expanding sales and profitability. After the losses of 1974 the Greene, Belfield-Smith Hotel Index show profits increasing by 11, 29, 18 and 27% in the years 1975, 1976, 1977 and 1978 respectively. As a result of this, the amount of investment undertaken by the industry climbed, and it was estimated in *Catering Times* (16 November 1978) that it exceeded the £100 million figure for renovating, and building rooms in 1978 alone. The major companies were well to the fore with Trusthouse Forte announcing investments that accounted for about 20% of that figure. Never the less, the NEDO report is still valid for many of our independent hotels in less favoured areas, for while sales revenue grew by about 60% in this period, it was a discriminating demand and the less favourably sited hotels survived by means of an 'overspill' process. Consequently, such hotels are vulnerable to any down-turn in business, particularly if modernization programmes widen the gulf between themselves and the more fortunate hotels, and should demand fall small hotels in poor sites will have great difficulty in sustaining profitability.

In addition to the costs listed above, there is a further cost, known to some as 'shrinkage', and to most as 'fiddling'. The Metropolitan Police's Hotel Collation and Intelligence Unit covers 860 hotels and in 1978 some 4715 crimes of theft were reported involving a value of £3.5 million. One estimate by this unit is that 'fiddling' deprived hotels of 10% of their gross turnover and that staff were responsible for nearly a third of all hotel crime. Approximately a further half of hotel crime involved prostitutes. Some of the London hotels are now using a computerized keyless locking system for bedroom doors, and have found that the system has had a dual advantage. First, it has meant a reduction of theft; and second, it has proved a good selling point to overseas customers. A further advantage has been a reduction of insurance premiums. The significance of these costs of crime can be realized in that the reduction of 'fiddles' could be the equal to a 20% increase in tariffs according to the Metropolitan Police (see the report of the *British Association of Hotel Accountants Conference,* September 1979).

Operating Costs: 2. Catering

The main constituent costs of catering are the same as those of hotels: namely materials and labour. Restaurants differ from hotels, however, in that their labour costs tend to be a small proportion of revenue than is the case in hotels, being, on average, 25% of revenue across a wide range of restaurant types. Kotas, in his survey of 90 London restaurants, found, on the other hand, a wide degree of variation, in that some establishments had over 35% of their revenue accounted for by labour costs, whereas in others it was as low as 14% (Table 8.5). In part,

TABLE 8.5 **Labour cost as a proportion of sales (%)**

	Highest	Average	Lowest
Restaurants	36.0	24.7	14.6
Speciality restaurants	30.1	23.7	15.6
National restaurants	45.0	26.8	16.0
Wimpy Bars	23.0	22.5	22.0
Other catering establishments	32.0	25.2	16.2

(Source: *Labour Costs in Restaurants*, R. Kotas)

the determinant of the importance of labour costs is the efficiency of the operation and the object of the establishment. To give an example: two Wimpy Bars may be equally efficient in many ways, but one will have labour costs as a higher proportion of total revenue due to maintaining a 24-hour operation.

Estimates indicate that a commercial 24-hour operation tends to have about 48% of its total costs attributed to labour, whereas commercial operations, aiming basically at one meal per day, spend about 28% of their expenditure in this way (Table 8.6). The cooking and preparation of meals does not absorb most of the labour cost in catering, for the costs associated with service and cleaning account for at least the same, and, in many cases, more than chefs' and cooks' wages. Serving costs can account for as much as 16% of total costs, and, consequently, the savings associated with a self-service form of catering can be imagined. This accounts, in part, for the familiar self-service image of non-commercial catering in staff restaurants, and the availability of only self-service at motorway restaurants outside normal hours when the

TABLE 8.6 **Catering costs by operation (%)**

	Direct				Indirect	
	Food	Cook	Serve	Clean	Labour	Other
1 meal/day for profit	43.6	5.3	9.6	7.1	6.3	28.1
1 meal/day at cost	49.9	8.6	7.0	10.2	2.2	22.1
2 meals/day for profit	47.2	17.3	8.5	4.9	3.3	18.8
2 meals/day at cost	52.4	5.8	2.7	5.0	10.8	23.3
24-hour operation for profit	47.6	16.1	16.6	8.7	6.4	4.6
24-hour operation at cost	52.0	18.8	15.3	6.5	3.9	3.5

(Source: *Convenience Foods in Catering*, NEDO)

overtime and 'unsocial hour' payments would be significantly higher than normal. Food accounts for the major part of a restaurant's total expenditure, and it is not uncommon that nearly half of a restaurant's outgoing will be on foodstuffs.

This means that the cost structure of a catering establishment is heavily orientated towards variable rather than fixed costs. In consequence this means that profitability begins at lower seating capacity and meals served points than would otherwise be the case.

For example, if in Fig. 8.1 variable costs (total costs minus fixed costs) remain the same and are proportionate to the number of meals served, then an increase in fixed costs giving a higher ratio of fixed to variable costs means a higher break-even point at OQ_2 instead of OQ_1, assuming that revenue remains the same and is also proportionate to the number of meals served. It was stated earlier that it is not uncommon for many caterers to lease rather than buy their equipment, and this is reflected in their cost structures where depreciation rarely comes to over 3% of total costs. But what is gained in this way means outgoings on leases as well as the other costs of rents, insurance, rates, etc., and thus these items can account for about a fifth of total costs.

There appears to be comparatively little difference in the distribution of costs between the commercial and non-commercial sectors of the industry, even though it might be expected that the non-commercial would be very cost conscious due to the usual aim of supplying low-priced meals to their clientele, with a consequential rigidity in

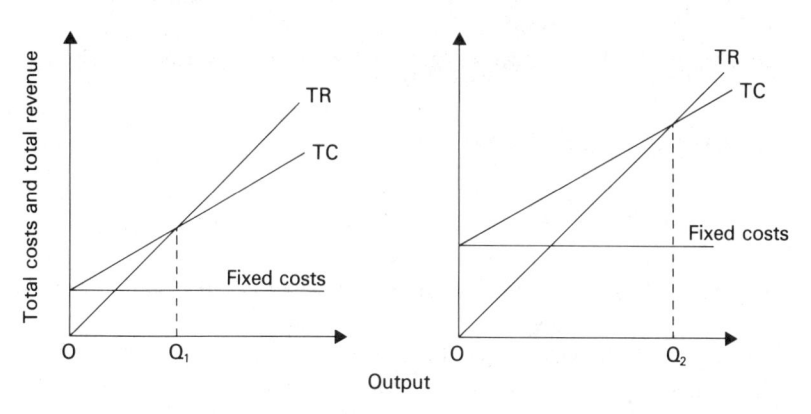

FIG. 8.1 **The importance of the ratio of fixed to variable costs**

pricing policy. In practice, non-commercial caterers may be comparatively free in that the subsidising authority may lay down very lax criteria. In 1977 the Industrial Catering Association stated that while 90% of companies give guidelines to their catering managers, many are simply 'nebulous'. Few have a set budget. Interestingly enough, of the 230 members surveyed by the association, two-thirds felt they achieved the targets given, but 40% of them were required to recover only the cost of the food; i.e. on the basis of our above figures, to cover about 50% of their costs. Where the target is higher, the rate of failure to achieve that target increases. Only a very few achieve the cost of food and 30% of the wage bill; and indeed where the target is one of the cost of food plus 1% of other costs, the majority (55%) fail to achieve this. This need not signify widespread inefficiency amongst non-commercial caterers, but rather reflects the wish of employers to provide low-cost meals for their employees. The objective is one of creating better staff relationships by providing a service, and, for some employers it is, in part, a means of increasing the real income of their employees at a time of wage restraint, whilst the losses on the catering operation may, in their eyes, be offset against tax. Industrial catering need not be a loss-making exercise. One of the largest contract caterers, the Bateman Catering Organisation, was one of the first to introduce a 'Management by Objectives' approach which, by definition, includes a number of specific targets, some of which are cost-based, and the whole process incorporates one of continuous review of progress against the targets. Indeed, some of the most demanding contract catering is for student unions who wish to provide a service for their far-from-rich membership while avoiding a great loss as this prejudices their other activities.

Economies of Scale

Large hotel and catering groups also have an advantage in that certain 'economies of scale' may be open to them. By the term 'economies of scale' is meant the tendency for average cost to fall as output increases. For example, a hotel will need sufficient staff for maintaining a good service at a given degree of occupancy. Suppose a hotel normally operates at 75% occupancy, for which it requires ten staff. If the occupancy levels fall below that level it will still be paying the wages of ten staff, so the average labour cost per client served will increase. If, for some reason, the hotel achieves occupancy rates far above 75% and still

OPERATING COSTS AND PROFITABILITY 189

maintains a staff of ten, then perhaps staff will have to be paid on an overtime rate; the possible loss of repeat bookings due to a poorer service (longer delays etc.) will mean an increased average cost per person served; and this gives us *diseconomies of scale* (i.e. an increase in average cost as output increases beyond a certain point). In Fig. 8.2 average costs fall up to output level OA (which could represent our example of 75% occupancy); beyond that level diseconomies occur. Amongst the major cost savings large groups have is the ability to buy furniture and fittings, linen, and foodstuffs (particularly convenience foods) in bulk, thereby getting discounts. In addition, the negotiating strength of such firms may mean favourable treatment from suppliers who will wish to obtain large orders and so quote a more competitive price. The major companies also have the financial resources to undertake technical improvements. Combined with the ownership of several hotels, a computerized reservation system means they can quickly offer a client alternative accommodation and in many cases the client will accept this. Consequently, the groups have obtained revenue that might otherwise be lost. This is particularly important in the hotel and catering industry for an empty room or empty table represents revenue lost for ever. They are not in the position of a manufacturing company which produces an item that, if not purchased by one customer, may be sold to another. The restaurateur or hotelier cannot sell last Tuesday's spare space next Thursday, even though he has entailed the costs of 'manufacturing' that item. The availability of a network of hotels, restaurants or pubs also represents a further economy

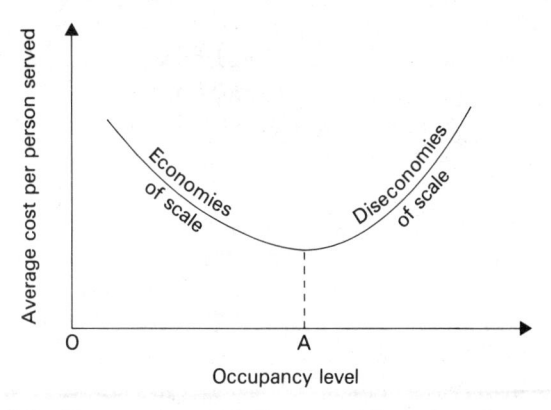

FIG. 8.2 **Economies and diseconomies of scale**

of scale through offering a risk diversification policy. If demand switches, say, from seaside resorts to country areas, the chain that owns units in both locations will be able to retain some revenue, whereas the independent seaside unit will be faced with the bleak prospect of a loss of business. Large chains also have a number of financial advantages, for they will generally find it easier and cheaper to borrow money for a number of reasons. First, they will have a 'name' which will gain immediate attention from bankers and the general public who may want to subscribe to a share issue. Second, they will tend to have greater assets to offer as security for a loan. Third, they will often be negotiating for larger loans for which various institutions compete, therefore gaining some advantage in interest rates, whereas the independent may have difficulty in finding someone from whom to borrow. All in all, the chains may achieve an economy in having to pay a lower cost per pound borrowed compared with smaller units. With these resources, the company is able to buy more modern equipment, as a result of which further cost savings can be achieved. On a large scale they can build new hotels which offer various opportunities for reducing average costs. For example, if one built to the dimensions 20 × 20 × 20 units, giving a cubic capacity of 8000 cubic units and then one built to double the external dimensions this would create an edifice 40 × 40 × 40 equallying 64 000 cubic units. In other words, for probably less than twice the cost of the original building, one has eight times the volume in our example, and, if this is reflected in the number of rooms, eight times the earning power. Similarly, a hotel or restaurant chain that is in the position of building a new hotel is able to plan it so as to include various cost-saving aspects. For example, corridors and spaces between cookers etc. can be standardized so as to be suitable for cleaning machines. Steps can be avoided that make the cleaning process easier. Kitchen layout can minimize wasted effort. Linen deposits are strategically placed. In older buildings that are converted by smaller businesses not having the finance available for new hotels, the opportunities for such cost-saving designs are more limited. The large breweries, hotels and restaurant chains may also gain from being able to fully employ specialized staff. The independent operator has often to fulfil many functions—sales manager, cost accountant, chef, waiter, chambermaid—a multitude of roles that means that he is unable to specialize in any one task. The chains can possibly benefit from specialized accounting and marketing skills that, for example, allow a combination of cost-saving and revenue-raising programmes to be operated. On the other hand, the independent does acquire the specialization of running his own business; he is quick to respond to change, personal contact is present and undue consultative processes are avoided.

The very size of the large chains creates problems as it lengthens the decision-taking process, and those at head office are very dependent on correct information flows from unit managers. Generally speaking, most of the main groups operate a highly centralized operation where for example, pricing and marketing decisions are taken by head office. However, as an indication of the degree of discretion that is allowed, a survey of bargain break pricing policies by 30 hotel groups, by the author in 1979, indicated that 30% of the managers in these groups considered that head office played no role in their pricing decisions. Yet, considering the stated policies of the firms involved, the figure should have been lower, thus illustrating the major problem that all large organizations have: namely the problem of faulty communication, and coordination. Yet, in spite of this problem, large firms gain. As Fig. 8.3 indicates, while there is no guarantee that the technical, marketing, financial and other costs will move together as the size of operation increases, it may be that the savings made possible by these factors will still outweigh the increasing communication costs and therefore produce a falling average cost per person served. It must be stressed that Fig. 8.3 is a hypothetical figure. Never the less, it is based on some observations. In the hotel and restaurant business, advertising and marketing budgets tend to be small, the exception being possibly Trusthouse Forte which accounts for about 40% of the hotel industry's advertising, and yet even in their case it is a small proportion of turnover. The communication and management curve is exaggerated to stress its tendency to rise. In the case of brewers, marketing costs will be higher than those shown. The 'financial costs' will also vary considerably, depending on how recently a unit was built or modernized. Those freehold premises not recently modernized may have little mortgage or interest charges on borrowed finance to pay, whereas a recently acquired site may carry heavy overheads in this respect. Consequently, the mix of properties belonging to a group will determine the nature of the 'financial' cost curve, as will the degree of self-financing undertaken. However, the figure overleaf does indicate how large groups may gain or lose when compared with their smaller

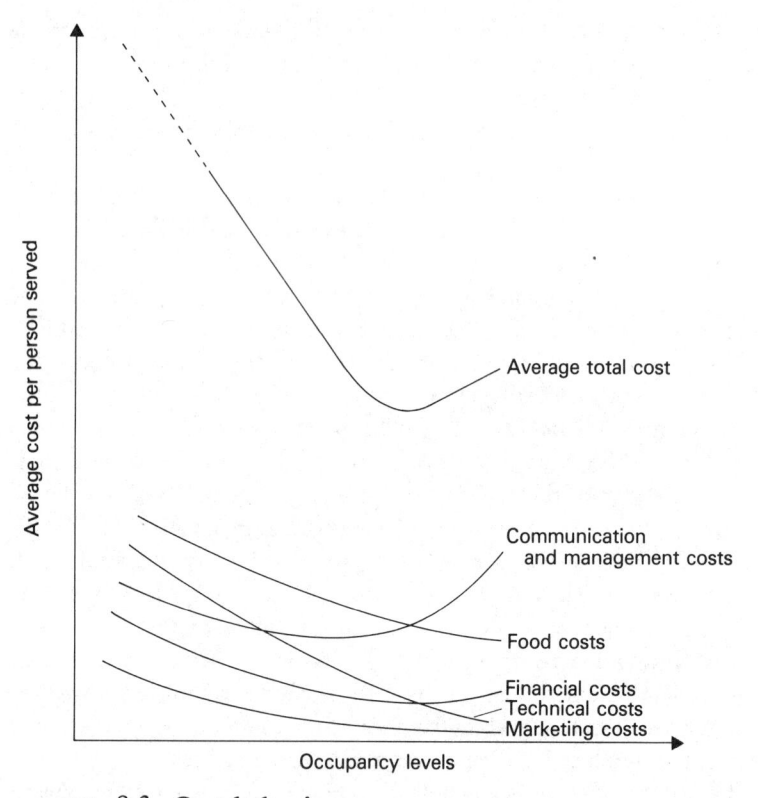

192 AN INTRODUCTION TO HOTEL AND CATERING ECONOMICS

FIG. 8.3 **Cost behaviour**

counterparts. In hotels and restaurants the diagram offers a plausible description of their situation. For breweries the position is less clear. As was explained in Chapter 7, the administrative overheads of the brewers allied with high investment charges and transport costs has meant a lower profitability compared with the smaller units. For them, the communication and management average cost curves have taken a definite upswing, for they may not be achieving as significant an average cost reduction in the financial and marketing spheres as hotels due to heavy investment and advertising costs, made in turn, possibly necessary by the competition created by the higher concentration curve in the industry, the slow growth in demand, and the attraction of CAMRA—an interesting combination!

9
Pricing Policies

Pricing policies in the hotel and catering industry range from looking in a crystal ball, crossing the gypsy's palm with silver, and then doubling her recommended price 'just to make sure', to calculations based on computer readouts of occupancy figures, recorded invoices and wage payments, all of which calculations are blended by the marketing manager's 'feel' for the market. In short, pricing policies range from the 'mad, bad guess' to the calculated mix of cost and market conditions. With such a situation it is difficult to be precise about the pricing policies companies adopt, but it is possible to postulate certain models and then make some general observations and look at some practices in outline that have concerned hotel groups. Consequently, various pricing techniques can be identified:

(i) **Marginal pricing technique**—This is drawn from the economist's models of the firm and, although not used by the industry, it does draw attention to some aspects of cost behaviour, and perhaps more importantly, concentrates attention on motivation.

(ii) **Cost-plus pricing**—This is a technique used very commonly in meal pricing and, consequently, for hotels, is incorporated into the pricing process for arriving at tariff levels.

(iii) **Target rate of return pricing**—This policy concentrates attention on assessing profit needs, and how profits might vary with different tariff and price levels.

(iv) **Contribution pricing**—This policy is derived in part from marginal analysis in that it too observes cost behaviour and recognizes the fact that revenue covering variable cost is the absolutely minimum acceptable level of revenue from a promotion.

We can describe each of these models in turn.

Marginal Costing Techniques

Marginal cost is defined as 'the extra cost involved in the production of one more unit of output'. Its revenue counterpart, *marginal revenue*, is the 'extra revenue gained from the sale of one more unit of output'. From these definitions it logically follows that it will add to profits to continue increasing output if marginal revenue is greater than marginal cost, for the extra revenue gained from the sale of that product is more than the cost of producing the extra item. Similarly, if the extra cost of making and selling an item is greater than the extra revenue involved in selling the item, then a reduction from the existing level of profits will occur. Therefore, applying our definitions, if marginal cost is greater than marginal revenue, it will pay the firm to reduce output. Consequently, it can be said that in Fig. 9.1 profits will increase as output expands to OA as marginal revenue is greater than marginal costs, and profits are at their maximum at output OA, whereafter, as marginal cost is greater than marginal revenue, profits decline as output is expanded above OA, and eventually losses will occur. Therefore, if a profit maximization policy is pursued, the formula of 'marginal revenue equals marginal cost' gives us the output at which profits are at their maximum. What then, does this tell us about price policies? To answer this we need to go back on stage and derive the revenue and cost curves.

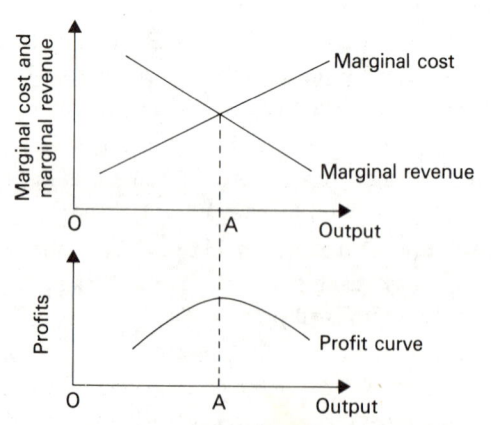

FIG. 9.1 **Profits, marginal cost and marginal revenue**

In Chapter 4 we looked at the demand curve. This indicates that, usually, as price is reduced, more is demanded. We can reproduce such a demand curve in Fig. 9.2, where the maximum price charged is £9, and the maximum quantity demanded is 9 units. Let us consider the position where 5 units will be purchased if the price is £4, and the

PRICING POLICIES 195

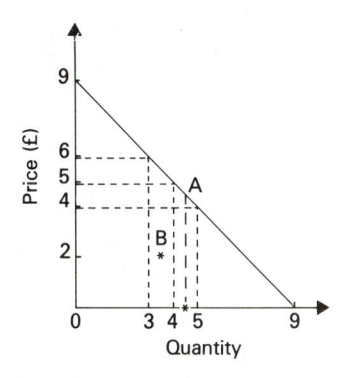

FIG. 9.2 **Deriving marginal revenue**

situation where 4 units are bought if the price is increased to £5. In both cases, therefore, the total revenue is £20 (£4 × 5 = £5 × 4).

Our definition of marginal revenue is the extra revenue gained from the sale of one more unit, and so in this example marginal revenue is zero. Because this marginal revenue arises from a change in output it is plotted at the halfway point between 4 and 5 on the horizontal axis of Fig. 9.2, i.e. at a value of 4.5. You might also remember from Chapter 4 that the elasticity of demand in the centre of a straight line demand curve joining the two axes is equal to 1. At point A elasticity of demand equals 1, and when this occurs, marginal revenue equals 0. Therefore, the point where marginal revenue equals 0 is immediately below point A on the horizontal axis. Now consider on Fig. 9.2 the situation when the price was originally £6, 3 units were demanded. This gives a total revenue of £18. When the price is reduced to £5, then 4 units are sold, and hence total revenue is £20. The marginal revenue gained from the sale of one more unit, the fourth unit, is, therefore, £2 and this is plotted at the position B where the coordinates are £2, and the quantity 3.5 (because this £2 arises from a change in output, and 3.5 is the average or midway point between 3 and 4). You will note that the marginal revenue is not equal to the price in this example. Marginal revenue will only equal the price if the price does not vary. In Fig. 9.3 we connect the two marginal revenue points by a straight line, and this gives us the marginal revenue curve, i.e. it shows that marginal revenue associated with every increase in units sold. Because we have assumed the firm is a profit maximizer, we must now ascertain the cost curves, as profit is, of course, a total revenue minus total cost.

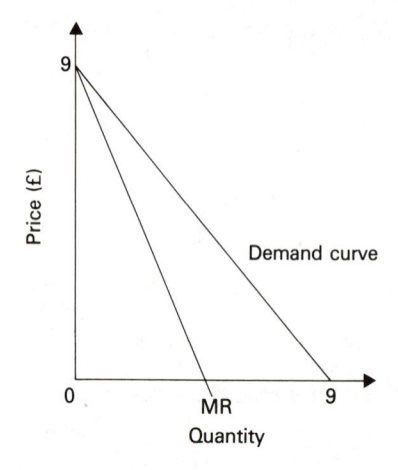

FIG. 9.3 **The marginal revenue curve**

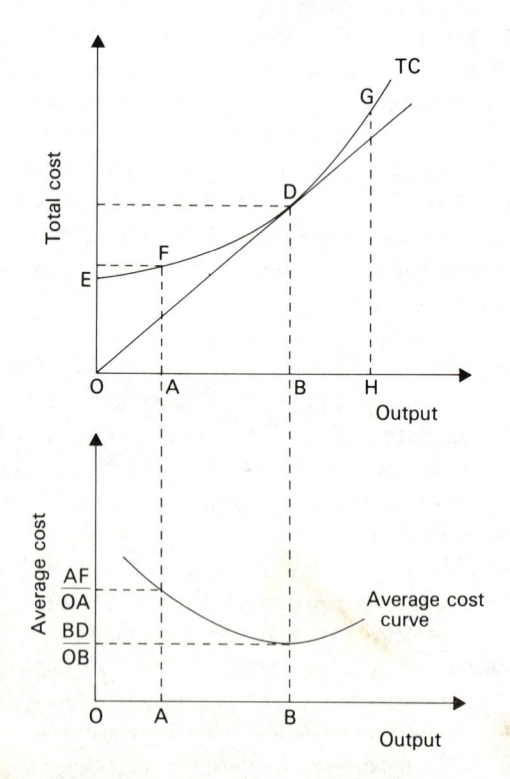

FIG. 9.4 **Deriving average cost curves**

PRICING POLICIES

Fig. 9.4 shows a total cost curve. You will notice that it is composed of two elements, fixed and variable costs, because even if nothing is produced, fixed costs of OE are sustained. The firm has to pay rents, rates etc. even if nothing is produced or sold. At an output of OA the total costs are AF. The average cost is calculated by dividing total cost by the number of units produced; i.e.

$$\text{Average cost} = \frac{\text{Total cost}}{\text{Number of units produced}}$$

Consequently, at an output of OA produced at a cost of AF, the average cost is AF/OA. If we gave values to these letters, all that we would be saying is if OA equalled (say) 10 units, and total cost equalled £30, then the average cost would be £30/10, i.e. £3 per item produced. Should output increase to OB, the total cost would rise to BD, and hence the average cost would now be BD/OB. Now this will have a lower value than our initial average cost, for as can be seen from the diagram, BD is not twice as much as FA whereas OB is more than twice OA. So giving these letters illustrative values, we could say BD is a total cost of (say) £50, and OB is 20 units, giving an average cost of £2 per unit. This will be the minimum value of the average cost as from this point onwards total cost begins to rise proportionately more than any increase in output. Thus, the distance BH is less than GH − DB, and therefore average cost will begin to increase.

Marginal cost is the additional cost resulting from the making of one more item. It is, therefore, the slope of the total cost curve, as is shown in Fig. 9.5. If we assume that IJ represents an extra item of output, then the addition to total cost of that item is KJ. If the line MN is drawn through the points IK we find it is tangential to the total cost curve.

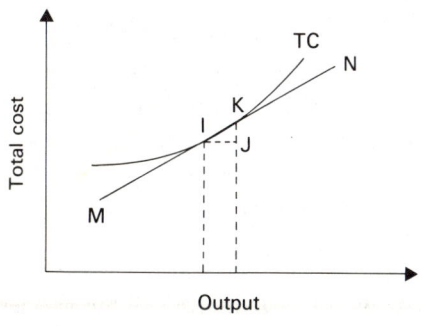

FIG. 9.5 **Deriving marginal cost**

198   AN INTRODUCTION TO HOTEL AND CATERING ECONOMICS

As we know, whenever we climb a hill, the slope of a line is the vertical distance divided by the horizontal distance, i.e. KJ/IJ. If IJ has a value of 1 (being the extra item), then the value of the slope of the total cost curve as the output increases from I to J is KJ, i.e. the value of the addition to total cost created by increasing output by one unit, which by definition is marginal cost. From Fig. 9.6 it can be seen that marginal

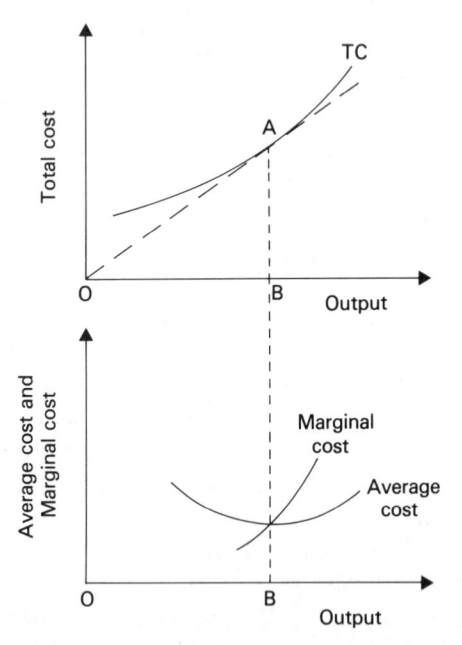

FIG. 9.6 **Deriving marginal and average cost from total cost**

cost is equal to average cost when average cost is at its lowest, for at the output OB the total cost curve has the slope of the line OA which is calculated by AB/OB, which is also the value of average cost. From the point A there is a more than proportionate increase in total costs; therefore, the average cost will increase, whereas marginal cost will have begun rising *before* the point A as the slope of the total cost curve becomes steeper.

We now have sufficient data to calculate the price a profit-maximizer will charge. If, as in Fig. 9.7, we impose the average and marginal revenue and cost curves upon the same figure, it can be seen that the

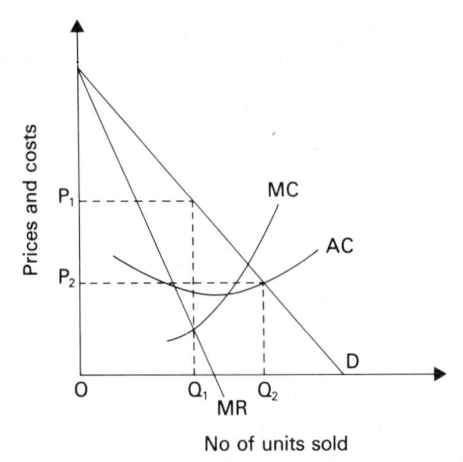

FIG. 9.7 **Profit and market share maximization prices**

price that results when the profit-maximizing output of OQ_1 is chosen is the price OP_1. It can be objected with this approach that firms are not necessarily profit maximizers for a series of very good reasons. The charging of such prices may attract the attention of governmental bodies such as the Monopolies and Mergers Commission; prices may anyway be subject to some form of government control; firms may wish to pursue an enlargement of market shares which would necessitate the reduction of price to encourage a growth in demand. In Fig. 9.7 such a policy could lead to a minimum price of OP_2 at output OQ_2, as this position is consistent with maximum sales and the avoidance of a loss in that the firm is operating at a breakeven point where average revenue equals average cost. In practice the firm will probably aim at a price level between P_1 and P_2, possibly at, for example, the level where MC = AR as this will give a profit without necessitating a price that would be unsatisfactory to the Monopolies Commission.

To undertake this pricing policy associated with a profit maximization presupposes that hoteliers and restaurateurs wish to maximize profit and that they know their marginal costs. Both are dubious assumptions. While companies wish to make profit the uncertainty of market conditions make it difficult to assess accurately the demand curve. Consequently, while estimates of demand at given prices can be calculated, and, with sophisticated statistical techniques, the probabilities of such demands could be incorporated, market uncertainty makes difficult the precise measurement of a marginal revenue curve.

Likewise, problems arise with marginal costs. As will be appreciated, the slope of our total cost curve is due to variable costs. By definition, therefore, costs vary with the amount of business undertaken, and a determinant of this is the price charged. In an inflationary period the calculation of costs is difficult, and, in the case of foodstuffs, is further complicated by the seasonable changes that occur. For a hotel, the problem of inflationary costs may be more pressing than for a restaurant in that brochures and sales material have to be prepared in advance, and consequently a price is fixed that needs to take into account not only present situations but also the situation in perhaps nine months time. Consequently, the profitability per client may be higher in the earlier part of that time sequence than in the later part. In this situation, the motivation for making maximum profits may be replaced by the one of making a satisfactory level of profits.

This is particularly the case where one is considering smaller, independent hoteliers and restaurants, where it would seem that the pleasure of giving service, meeting people, being one's own boss, is as great an incentive (if not a greater incentive) than the thought of making a maximum profit. For small businesses, the business aims may be expressed more in terms of acquiring high occupancy levels than in estimating profit levels. This has certainly been evident in any survey undertaken of hotel pricing methods: both A. Rogers (*MPhil Dissertation*, Surrey University, 1976) and the present author (unpublished work) have found examples where independents have strongly stressed the service factors. Never the less, in the author's research, it does appear that while the motivation of maximizing profits is not sought, a more easily identified target of maximizing revenue may be important for smaller hotels. Thus, in a questionnaire of 135 hotels, 78% stated that giving the best possible service to customers was very important, and 86% stated that maximizing revenue was very important. Possible objective conflict was not perceived by many of the smaller hotel units, whereas larger organizations do argue that the provision of a good service helps create the revenue and hence profits. But the service must be paid for by the customer.

Cost-plus Pricing

The cost-plus system of pricing has great appeal, because calculations are much easier than with marginal costing. Certainly, in a survey of

135 hotels by the author, less than a third stated they took into account marginal cost, whereas 89% stated that they adopted average cost-plus mark-up pricing techniques in determining at least some of the prices—notably meal prices, and in many cases tariffs as well.

Under this method the price is calculated by adding to the average cost a mark-up that is often expressed as a percentage of the average cost. Thus, an average cost of £1 plus a 25% mark-up yields a price of £1.25 (i.e. £1 + 25% of £1). However, this apparently simple pricing method is not so simple in practice. Firstly, it depends on how the average cost is calculated. Does one use actual costs, expected costs, or some mix of both, to create a standard cost? If one is using a standard cost, then this entails an estimate of an optimum level of output. Further, in the calculation, are only direct costs involved, or does one also include overheads? If overheads are included, how then are they allocated? A common variant of this system is used in meal pricing. The cost of foodstuffs is added, and then divided by the number of portions, to arrive at average cost. A mark-up is added to arrive at the price. It is common to express this mark-up as a gross food profit margin. For example, the average food cost of a portion of roast topside of beef with Yorkshire pudding plus frozen peas, potatoes and gravy etc. may cost 59p, but will be retailed at a price of £2.50. The food cost is, therefore, 23.6% of the retail price, giving a gross food margin of 76.4%. The less common alternative is to state the food cost is 59p, and to this is added a mark-up of 423%, giving the price of £2.50. But, of course, the gross food margin is not all profit, because from it must be deducted the direct costs of labour and energy; also the overhead costs of depreciation and replacement of equipment, rates, rents, interest payments on loans, capital repayment etc. must be met. The difficulty of attributing these costs to a meal means that the caterer adds a high gross food profit to something like roast beef etc. which does have a high labour content in preparation. In practice, then, one can seriously question whether this pricing technique is as cost-orientated as it appears at first sight. The need for high gross food margins to generate sufficient income to meet all the costs not included in the calculation means effectively setting a price which is acceptable to the market. This highlights the precarious nature of this seemingly safe way of pricing; seemingly safe because the price covers the cost. The average cost is based on an estimate of the number of portions sold. So, in Fig. 9.8 OD represents the price charged, and OC the average cost per portion, based on the assumption

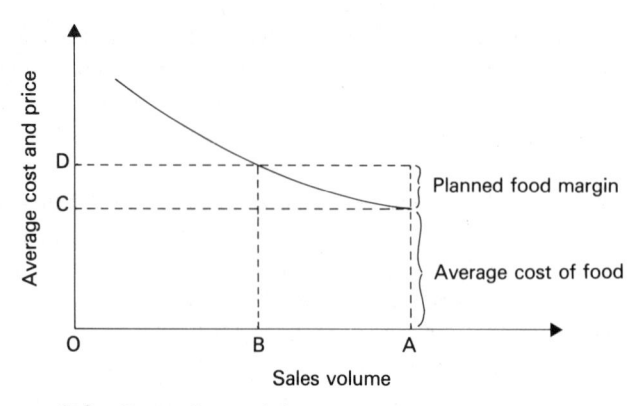

FIG. 9.8 **Cost-plus pricing**

that OA portions are made and sold. If sales are at a level of OB the caterer will break even. If sales are below OB he will make a loss. His expectation of OA sales lead him to base his price on an average cost of OC. If he had expected only OB of sales, then what was his price then becomes the base of his costing, and, if he wished to maintain the same money profit per portion sold, his price would have been OD + CD. But one of the main determinants of demand is price, and his calculation that OA would be sold assumes that the price OD is acceptable to the public.

In the pricing procedures often adopted for meals where gross food margins can vary from about 40–80%, the acceptablility of the price to the customer is a more important aspect of the pricing policy than the

TABLE 9.1 **Mark-ups (%) on weekend break tariffs 1978–79**

Mark-up	Absolute frequency	Cumulative frequency
Break even	19	19
0–5	21	40
6–10	19	59
11–15	17	76
16–20	7	83
21–25	7	90
25+	9	99*

*Not 100% due to rounding.
(Source: Present author's study on weekend break prices, Trent Polytechnic, 1979)

calculation of mark-up on food costs. Consequently, one suspects that, although many restaurateurs and hoteliers say they adopt a mark-up system of pricing, they in fact do not. Rather they adopt a policy of charging what the market will bear. This in part determines the wide variation of mark-ups found in the present author's own study of bargain break pricing, shown in Table 9.1.

It will also explain the wide variation in discounts given for party bookings, etc. In short, in practice, what may seem to be cost plus pricing is really our third type of pricing.

Target Rate of Return Pricing or Backward Pricing

Under this form of pricing one looks at what the market will bear. Competitors' prices are assessed, one looks at the differences in the quality of service offered, one tries to see how one's own hotel or restaurant fits into the general provision of services, and the price is estimated. To some extent the major five-star hotels are in this position because of the way in which customers view prices as an indicator of quality. Consequently, if (say), the London Hilton Hotel suddenly started advertising 25% off with announcements saying 'buy now, summer sale', they might even tend to lose business as their existing customers might feel that the quality of service was being threatened. This trivial example does, however, highlight a more serious point. If price is to serve as an indicator of quality, then the price becomes part of an overall marketing strategy aimed at establishing the quality. In retailing this may be done through various forms of advertising, packaging etc. that creates an aura of 'style'. Look at the way perfumeries are sold. Likewise, for a hotel and restaurant, the decor, politeness, speed of service and the attention to fine detail are all important; and although adding to costs, they justify, in the public's mind, the higher price that is charged. None the less, even fine-quality hotels can over-charge and find that at a given level demand will tail off. Much of the marketing effort of organisations goes into assessing the public's 'thresholds', i.e. what is the lower price limit below which the public suspect the quality of the product and what is the highest price that the public will pay before they consider they are being overcharged. Having determined the price that will be charged by these market considerations, one must next assess the likely demand and the sales revenue it will generate. This may be estimated by looking at past levels of demand and the general factors in the economy affecting disposable income. Again, there is an emphasis on marketing knowledge and an ability to be sensitive to changes in demand. Having assessed the volume of demand, one then assesses the variable costs involved in meeting this demand and adds them to fixed costs. By definition, fixed costs are usually known, and, given a reasonable accuracy over the rate of inflation, variable costs are possible to forecast within an acceptable degree of error. Once total cost and total revenue is assessed, the question is whether or not the profit is satisfactory. Does it meet a required rate of return on capital employed? Does it generate sufficient funds for investment purposes, dividends, etc.? Should the profit be insufficient then the nature of the service is carefully analysed to see where cost savings can be found. 'Special features' introduced to appeal to customers may be abandoned if it is felt that their contribution to total cost is greater than their contribution in eliciting revenue and sales. In short, the nature of the product is trimmed to fit the price.

This pricing policy has gained some support within the industry, particularly where a group is in a position to build hotels or motels which are designed to operate at a given level of costs. In their annual report for the financial year 1973-74 Centre Hotels stated that 'Bedroom selling prices are directly related to capital costs, and this means investment and pricing policies are bound together. Success lies in an accurate indentification of consumer needs and potential demand.' Where there is a standardization of buildings such as in the motel type of accommodation, a tight control over variable costs can be maintained and a uniform pricing policy for all units can be attempted on this basis.

Contribution Analysis of Pricing

This method of pricing has attracted some attention in the hotel industry for the pricing of special packages such as weekend breaks, and is derived in part from marginal costing techniques. It rests on making a distinction between fixed and variable costs associated with a given volume of business. First, there is again an assessment of possible response to a given price level, thereby producing estimates of total revenue. From this is deducted the fixed costs involved in the product. The scheme being considered will be worth considering if the revenue it generates more than covers the variable costs involved and therefore makes a contribution to fixed costs that would not otherwise be forthcoming. This approach will also explain why for some it is not profitable to launch a weekend bargain break programme. The hotel will have to pay the fixed costs it has such as rents, mortgages, rates, capital and interest repayments, whether or not it opens for business. At weekends in the off-peak season, many hotels will find that from Friday to Sunday evening, occupancy levels will fall as businessmen leave for home. Consequently, the obvious solution seems to be to attract tourist demand for those hotels so as to fill empty beds that would otherwise remain empty, and generate revenue that would not otherwise be gained. Hence, the special 'bargain' price to attract these people. However, in doing so, various costs will be involved. Firstly, there will be advertising costs. Generally speaking, these tend to be comparatively low, for the independents will use *Let's Go* as do the large companies, and the majority of hotels will print brochures to be picked up by existing customers. Few are involved in press advertising. At first sight, it appears that there is little additional variable cost involved in weekend break schemes and hence profits are forthcoming. However, much depends on the level of weekend occupancy before the scheme is launched and the policy towards staffing. There is some evidence to suggest that if the weekend occupancy is below 30%, then a hotel would do well to carefully consider its weekend break scheme. At such an occupancy level the promotion of the scheme may generate additional demand that requires additional staffing, the cost of which, coupled with the additional promotional, linen, depreciation costs etc., is greater than the revenue gained. (Note though that since food costs are usually costed separately on a mark-up basis, meals will normally show a profit.) Particularly important is the staffing cost.

If part-time labour is being used the weekend break may mean employing this labour at an 'overtime' rate. Consequently, the addition to total costs may be greater than the addition to total revenue gained, as it is by discounted tariffs. On the other hand, if staff is already employed full time, then no additional variable cost is involved in these schemes. It can be seen that under certain conditions a minimum occupancy level is required before bargain breaks are offered. For example, Mercury Hotels Ltd (now taken over by Ladbrokes) did not offer bargain breaks until about 1976 because for a long time it was more profitable (or rather avoided most loss) to avoid employing staff at weekends than attempt to generate more demand. However, once weekend occupancy levels reached a level where staff were required to

TABLE 9.2 **Ratio of fixed to variable costs and contribution pricing (1)**

	Scheme X	Scheme Y
Tariff	£8.00	£12.00
Full cost	£7.00	£10.50
Profit	£1.00	£1.50
Net profit on sales	12½%	12½%

meet existing need levels, yet could also serve additional clients, the prospect of weekend breaks then became a more profitable proposition, and hence Quicksilver bargain breaks were launched; for now the additional revenue generated was greater than the costs involved in meeting and generating that demand. In due course, the contribution to fixed costs became such that total costs were covered and weekend occupancies became profitable.

Making this distinction between fixed and variable cost can be important. Assume, for example, that a hotel group is faced with two alternative schemes, X and Y as shown in Table 9.2. It might choose scheme Y in that it yields a higher value of profit, but an analysis of the variable cost content of the full cost could induce a change of mind, as illustrated in Table 9.3. Here it is seen that because variable costs are £5, scheme X makes the highest contribution to fixed costs, of £2 (full cost £7 less variable cost £5).

Scheme X makes the highest contribution to fixed costs. Hence, if there is uncertainty about the success of the schemes, and the possibility that demand may not reach the anticipated level, that scheme with the greatest contribution to fixed cost and profit is the better. You might wonder why, in a hotel group, the element of fixed cost should differ. However, within a group, hotels may be of differing ages or may have had more recent investment, and consequently one hotel may be carrying more interest and capital repayment charges than another, and

TABLE 9.3 **Ratio of fixed to variable costs and contribution pricing (2)**

	Scheme X	Scheme Y
Tariff	£8.00	£12.00
Variable Cost	£5.00	£9.50
Contribution	£3.00	£2.50

hence the difference. This factor does mean, therefore, that any hotel chain attempting to market a package at a standard price spread over a number of its hotels will have to accept that different hotels will achieve different levels of profit at the standard price.

Profit Sensitivity Analysis

The awareness that competitive pricing rests on a thorough knowledge of the market and cost behaviour has led larger groups to adopt, as a guide to pricing decisions, the technique of profit sensitivity analysis. This approach does help in that it concentrates upon the key areas of a hotel or restaurant operation and forces people to ask the right questions, and hence, hopefully, arrive at some solutions. It is easier to explain the technique if we look at an example. Let us suppose that a hotel manager decides that in his unit the key costs are food and beverage costs, labour costs, which are in turn divided into fixed and variable costs, other fixed costs meeting rates, interest charges etc., and sales costs, while the other important factors are occupancy rates and tariffs. Having identified these areas, one then assumes that a small change occurs in one of the variables, and, holding the other variables constant, one can assess how the change influences profits. This is done in Table 9.4, which is based on annual figures.

TABLE 9.4 **Profit sensitivity analysis**

Key factors	Base	5% change in price	5% change in occupancy	5% change in F & B costs	5% change in labour costs	5% reduction in all costs
Tariff (£)	10.00	10.50	10.00	10.00	10.00	10.00
Number of rooms occupied	2 000	2 000	2 100	2 000	2 000	2 000
Total revenue (£)	20 000	21 000	21 000	20 000	20 000	20 000
F & B costs (£)	6 000	6 000	6 300	6 300	6 000	5 700
Labour—variable (£)	1 000	1 000	1 050	1 000	1 050	950
Labour—fixed (£)	5 000	5 000	5 000	5 000	5 250	4 750
Other fixed (£)	3 000	3 000	3 000	3 000	3 000	2 850
Advertising (£)	1 000	1 000	1 050	1 000	1 000	950
Total cost (£)	16 000	16 000	16 400	16 300	16 300	15 200
Net profit (£)	4 000	5 000	4 600	3 700	3 700	4 800

TABLE 9.5 **The profit multiplier**

Variable factor (1)	Change in factor (%) (2)	Change in profit (£) (3)	Change in profit (%) (4)	Profit multiplier (4)÷(2)
Tariff	+5	+1000	+25	+5
Occupancy	+5	+ 600	+15	−3
F & B costs	+5	− 300	−7.5	−1.5
Labour costs	+5	− 300	−7.5	−1.5
All costs	−5	+ 800	+20	+4

The next step is to base these calculations on a common footing to ease comparison. This is done by dividing the change in net profit by the change in the key factor, so calculating what is termed, the profit multiplier. This is done in Table 9.5.

The example shows that, assuming that nothing else changed, profits are best increased by increasing prices, and that increasing occupancy rates in this particular instance, because of the pattern of costs, is not a satisfactory alternative. Nor either is cost reduction a more profitable path in that overall reduction of costs generates less additional profit than the increase in price. For this particular hotel then, and in general for most of the hotel industry, increased profitability lies in increased tariffs rather than cost reduction policies. Consequently, an emphasis on marketing is required to fill the requirement implied by the analysis; that is to say, increased profits will come *if* levels of demand are maintained. The concept of the profit multiplier indicates where the manager may most profitably spend his time; but it should not be assumed from this that cost reduction is unimportant. Under given market conditions, increased tariffs may be self-defeating as a hotel or restaurant prices itself out of the market. Consequently, the only way to achieve profits will lie on an ability to keep price rises to the minimum and cut costs wherever possible, without affecting the quality of the product offered too adversely.

The Importance of Price—A Case Study: Weekend Breaks

The price of a product has to be regarded as part of the overall marketing mix and strategy, and of the product. People are not adverse to spending money; what they do object to is poor value for money. Yet the price must be realistic for the target market. While the Rolls-Royce may well represent value for money, if every car manufacturer made cars equivalent to the Rolls, then the incidence of car ownership would rapidly decline. It is very difficult to isolate the importance of price in determining occupancy levels; in part, for example, the demand from some sections of the market is inelastic. Businessmen will continue to need to travel and hence to stay at hotels even if the tariffs increase further. Consequently, attempts at isolating the importance of the tariff as against decor, location, quality of service, etc. are bound to run into a number of research difficulties which statistical techniques cannot entirely overcome. However, in the area of bargain break holidays, in as much as these are aimed at fulfilling a specific purpose, it may be possible to use this example as a case study to see how important prices are in this particular market. The main motivation behind bargain break holidays is to increase hotel occupancy between Friday and Sunday night when occupancy levels fall due to a loss of business demand. It is a classic example of an application of price elasticity of demand; i.e., when one is looking at a discretionary element of spending, a reduction of prices may increase revenue if one assumes there is a responsiveness to price charges. As such, bargain break weekends have been in existence for some time.

In 1964 Grand Metropolitan, in conjunction with British Rail, launched Stardust holidays which offered a weekend in London for £9 7s 6d (£9.37½) including rail fare. Backed by an advertising campaign costing £1000 it gained 300 bookings, and by the early 1970s a profit was being made in as much as the marginal cost of the scheme was primarily the advertising and the travel since the hotels would have been open anyway. However, it was not until 1973 that practically all of the major groups were offering similar schemes, and then it was prompted by: (i) the existence of surplus accommodation that had been created by the investment carried out under the Hotel Incentive Development Scheme that ran between 1968 and 1973, and (ii) a fall of demand as the economy moved into a recession with increasing inflation (not eased by the industrial unrest, in part caused by the industrial relations legislation and the poor relations between the Government and the trades unions). Falling occupancy rates meant that the additional revenue generated by comparatively little promotional cost was more than welcome to the industry. Since then, the weekend bargain break has become an accepted part of the hotel industry's promotional activity, and each year the English Tourist Board's publication *Let's Go* lists more and more hotels anxious to gain this business. In addition, for some, the weekend special off-peak rates have been extended into year-round weekend promotions, and into other parts of the week, while in 1979 the idea of activity or interest holidays, which have long been run by universities and various educational trusts, was taken up with gusto by the industry. Certainly, for the small independent hotel, the comparatively small cost of advertising in *Let's Go* (about £70) would seem to repay dividends. It is, of course, difficult to judge the success of any scheme in that one is comparing what is with what might have been. One attempt was made by the author (*Hospitality*, Jan. 1980, p. 60) who compared the occupancy rates of hotels offering schemes with the occupancy rates recorded by A. C. Neilson in his surveys for the English Tourist Board for the winter of 1977–78. This was not entirely satisfactory in that an unknown number of the Neilson sample also offer weekend breaks, but in the period considered, such hotels, due to the wide sampling methods of Neilson's, were a minority of the sample.

A summary of the results shows that small hotels offering these schemes did significantly better than small hotels who did not, whereas the impact of these schemes, while beneficial for larger hotels, did not increase bed occupancy rates quite so dramatically. Table 9.6 indicates locational differences, but before attributing the higher occupancy of seaside hotels offering these schemes to those who did not, you must take into account the varying situations such hotels might find themselves in due to the common practice of many seaside hotels to close during the winter.

TABLE 9.6 **Comparison of hotels offering (O) weekend breaks and those not offering (NO) such breaks, winter 1977–78 (bed-occupancy)**

	\multicolumn{8}{c}{Location type}
	Seaside		Rural		Small town		Large town		Average	
Size (rooms)	O	NO	O	NO	O	NO	O	NO	O	NO
1–15	48	22	42	31	55	42	n.a.	36	45	33
16–50	40	34	43	42	48	47	52	50	44	43
51+	42	34	45	39	53	42	55	48		
Sample size	37		41		8		25			

(Source: *Hospitality*, Jan. 1980)

Since the schemes seem to be successful it could be thought that their competitive pricing must be an element. Earlier studies had indicated that discounts on tariffs given had ranged from 10 to 60%. By 1977 the range of discounts given had shrunk so that the average discount given was about 14%, the maximum being about 55%. The survey indicated that price, however, was possibly a secondary factor. A major element in the success of these schemes was location and style of the hotel (particularly age), and that price may have been a factor as a means of choosing between hotels once customers have, as it were, drawn up a short list that meet their criteria of the type of hotel they require for a short break. Thus, the success of the smaller hotels in these schemes is not just one of price but a strong reflection of the fact that larger hotels are often in city centres which are not wanted by the person who wishes to have a get-away-from-it-all holiday. Such a finding supports earlier research by the English Tourist Board surveys among holiday-makers. Consequently, it would appear that hotels should not depend on the fact of a discounted tariff to 'pull in' weekend occupancies on these schemes, but care must be paid to the means and packaging of these schemes.

Current Problems in Tariffs and Marketing

There are a number of surveys of tariffs and sales movements, some undertaken by the Central Statistical Office, some by management consultants such as Green Belfield-Smith, some by individual researchers, and by some booking agents such as Exp-o-tel. Table 9.7 is based on an amalgamation of these sources, and estimates the movements of tariffs, profits and sales compared with movements in the retail price index. From this table it can be seen that meal prices

TABLE 9.7 **Annual movements in tariffs and meal costs (% annual change)**

	1973	1974	1975	1976	1977	1978	1979
Tariffs	4	14	23	8	23	21	23
Profits	2	-20	12	30	24	23	22
Sales	5	4	13	20	28	15	12
Meals out	4	12	19	23	18	16	10
Retail Price Index	9	16	24	17	16	8	10

(Sources: *Annual Abstracts of Statistics, Green Belfield-Smith, Exp-o-tel, private surveys, Department of Trade and Industry*)

adapt very quickly to changes in costs, and correlate very closely with the rate of inflation. The forward advertising of tariffs, however, presents a greater problem, though the discrepancy between tariffs and the inflation rate can probably be explained by demand conditions. The resistance to tariff increases in 1974 and 1975, as indicated by the sales figures, meant that hoteliers in 1976 increased tariffs by less than the rate of inflation, and subsequent increases above the inflation rate were then supported by a growth in demand. By 1979 that growth was diminishing, particularly in that the 12% sales growth was being increasingly explained by tariff rises rather than by an increase in the volume of business.

At the beginning of the 1980s the industry faces a situation akin to that of the period 1974–75; with an increase in costs and uncertainty as to the response of both the domestic and international markets to an increase in tariffs. In 1979 the Licensed Residential Wages Council awarded pay rises of about 25%, while property rates, food prices, interest rates, etc. all showed an increase as the rate of inflation accelerated from just under the 10% per annum mark to over 16%; all of which meant that tariff increases were unavoidable. However, at the same time, customer resistance to price increases was present, with the North American market showing sensitivity to London hotel prices as adverse publicity recurred in 1979, allied with a fall in the value of the American dollar. In addition, the increases of VAT to 15% further increased tariff prices. For example, if a hotel charges a tariff of £15 plus VAT and decides to increase the tariff to £19, the final price the customer pays is £21.85, compared with the original tariff of £17.25, an increase of 26.6%. At a VAT rate of 8%, the level existing before the 1979 budget, the VAT-inclusive tariff would have been £20.52, i.e. £1.32 less. The position is not aided by the common usage of a mark-up form of pricing, as Table 9.8 shows. Rows (a) and (c) show the tariffs we

TABLE 9.8 **The effect of mark-up pricing and VAT on tariffs (£)**

	Average cost	Mark-up at 25%	Total	VAT at 15%	Tariff
(a)	12	3	15	2.25	17.25
(b)	16	4	20	3.00	23.00
(c)	16	(3)	19	2.85	21.85

have already noted. But let us suppose that the original tariff of £15 was calculated on a mark-up basis of average cost plus 25%. When average cost increases from £12 to £16, the maintenance of the 25% profit margin increases the VAT exclusive tariff to £20, which, with VAT, increases the final tariff to £23. Consequently, an original cost increase of £4 is converted to a £5.75 increase for the customer. The hotelier has thereby contributed to a maintenance of the inflation rate, whereas the retention of the money value of the mark-up, as in Table 9.8, row (c), helps to hold down the price increase to the customer, as the resultant tariff is £21.85; i.e. an increase of 'only' £4.60 compared with the previous increase of £5.75.

The implications of this example are that, faced with a situation of increased costs and consumer resistance to too high a tariff increase, hotels may be able to preserve money profits by accepting a lower profit margin on tariffs, as in example (c), and retain a price competitive edge to attract customers if other hoteliers are adopting the strategy outlined in row (b). The extension of the competitive edge is required if a growth in profits is to occur, for such a growth is necessary if the real value of profits is to be maintained in an inflationary period.

For the buying power of profits to be preserved, profits must increase by an amount equal to the rate of inflation. Other policies are also possible. Resistance to increased tariffs may be weakened by successful marketing. The purpose of advertising is not simply to sell more; it can be argued that it is to sell more at a higher price! The successful establishment of a brand name will, for example, mean that customers willingly pay more for the brand product than for another, possibly, equally good, product. Bearing this in mind, it can be regarded as more than fortuitous that in 1980 three companies, Thistle, Centre and Embassy, launched a joint marketing operation of weekend break holidays under the name of Highlife. The marketing effort involves not only increased advertising, but also a sales team of 35 who planned to approach 3572 travel agents who were offered 10% commission on sales. At the same time both Grand Metropolitan and Trusthouse Forte, increased their marketing of similar holidays. Another tactic that can be operated in a stringent financial climate is to control costs carefully. Obviously, there are various stages that can be envisaged. The first is waste avoidance. Once that is achieved, further cost reduction can only be achieved by a reduction in the quality of service. Thus, room service may be minimized, breakfast may become a self-service operation, and a buffet-style meal may become more common. Yet, again, there is a minimum that can be achieved. For some hotels it may well be more cost-effective to close during the off-peak season, and, depending on the ratio of part-time to full-time staff, it may aid profits not to offer weekend breaks. The increasing, almost frenzied competition in this market may mean that there is greater competition for what may be a non-growth market. In the 1972 British Tourist Authority statistics it was reported that only about 20% of the sample population had two or more holidays away from home, and the same figure was true in 1979.

While these figures refer to people being away from home for over four nights, it may be a valid indicator of market size. It would seem, therefore, that the weekend break holiday will only raise occupancy rates in more hotels if they can attract people away from alternative forms of accommodation. For many people this might represent a change in social habits, and those involved in the marketing of hotels have to discuss the extent and desirability of penetrating the C1 and C2 markets. If marketing does generate a greater demand from this segment then, particularly as it is a part of the population that has acquired a fast increase in incomes over the past two decades, the problem might well be that of a shortage of rooms!

The problem of over-pricing is forcing hoteliers in the early 1980s to examine costing techniques and marketing strategies. In addition to the possible courses of action outlined above, two others exist. One is to shorten the period of forward pricing. It is common for tariff prices in the autumn to spring period to be determined in the early summer. This allows time for the calculations and publicity etc. before the rush of the peak period. Thus a price may be set in (say) June for a period of eleven months into the future. Consequently, if consumer resistance to tariff increases is strong, autumn bookings may be the most adversely influenced. If a hotel is confident in its ability to attract custom, it may be prepared to possibly double promotion costs by charging a lower tariff in the earlier part of the period and a higher tariff later. To obtain the highest possible revenue from this successfully necessitates two separate promotions, as the advertising of the twin set of tariffs in the initial period may simply switch tourist demand from the spring to the autumn, thereby creating a situation of having the hotel open in the spring to meet a lower demand and so incurring higher costs and less revenue at a time when inflation is that much higher. The markets must be kept separate. It may be argued that the decision to take a short secondary holiday is often taken not more than a month before the holiday, but the pattern may be disturbed if people feel that by delaying that decision a higher cost will be incurred. A further approach is to try and extend stays at the hotel. Extended stays achieve a greater security of higher occupancy ratings in hotels more dependent on tourist demand, while marginal cost savings may be achieved. Examples of the latter may be a slightly reduced linen bill, some savings in food in that restaurant demand may be better forecast, and administration costs may be marginally saved, e.g. in terms of numbers of invoices. A careful analysis of such costs may allow some discount for extended stays.

Whether or not a hotel needs to adopt these policies will depend on the existing occupancy levels. A hotel with high occupancy that can maintain those levels, implying an inelastic demand, will be able to increase tariffs to compensate for higher costs without too much concern. However, few are in this situation, and although the period 1976–78 was generally one of high sales, this was not evenly distributed. London hotels did very well, but some hotels in the smaller traditional seaside resorts fared less well. For them, a period of a slowing in the growth of demand may prove too difficult to overcome. Neither will they be helped if the work of the public tourist agencies is adversely effected by the Government reducing public expenditure in an attempt to control the money supply. Some may say the industry has been in a similar position before. The early 1970s were years of marginal profits and uncertain demand. If it survived then, it will survive now. In many ways the industry is perhaps *better* prepared. Marketing awareness is greater, and, for the major companies, more assets are now available for each company after some five years of amalgamation, take-overs and diversification. In addition, just as the gloom of the early 1970s gave way to the better period of 1976–79, so too forecasts for the middle 1980s are bright. It may well be too easy to exaggerate the difficulties of 1980–81, for after all, while 1979 was forecast by some to be a poor year, the number of foreign visitors was higher than in Jubilee year, the increase in profits was near 1978 levels, and records were achieved for occupancy levels associated with various promotions. In an inflationary period, people expect prices to rise, and so long as tariff increases are controlled the industry can expect to maintain progress. There are also grounds for longer-term optimism since surveys undertaken by the National Economic Development Office and the British Tourist Authority indicate a future growth in demand; so much so, that there is a fear of a shortage of capacity in the London area for meeting peak periods of demand. A shortage was forecasted of 20 000 bed-spaces by 1985 and of 50 000 by 1990. Consequently, because of the delays involved in obtaining building permission, actual design and construction, the industry in London is being faced with the need of undertaking investment even while there is currently a slowing down in the rate of growth. Conversion of existing premises can offer a cost-effective approach, and, coupled with the different attitudes by the London boroughs, may be one reason why the office premises of J. Lyons at Cadby Hall, Hammersmith is going to be converted to a 910-bedroom hotel. Likewise, investment is also required by other hotels as, faced with possible consumer resistance to higher tariffs, hoteliers will need to offer good facilities to justify those tariffs and to attract business. Such facilities may also offer possible additional business, for example, through the business conference and seminar market.

At no time since 1974 has the pricing decision for hotels been so vital as in the early 1980s, but in many ways the industry is now better prepared than it was in the early and middle 1970s.

10
Government Economic Policy and the Catering Industry

The Aims of Government Economic Policy

There is considerable agreement about the aims of government economic policy between economists, politicians, journalists and other commentators. But as to the means of achieving them, there is dreadful confusion as economic prophets of varying opinions create a cacophony rivalling that at the Tower of Babel. Fortunately, our brief is a limited one, but a start must be made by indicating the aims of policy and how the possible means of achieving those aims could affect the industry.

Since the end of the Second World War there have been four main themes with subsidiary ones in British economic policy, each coming to the forefront at some particular period or other, but none showing signs of being conclusively achieved. Taking these themes in no particular order, we can start thus:

(1) **To maintain full employment**—This, until comparatively recently, has tended to be the major concern of politicians, perhaps because of the British experience of the late 1920s and the 1930s when unemployment was over three million and in a number of areas (particularly Wales, the North-East and Central Scotland) local unemployment rates were well in excess of 60% of the working population. It was this experience that prompted many of the leading politicians and trade unionists of the 1960s and early 1970s to enter their political careers, and the vividness of their adolescent experiences in part stayed with them. At the same time, the economic theories of Maynard Keynes, published in 1936, indicated how government could avert unemployment, and his theories generally served government well for nearly 30 years after the end of the Second World War. Thus, both political and economic opinion were, at least at a popular level, slanted towards the unemployment problem.

(2) **The maintenance of price stability**—In recent years, however, and in spite of increasing unemployment, more has been spoken of inflation. This is no new thing, for there were credit squeezes at the beginning of the 1960s to avoid inflation, but since 1973 Britain has experienced its worst rates of inflation this century. The plight has been compounded by a growing uncertainty as to how to tackle the problem, since the Keynesian theory of holding back demand meant increasing taxes, which move added to prices and fuelled wage demands which, in Keynesian terms, increased demand and thus helped inflation. At the same time, other theories found favour, particularly Friedmanite monetarism, named after Milton Friedman, an American who argued that the main force in the economy was the supply and flow of money. A confusion over theories has not been helped by the thought that much of the source of inflation has been due to sharp increases in the prices of world commodities (particularly oil) since 1973. Consequently, the Government sought to solve the problem by tackling symptoms and imposing restraints on wages and prices, and this, aided by increased stability in world commodity prices and tighter control of money supply, bought some relief in the period 1975–79.

(3) **The balance of payments**—The balance of payments is divided into three sections: (i) the *Visible Balance of Trade* which is concerned with the overseas buying and selling of physical goods; (ii) the *Invisible Balance of Trade*, i.e. the overseas transactions concerning services such as tourism, shipping, insurance and banking, and (iii) the *Capital Account*, which is concerned with the flows of currencies involved with investment overseas and inter-governmental borrowings, and also with regard to transactions undertaken with international monetary bodies such as the International Monetary Fund, or the Bank of International Settlements.

The British problem is that we rarely have a surplus on the Visible Trade Balance (indeed there have only been ten surpluses in the last 187 years), and thus we have to make a large enough surplus on the Invisibles to cancel out the deficit on the Visibles. In the years since 1971 there have been difficulties in achieving this, and consequently borrowings from overseas have been made, while at the same time, the need to attract overseas currency has meant that the interest rates have tended to be high, even though this has perhaps prejudiced investment in the UK by British companies. The historical difficulty in achieving a surplus on Visibles was a lack of raw resources other than coal. The UK imports approximately half of its food, and for a long time was dependent on overseas supplies of raw commodities such as oil. Part of the importance of North Sea Oil is due to the impact it will have on our balance of payments—not so much because the UK may export large quantities, but because it will save a proportion of oil imports. Increasingly, however, the UK has begun to import manufactured goods which effectively compete with British goods, and one of the best publicised examples of this is the car industry where foreign imports are catching larger shares of the home market.

Balance of payments problems are not new to the UK, and in the 1950s and 1960s a feature of the British economy was that, when it was expansionary, it sucked in increasing amounts of raw material imports and thus, since exports did not increase so rapidly due to growing home demand taking up home output, the balance of payments moved into deficit. The governments of that period then took corrective measures to move the balance back into surplus, and in so doing upheld the international value of the pound sterling. Unfortunately, such action usually required a damping down of demand and thus halted the economic growth. In 1967, however, the Government sought to improve the balance of payments by devaluation, which makes exports more price-competitive by making them cheaper. This did work, but when the balance again moved into a deficit at a later period (and because of unrest in the international currency markets generally due to pressure on the American dollar to devalue, and pressure on the German mark and Japanese yen to revalue) the pound was floated in 1971, and continued to fall steadily until the summer of 1977 when it began to gain marginally. By this time it was worth about 70% of its 1971 level in international currency dealings.

The movement of the pound, allied with general economic conditions, has had an influence on tourism, and as a result tourism has become an important earner of foreign currency in the British balance of payments.

(4) **To create economic growth**—In the 1950s governments were re-elected on the philosophy, 'You've never had it so good', and this was not only true in terms of increasing income per head of population, but it also showed how important economic growth had become to the ordinary person's consciousness. Economic growth has been seen as the cure for many problems. It has been argued that increasing demand and output creates a need for more jobs and thus is a solution to

unemployment. Economic growth can also cure inflation in that additional productive capacity can meet demand. Indeed, British economic policies of 1962-64 and in 1971-72 had some aspects of a belief of curing inflation by aiming for economic growth by tax-cuts and a stimulation of demand. And, in as much as it can be claimed that a growing economy is a strong economy, the balance of payments problems may be cured, as we may see from envious glances at Germany and Japan. Certainly, while the UK consistently had economic growth in terms of increasing income per head and thus increased material standards of living up to 1973-74, our record has not been good compared with many other industrial countries. In part, however, perhaps the difference has been one of maturity, as the divergence between British and American growth rates has not been over-great, and as other European countries progress their rates of growth too have fallen. None the less, there has been grave concern as to why the British rate of economic progress has not matched that of others, and, in the post-oil-crisis world of the middle and late 1970s and early 1980s it has been the case that while the rate of growth in many European countries has slowed down to one or two percentage points a year, in Britain, there has been zero growth, and indeed at times a slight 'negative growth' (if such a phrase is not a contradiction in terms!).

At the same time, there has been increased criticism of the narrow concept of economic growth, and it has been argued that increasing standards of living cannot be purely equated with increased income, and commentators have expressed concern over 'the quality of life', and have pointed to facts such as increasing crime to indicate that economic growth is not a panacea for all ills. Unfortunately, in the period since 1974 when, in Britain, economic growth has all but stopped, those social ills still continue to grow, only now many commentators ascribe growing juvenile crime, for example, to unemployment caused by a lack of economic growth! At the same time, the economic difficulties have prejudiced many social services that hitherto had begun to be taken for granted. Thus, the objective of restoring economic growth is again valued. None the less, there is a long-term major problem, and that is the finite supply of resources that is used in the present means of obtaining such growth. While we may all seek to emulate American standards, the fact is that known present energy sources do not permit this and thus the problem is how to attain the desired growth by a means that does not premeditate an ecological, social and economic disaster. Some are optimistic, others less so.

(5) **To solve the regional problem**—'The regional problem' has been a part of British economic policy ever since the Government began to play an active economic policy making role 50 years ago, and, it is true to say, the problem is still with us. The difficulty is that some areas consistently have rates of unemployment that are higher than the national average, and if the differences have closed slightly in the middle 1970s then, according to some, it is due only to an all-round increase in unemployment. The problem regions are those declining industrial areas of central Scotland, the North-east, the North-west, Merseyside and S.E. Lancashire and rural areas, including the South-west and Wales, because there, lack of opportunity has meant a drift from the land and rural areas that once supported industry, and so, in a sense, has caused a hidden unemployment. Nor does the problem cease with simply recording higher levels of unemployment. The lack of income means other deprivations. There is the expected result that car ownership and the ownership of household durables is proportionately less in these areas than in the South-east. But, in addition, a comparison of exam results and infant mortality rates will show that the North-east (say) is not so well favoured as the richer South-east. Such statistics indicate that degree of urban deprivation that exists, the poor housing and poor social capital. Doctors in the South-east, for example, tend to have shorter lists of patients than elsewhere. This is not to say that large areas of the regions are slums—slum clearance plans have made considerable headway and new centres adorn many of the towns in these regions. But the problem does persist in spite of government grants and attempts to attract new industry to these areas. In addition, there are signs that the attempted solutions have themselves created problems as London has lost many thousands of manufacturing jobs with the consequence that unemployment rates in London boroughs such as Tower Hamlets are now as high as many regions in the 'development areas'. It is symptomatic of the problem that under the 1972 Industry Act, 53% of the land area of the UK was designated as an area receiving some form of government regional aid, and an even greater part of the UK qualifies for EEC regional grant aids.

We have now examined some of the generally agreed economic policies. There are others that depend upon the political hue of the

Government. Some are a reflection of differences of degree; others are more basic. For example, while many politicians of the two main parties recognize a need for some redistribution of income, there are considerable differences of opinion as to how far to go, with various principles which, though seemingly valid in themselves, can and do clash in practice. The principles of reward for effort, equality of opportunity, freedom of choice and no discrimination on the basis of prejudice illustrate such difficulties. In the extreme such arguments mean a basic difference between politicians on such subjects as nationalization, with both proponents and opponents of nationalization claiming that their ideas would aid economic growth.

The hotel and catering industry is affected by government policies that seek to achieve the above aims: sometimes to its benefit, at other times not. At the same time, the hotel and catering industry is able to make its own contribution towards the fulfilment of these objectives, of which the best example is in the achieving of higher rates of employment and the aiding of the balance of payments through tourism.

The Industry, Its Employment Policy and Relations with Government

The commercial sector of the industry employs approximately 860 000 and is the eighth largest industrial employer in the country. Consequently, it cannot help but be intimately concerned with employment policy, and has indeed been adversely influenced by government attempts in the 1960s to switch labour from the service industries into manufacturing by the introduction of Selective Employment Tax. The tax was abolished in 1970 and was generally conceded to have been (at best) of a dubious success since it increased the tax burden on service industries and made them more wary of employing staff, while the problem for manufacturing industry was one of investment and productivity levels rather than one of attracting employees. The result was that in the hotel and catering industry, employment actually fell from 730 000 in 1964 and did not regain this level until 1972—although one cannot blame the whole of this upon SET. Another factor at this time was the growth of UK demand for holidays overseas, as will be seen later in this section when looking at the industry's impact on the balance of payments. To recap from Chapter 5, it was seen that the industry employs approximately 3.6% of the working population, and that approximately two-thirds of its labour force is female. Probably the most important contribution to employment that the industry can make is in terms of the regional problem because so many hotels are situated in the rural and seaside sites of the development areas. Indeed, one aspect of many of the development regions such as Scotland, Wales, Yorkshire, Cumbria and the South-west is that they are important tourist regions, and consequently tourism does provide many important employment opportunities. One means of measuring the contribution of an industry to employment is by a *location quotient*. This is calculated by the percentage of the total working population in an area employed by a given industry, divided by the percentage of the national workforce that that industry employs. Thus, if the regional employment of the hotel and catering industry were equal to the national proportion of the employed in the industry, then the resultant of the calculation would have the value one. If the value of the calculation is more than one, the industry in that area is employing proportionately more than the national average. The higher the figures, the more important is the industry as an employer in that area. This method of calculation, therefore, takes into account the relative importance of the hotel and catering industry as an employer in each area, and so it can be said that whereas the industry employs more people in the South-east (about 250 000) than in the North (where the industry employs less than 50 000), it is more important an employer in the North than in the South-east.

Table 10.1 shows that in the development regions of Wales, Scotland, the South-west, the North and Tyneside, the industry is a proportionately more important employer than elsewhere in the country; but even in these areas the industry rarely employs more than 3.5% of the total working population. Only in one part of the country is the industry a major employer and that is on the N.W. Welsh coast where the hotel and catering industry accounts for about 9% of the total working population. It is also interesting to note that in most regions the location quotient has fallen, although usually only marginally. The three regions where it has increased have been East Anglia, Wales and Scotland, with only the first having any significant change; but the changes are all the more significant in Wales and Scotland because they are development regions.

It can therefore be stated that, as a labour-intensive industry, hotel and catering can play a constructive role in regional development

TABLE 10.1 **Regional location quotients**

Area	1966	1971
North	1.11	1.13
Tyneside	1.15	1.03
Yorkshire	0.88	0.55
West Yorkshire	0.78	0.76
North-west	0.94	0.89
S.E. Lancs Conurbation	0.80	0.82
Merseyside	0.91	0.86
East Midlands	0.92	0.79
West Midlands	0.84	0.79
West Midlands Conurbation	0.70	0.69
East Anglia	0.66	0.89
South-east	1.07	1.00
Greater London	1.08	1.03
Outer Metropolitan	0.77	0.75
South-west	1.36	1.31
Wales	1.05	1.09
Scotland	1.08	1.13
Clydeside	0.80	0.84

(Source: *Census of Population*, 1966 and 1971)

policy. Certainly, the industry itself has not been slow to realize this and has pressed its claims continuously, and in July 1977 the National Enterprise Board was reported as supporting a growing tourist industry for the North-east, one of the development areas, as a means of creating employment. Unfortunately, government regional policy of grants and tax allowances has tended to be concentrated on manufacturing industry, and consequently neither hotels nor catering have automatically qualified for these grants. The UK does not have special tax arrangements on depreciation for hotels as other European countries do—namely, Denmark, France, Spain, Germany and Switzerland. Indeed, a 1974 NEDO report concuded that the UK offers less assistance to hotels to invest in development areas than any of the other countries it studied, with the exception of Switzerland. For example, it has been noted that one of the major costs in hotel developments is the cost of land, but no expenditure on land is eligible for capital allowances. Likewise, if a building is not 'industrial' it does not qualify for a grant under the 1972 Industry Act. The industry may however obtain grants upon the purchase of equipment and under the current regional legislation, which lapses in 1980, 22% grants may be available. Likewise, it is possible for hoteliers and caterers to obtain some tax concessions for the replacement of china and cutlery, but such tend to be special arrangements. A major inducement to industry to employ people in the development areas was the regional employment premium where firms were given a direct payment on the basis of the number of staff they employ; but this too referred *only* to manufacturing industry. A 1979 report by the management consultants Horwath and Horwath took up the same theme and compared the assistance given with their respective hotel and catering industries by the UK, France, Greece, Spain, Austria and West Germany. Of the six countries, it was the UK that received the least government assistance and faced the greatest difficulties in securing long-term loans. Yet, in comparing the rate of return on investment for similar types of hotel buildings, the English hotels showed the highest rate of return, a return of 13.5% as against the next best of 9.5% for Austria. Against that, however, the rates of inflation in the UK were higher than those of Austria and West Germany, and consequently investors required a higher rate of return. This is not to say that the industry has not received *any* government aid. As indicated previously, the industry has received government aid and monies from the EEC, and the major avenues of revenue are through the British Tourist Authority and through institutions such as COSIRA, SICRAS, ICFC, etc.

The major scheme that existed in the past for government aid to the industry was the Hotel Development Incentive Scheme which operated between April 1968 and March 1973. This was introduced partly because of the criticisms of a lack of government aid. At the time, the Spanish government was providing loans on easy terms of up to 40% of the cost of building a hotel, in Portugal there were 50% loans, and in France over £14 million had been lent by the government in 1966 to their hotel industry. At the same time, the British government became aware, following the 1967 devaluation of the pound and the consequent attraction of the UK to overseas tourists, of how the industry could benefit the balance of payments. The Hotels Development Incentive Scheme was preceeded by an experimental Hotel Loans Advisory Committee which operated between 1967 and 1968 and which allocated £2.4 million out of the £5 million made available to it. While this would not seem particularly successful at first sight, it did give both parties, government and hoteliers, experience of dealing with each other, and, since in part the 'low' response was due to a need for a longer time period for loans, the scene was set for the Hotels Development Incentive Scheme. To qualify for the scheme a hotel had to have a minimum of 10 bedrooms (25 if in Greater London), have a lounge and provide an evening meal in addition to breakfast. Under the scheme, there were 20% grants on buildings and fixed equipment up to a maximum of £1000 per letting bedroom, with slightly higher figures of 25% and £1250 for hotels in Development Areas. A total of £43 million was made available. This had a significant effect on hotel profitability. Rates of return, on a post-tax DCF method of calculation rose from under 10% to about 12% for large hotels, but with the removal of the scheme in 1973, rates of return fell back to their previous level; and fell further in 1974 and 1975 as the scheme created a surplus of hotel rooms with the slow down in the growth of tourist demand.

Certainly the scheme had a considerable impact on the stock of hotel accommodation. It was estimated that the loans generated some £300 million of investment by the industry from its own funds and created 1300 new hotels and extensions with over 50 000 bedrooms and 100 000 new bed-spaces. Of these figures, 20 000 bed-spaces were in London. For many small hotels it made possible the attracting of entirely new conference, seminar and functions business, while all types of new equipment ranging from wash-basins, freezers, air-conditioning and central heating were installed. The question is: how much of that increase would have taken place without the scheme, and how much took place because of it? There is some evidence to suggest that while for smaller, proprietor-managed hotels, it did generate entirely new projects, for larger companies and chains it tended to simply bring forward projects that were already in the planning stages. Also, for such companies, the provision of government funds meant a reinforcement of the wish to trade up-market, even though the maximum limits on loans had been designed to provide an expansion of medium tariff accommodation. Yet, in as much as there was an increase in new rooms, and as profitability could be said to have been 20% higher during the period of the scheme when comparing pre-1968 and post-1973 profit levels, the scheme must have made a significant impact, particularly since the higher grants for hotels in development areas meant that the hotels were making profits marginally better than those of manufacturing industry, which record should have attracted some investment capital. If, therefore, the scheme was successful, why was it dropped?

To a degree the answer lay in the fact that the Government recognized part, but not all, of the problem. On the one hand, it saw an industry that could potentially make a significant contribution to employment and the balance of payments; yet which, due to previously poor profit levels, had difficulty in attracting long-term loan capital. On the other hand, it perhaps failed to recognize that most of the new overseas tourist demand would be centred in London, and that there was a need for a national tourist strategy. Locational considerations as a basis for grants was not really analysed apart from the extra 5% grant given to Development Areas. In part, it could be argued that it was not for the scheme to develop a 'tourist policy', this being the business of the bodies set up by the 1969 Development of Tourism Act; but in this case a rejoinder could be made that the two attempts could have been better coordinated. Another argument for the scheme not continuing may have been some disappointment over the industry's seeming inability to contribute towards employment.

While it is agreed that the industry is labour-intensive, it is becoming less so with the passing of time due to increased technology. Yet, it can be objected that this is not true of hotel and catering only, and in this respect the industry is simply partaking in a general trend. And indeed the industry is still more labour-intensive than most, and is becoming less labour-intensive at a far slower rate than manufacturing industry which attracts most of the grants at present (Table 10.2). Indeed, in manufacturing it is not uncommon for each new job created to cost about £60 000 due to the heavy capital investment required. A

TABLE 10.2 **The estimated numbers of workers per £1000 worth of value added**

Industry	1961	1971	% change
All manufacturing	1.03	0.74	28.2
All services	0.96	0.77	19.8
Hotel and catering	0.95	0.79	16.8
Hotels	n.a.	1.25	n.a.
All industries	1.02	0.77	24.5

(Source: *Census of Production*, 1961, 1971)

comparable figure for a hotel must be less, particularly for small hotels where, for example, a new small 30-room hotel would cost £600 000 at £20 000 per room, and would create a few more than ten jobs, the exact number depending on the number of part-time (female?) staff that would be employed. However, because the industry tends to have a lower degree of inter-relatedness with supplying industries compared with many others, and because, at least for male labour, it tends to be a below-average wage-payer, it tends to have a low multiplier effect in the region. What is meant by this is that the money paid by an employer is income to his suppliers and employees, who in turn spend it, thus providing income for a third party, who, in turn will spend it, and so on, continuing the process.

TABLE 10.3 **The multiplier process**

	\multicolumn{9}{c}{Periods of time}
	1	2	3	4	5	6	7	8	9
Spending		80	64	52	41	33	27	21	16	12
Retained		20	16	12	11	8	6	6	5	4
Initial injection	100	80	64	52	41	33	27	21	16	12

This process is simply illustrated in Table 10.3. An initial injection of £100 when received is passed on, in that the first recipient retains £20 as profit and buys £80 of goods. In turn, the next person keeps about 25% and spends 75%. If each does so, after nine time periods the initial injection has created an additional expenditure of £(80 + 64 + 52 + 41 . . .); i.e. a total of £346. There is, therefore, a multiplier of 3.46 (£346 ÷ £100) after nine periods; and, if we traced the pattern through we would find that the final expenditure created would be approaching £400 to give a multiplier of four. This is because the multiplier is calculated normally by taking the reciprocal of the proportion of increased income that is retained. So, in applying this to our example, we find that

$$\text{Multiplier} = \frac{1}{\text{Proportion of change in income that is not spent}}$$

$$= \frac{1}{25\%} = \frac{1}{1/4} = 4$$

and the final income generated is given by the formula

$$\text{Generated income} = \text{Injection} \times \text{multiplier}$$

In our example £100 injection multiplied by four equals £400.

It will be realized that another way of calculating the multiplier would be to involve expenditure rather than savings. If you receive an increase in income and spend part of it, and save the remainder, then the savings plus expenditure equals the change in income. So, if in the above example, people save a $\frac{1}{4}$ of their increased income, they spend $\frac{3}{4}$. So the multiplier can be calculated by the formula

$$\text{Multiplier} = \frac{1}{1 - \text{proportion of change in income that is spent}}$$

which in our example is

$$= \frac{1}{1 - 3/4} = \frac{1}{1/4} = 4$$

The answer remains the same. For various statistical reasons it may be easier to calculate expenditure rather than savings, and consequently tourism multipliers are usually on this basis. A first step to calculating tourism multipliers may be the formula

$$\text{Tourism multiplier} = \frac{1}{1 - A \times B}$$

where A is the proportion of tourist spending that local people spend on local goods and services, and B is the proportion of that expenditure of local people that accrues as local income. The formula would then be multiplied by the value of spending by tourists in an area.

But once started, the process will eventually die out because at each stage someone will retain some money as savings, though, if the savings are channelled through institutions such as banks, these will come to be used in investment lending. Therefore, an industry that uses many suppliers on a continuous basis and is a payer of above average wages will have a greater multiplier effect upon the region to the benefit of other industries and employment. Generally speaking, the hotel and catering industry tends to have a lower dependence on suppliers than many other industries once the capital equipment is purchased. If we remember, it is labour which is the main cost in the industry, particularly for hotels, and yet, for male labour, the industry pays below-average wages. Consequently, the multiplier effect of the hotel industry is lower than the average for all industries according to estimates by the NEDO in 1974. These give a figure of 1.38 for hotels, as against a manufacturing industry average of 1.60, and an all-industry average of 1.52. These, however, are output multipliers, and it is also possible to estimate multipliers for income generation effects and for employment. It can be argued that for Development Areas these are even more important, and that the low degree of inter-relatedness of the industry referred to above may even help as it means that its income and employment creating effects are less likely to be dissipated outside of the region. One of the earliest studies of tourism multipliers was in the 1972 report *Tourism and the Economy* by G. Richards of the University of Surrey. He calculated that if the indirect effects were included, the income multiplier of tourism was 1.6 and the employment multiplier was 2.4. In other words, a £1 million of tourist expenditure created income flows of £1.6 million, and 2400 man-hours of labour was induced by a £1 million tourist expenditure. Dr. Richards referred to 1965 statistics, and to the UK as a whole. More recent studies tend to refer to more localized areas, and consequently the multipliers are considerably smaller (Table 10.4). The mechanics of the multiplier process were illustrated by a study of tourist spending in Eastbourne undertaken by the English Tourist Board, and the example also indicates how the discrepancy between national and local multipliers can occur. Fig. 10.1 indicates that out of every £100 spent by tourists at Eastbourne hotels and guest-houses £72 is spent by the hoteliers on goods, services and labour. In turn, the recipients of this income spend

TABLE 10.4 **Income and employment multipliers for tourism**

		Income	*Employment*	*Source*
Anglesey	(1973)	0.25	0.48	1
Gwynedd	(1973)	0.37	n.a.	1
Tayside	(1975)	0.46	0.47	2
Skye	(1974)	0.32	n.a.	3

1. Dr. Brian Archer, Bangor University
2. Henderson and Cousins, Edinburgh University
3. *The Economic Impact of Tourist Spending in Skye* (University of Stirling)

GOVERNMENT ECONOMIC POLICY

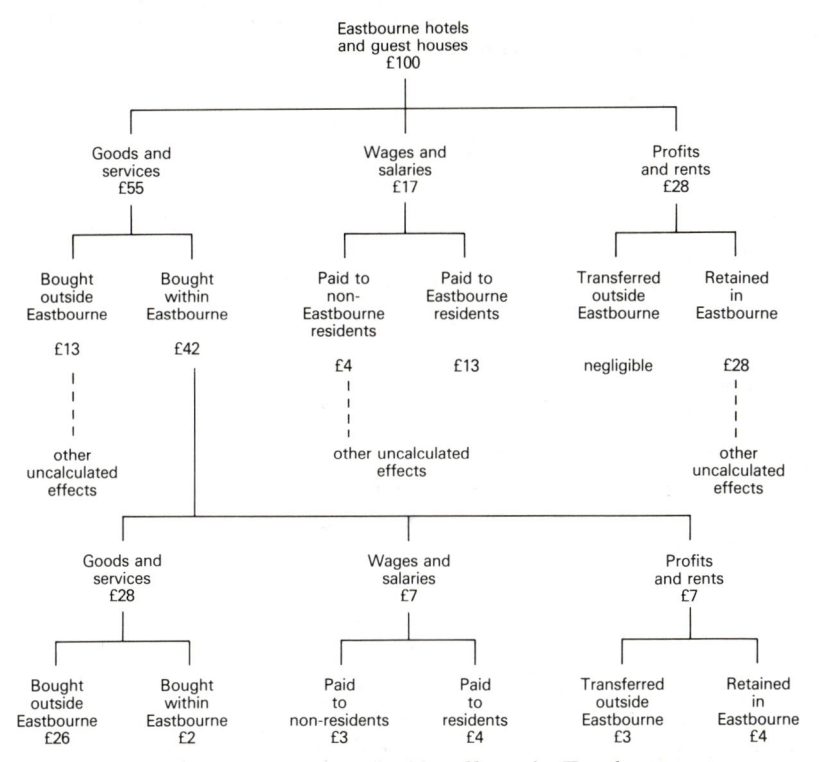

```
                    Eastbourne hotels
                    and guest houses
                         £100
        ┌────────────────┼────────────────┐
   Goods and         Wages and         Profits
   services           salaries        and rents
     £55                £17              £28
   ┌───┴───┐         ┌───┴───┐         ┌───┴───┐
 Bought  Bought    Paid to  Paid to  Transferred Retained
 outside within    non-     Eastbourne outside    in
Eastbourne Eastbourne Eastbourne residents Eastbourne Eastbourne
   £13    £42      residents
                    £4       £13      negligible   £28
    |                |        |                     |
    |                |        |                     |
  other          other uncalculated              other
uncalculated         effects                   uncalculated
  effects                                        effects
        ┌────────────────┼────────────────┐
   Goods and         Wages and         Profits
   services           salaries        and rents
     £28                £7               £7
   ┌───┴───┐         ┌───┴───┐         ┌───┴───┐
 Bought  Bought    Paid     Paid    Transferred Retained
 outside within    to       to      outside      in
Eastbourne Eastbourne non-residents residents Eastbourne Eastbourne
   £26     £2       £3       £4       £3         £4
```

FIG. 10.1 **Tourism multiplier effects in Eastbourne**
(Source: *ETB Eastbourne Tourist Study*, July 1977)

the money, until eventually the injection of £100 creates a further £137 of expenditure, thereby giving a multiplier of 1.37 after two 'rounds'. This figure is calculated by taking the £72 spent by hoteliers. Of this figure, £7 is retained in profits and rents, and hence £65 is spent in the next 'round'. The two figures of £72 and £65 are totalled, and then divided by the initial injection of £100, thereby obtaining the multiplier. Obviously this is a crude multiplier, but it serves to demonstrate the process. However, of the £137 so created, only those sums underlined actually remain in Eastbourne, so giving a 'local' multiplier of 0.51. As you will appreciate, the final figures will be higher as the process of recipients of income go on to spend, in turn, but the main impetus has been recorded in these early rounds. As you will also notice the 'local Eastbourne multiplier' is lower than the 'total multiplier' effect of tourist expenditure.

However, although there is now a much greater awareness of the income-generating effects of the tourism industry, it is difficult to assess fully the industry's contribution to the creation of employment. It is a provider of many direct jobs in that it is a labour-intensive industry, but it would seem it does not indirectly create as many other jobs as some other industries. The question is: does it create in total as many other jobs as do other industries? It is probably true to say that it does for female labour, but the position is less clear for male employment. Consequently, the effectiveness of the contribution of the industry towards the regional problem will in part rest with the willingness of females to join the labour force. Yet, at the same time, the hotel and catering industry is facing a growing competition from offices and light industries such as electronics, simply because these alternatives offer less strenuous manual tasks.

Probably the main reason why the hotel and catering industry has not attracted all the support it deserves in creating employment, in spite of its importance as an employer in the country, is that compared with manufacturing industry as a whole, it employs a smaller number. While it is true to say that the commercial sector of the hotel and catering industry employs over 3% of the whole active labour force, and therefore more than (say) the car industry, the chemical industry, the iron and steel industry etc., all these other industries can be covered by the same set of tax regulations and the like as part of 'manufacturing industry', and together they and the other manufacturing firms employ more than hotel and catering. If the hotel and catering industry is to receive the tax allowances and other aid, it perhaps needs to stress its differences from, rather than its similarities to, other service industries such as banking, transport, retailing, advertising, and hairdressing. Perhaps in any case the service industries still suffer from an image of being non-productive in the sense that they do not make some 'thing', but such an image is probably out-moded for it is true to say that tourism makes a greater contribution to Britain's economy than many of the prestigious manufacturing industries.

Whatever the pros and cons of the arguments, the industry in 1978 seemed at last to have achieved a fuller recognition of its needs and its contribution to the economy. In that year there were tax allowances of 20% granted in the budget on buildings and equipment to hotels that met the same specifications as laid down by the earlier Hotel Incentive Development Scheme. This was below the 50% allowances given to manufacturing industry, but before the 1979 elections it was strongly rumoured that the Government was going to place hotels on the same basis. Certainly, the Labour Government of 1974–79 had begun to recognize the claims of the industry for aid, for not only were budget concessions granted but an extension of aid under Section 4 of the 1969 Development of Tourism Act was also granted. By 1979 Cumbria, Northumbria, and the West Country were each in receipt of over £2 million from the Government. In addition, the Government had decided, following the Prior report on motorway catering, to offer, in April 1979, incentive schemes for all 42 motorway service areas and to employ the management consultants Green Belfield-Smith to aid the respective managements. In addition, as will be later described, the work of the Tourist Boards was also encouraged. However, with the change of Government in 1979 there was a change in attitude and subsidies, particularly for the large companies, which came under scrutiny. In part, this scrutiny seemed well founded. In the years just before 1979 the industry had increased its profits and longer-term prospects were still considered bright. At the same time, while the regional Tourist Boards had been trying to encourage investment, some areas had lost government aid because the industry had shown insufficient interest in putting forward proposals. In 1977 the Government established three tourism growth points, one of which, the Bude and Wadebridge area of North Cornwall, lost its right to £1 million of guaranteed government and ETB aid due to insufficient local support.

In addition, not all of the firms in the industry shared the view that government aid was a 'good thing' in that it was felt that such aid could compromise the freedom of the industry to act as it saw fit. The industry was also adversely influenced by the increase in VAT and the change of status of the Development Areas, which meant that by 1982 areas such as Yorkshire and Humberside would no longer be eligible for tourist aid. On the other hand, the 1979 budget and other government actions will help some sectors of the industry. Areas such as Torbay and Dartmouth are now eligible for aid where previously they were not, while the abolition of the Prices Commission means that for organizations with a turnover of over £10 million there is no longer need to be involved with the delays and paperwork created by the need to justify tariff increases. Certainly, there was little evidence that generally the Prices Commission found the industry overcharging. Similarly, proposals for easing the problems of small businessmen would be of significance to an industry where, particularly in catering, a large proportion of businesses are proprietor-managed.

The Industry and Inflation

The hotel and catering industry can do little to aid the Government in maintaining price stability other than try and minimise price increases. In view of its historically low rates of return, it cannot be said to have had prices that were sufficiently high to exploit consumers with the possible exception of alcoholic drinks, in that the brewers have been the subject of adverse criticism by the Monopolies Commission in 1967. Yet it could be argued that for alcohol a reduction in tax would more effectively reduce prices than a reduction in public house profits! Nor, because of the wage structure of the industry, can hotel and catering be said to have encouraged inflation by creating wage explosions! No doubt some of its employees only wish it could! This is not to say that the industry has a totally unblemished record. There has been some criticism that the practice of levying a service charge of 10%, which is above the level of tips that would voluntarily be left by the customer, is a form of price increase which also helps to maintain wage levels below what they should and would otherwise be. More seriously, in the summer of 1977 the Prices Commission ruled that tariff increases in the South-west were not to be allowed. That this ruling attracted as much attention as it did perhaps implies that it was exceptional. The competitive nature of the industry would tend to keep prices at a reasonable level since any hotel raising prices beyond current market levels would probably lose its clientele. However, from Table 9.1 (page 202) it could be argued that the industry has tended to follow inflationary trends rather than cause inflation, and since it is competing for discretionary expenditure, it is against its own interests to have prices that increase faster than the rate of inflation.

The Industry and the Balance of Payments

The industry has an increasingly important role to play in the balance of payments because it caters for a demand which is growing as leisure spending becomes an increasing proportion of total consumer expenditure. The industry has two roles: it is an import-saving industry if British citizens can be induced to take their holiday in the UK; and it is an export-earning industry if it can attract overseas visitors. Since 1968, with one exception, tourism has been a surplus item on the balance of payments figures for the UK, and generally speaking, about half of the overseas expenditure is on hotels and catering. Of course, one cannot attribute the whole growth of overseas earnings from tourism to the British hotels and restaurants, and to do so would be to malign the efforts of the BTA and the various Tourist Boards and other bodies such as British Airways who have so effectively sold holidaying in Britain to overseas residents. Yet the industry has undoubtedly played its role by providing satisfactory accommodation for holiday-makers. If we concentrate on tourism as a whole then it can be seen from Table 10.5 that the trend had been towards an increasing surplus on the balance of payments. It will be noticed that the 'turn-round' point came in the period 1967–68, and in part this was due to the November 1967 devaluation of the pound sterling, which fell from American $2.79 to $2.41. Indeed it can be suggested that the value of the pound, when allied to home economic conditions, is an important factor in the existence of a surplus on the tourism balance of payments. In the period 1967–70 the British economy was in a period of restraint while the Government sought to correct an adverse balance of payments, and, from its devaluation level, the pound sterling fell marginally to $2.39 until 1971. In that period, which also saw limitations on the amount of currency British citizens could take overseas, expenditure by the British overseas was at first static; it only began to rise in 1969 when economic conditions improved. But price competitiveness induced by the devalued pound, whereby overseas residents could buy more for their money, meant an

TABLE 10.5 **Travel as an invisible export and import (£ million)**

Year	1961	1962	1963	1964	1965	1966	1967	1968	1969
Receipts	176	183	188	190	193	219	236	282	359
Payments	200	210	241	261	290	287	274	271	324
Balance	−24	−27	−53	−71	−87	−78	−38	+11	+35

Year	1970	1971	1972	1973	1974	1975	1976	1977	1978
Receipts	433	500	576	726	898	1218	1768	2352	2502
Payments	385	442	535	695	703	917	1068	1186	1548
Balance	+48	+58	+41	+31	+195	+301	+700	+1166	+954

(Source: *Annual Abstract of Statistics* and *Trade Gazette*)

almost doubling of their expenditure in Britain between 1967 and 1970, as against a 40% increase in spending overseas by the British. In the period 1971–June 1972 the value of the pound climbed to $2.60, and at the same time a policy of economic growth had begun to succeed, meaning less unemployment and higher incomes. The result was that British expenditure overseas now rose faster than overseas tourist earnings, and the surplus fell, until indeed, by 1973 it returned to 1969 levels. However, 1973 was to prove to be the start of another recession in the British economy with industrial disputes and the oil crisis. The successful high wage claims which had in part enabled people to holiday overseas also came to an end with the imposition of a wages policy. The result of the balance of payments crisis meant that in 1974 the value of the pound fell to $2.34, which, combined with restrained income growth, restricted the growth of overseas tourism by the British to a mere 0.2% increase in expenditure. But what was bad for the British tourist proved beneficial to the overseas visitor, and in the same period of 1973–74 the expenditure of the foreign visitors to Britain rose by over 20%. Since 1974 the continued combination of high inflation and high unemployment has meant that in 1976 some 400 000 less British citizens went overseas than in 1973. At the same time, the continued stress of a balance of payments deficit has meant a further fall in the value of the pound, and in 1975 it averaged $2.20 Then in 1976 speculation also took place and the pound fell from $2.03 in January 1976 to $1.70 by the end of the year, and throughout the greater part of 1977 it remained at that level. The result for the overseas resident was that the UK offered even better value for money, and between 1975 and 1976 British earnings from tourism increased by 45%, and, in 1977, Jubilee Year attracted even higher earnings.

The result is that today tourism accounts for approximately 12% of total invisible earnings, and about 4% of total British exports. The importance of tourism compared with other industries as an export-earner for Britain can be gained from the ratio of exports to imports, and where the figure is over one in value, it can be argued that the industry should be supported because it earns surpluses on the balance of payments. By this criterion it can be seen that tourism makes not only a positive contribution to the British balance of payments but an increasing one. It is also interesting to note that although other financial services—the motor vehicle industry and manufacturing generally—make a positive contribution to the pattern of trade for

TABLE 10.6 **Estimates of export/import ratios**

	1969	1977	% change
Tourism	1.10	1.98	+80
Chemicals	1.49	1.52	+2
Machinery and transport equipment	2.29	1.28	−45
All manufacturing	1.51	1.15	−24

(Source: *Annual Abstract of Statistics*)

Britain, since 1969 it has been a declining one, with the consequence that tourism has become increasingly important in both absolute and relative terms (see Table 10.6).

The question is how long this can continue, for it does seem to be the case that the increased importance of tourism from this viewpoint has been due to British economic ill fortune with the value of the pound declining, and the number of UK residents holidaying overseas falling due to pressures on their incomes. It could be argued that a revival of the UK economy would recreate the same position as that of the middle 1960s when tourism was a deficit item on the balance of payments. In part, the answer will depend on how effectively holidaying in Britain is promoted, and how well the potential overcrowding of well-known beauty spots is avoided. At the same time, it may be that financially enforced holidaying in the UK by the British may create new habits when combined with the increased growth of leisure activities including hiking, pony trekking, and such like. None the less, surveys of the early 1960s show that the British were amongst the most travelled of the Europeans, so with improved economic fortune they could once again take to overseas travel.

The Industry and Economic Growth

The determinants of economic growth are many and include the availability of natural resources, the flow of savings and their use in investment, to government economic policy, the absence or presence of the right psychological atmosphere of confidence, and, in western societies, an entrepreneurial spirit. Obviously there are some means of achieving economic growth that the hotel and catering industry can do little to influence, at least by direct means. For example, the industry tends to use rather than create a technology, and it can do little about creating natural resources, although it may service those who extract them from the earth. The ways in which the industry can contribute to economic growth are by creating employment as we have seen, or by its own investment, and this will create a multiplier effect as has also been discussed. In order to do this the industry must achieve its own growth through increased sales. Indeed, the industry has a record of increasing turnover at current prices in successive years to the present, and Table 10.7 shows that the industry has achieved over a doubling of turnover in the period 1969–78 at current prices. However, this is a slower growth than that of gross domestic product, and, in this respect, the industry is continuing a trend from the beginning of the 1960s.

TABLE 10.7 **Economic growth and the industry (£ million)**

	1969	1978	% change
Gross domestic product (at factor cost)	39 483	140 889	+356
Catering trades turnover	2 533	7 269	+286
Manufacturing	12 813	35 279	+208
Construction (new work)	2 699	8 957	+331

(Source: *Annual Abstract of Statistics: Monthly Digest of Statistics*)

From that time until 1975 the industry has consistently deviated from the growth in gross domestic product by a small negative amount each year (with three exceptions) of about one to three percentage points. This is in part a reflection of the difficulties experienced in the 1960s and the resultant low profitability and investment programmes in the period leading to 1968. However, if the most recent period from 1974 is taken, one finds an improvement: in 1974–76 the gross domestic product increased by 46% in current price terms (or a fall of 1.5% in real terms), whereas manufacturing, construction and catering trades turnover increased by 25%, 24% and 35% respectively, and in the period 1976–78, the respective figures were 27%, 25% and 16%. Consequently, we find that the industry has maintained its growth more successfully in a period of economic recession than other industrial sectors, probably in part due to the tourist boom.

An implication of this is that the hotel and catering industry assumes a greater importance at times of economic recession and may be of use in escaping from that recession, whereupon it declines in importance. The histories of such countries as Greece and Spain bear this out to some extent.

Miscellaneous Contributions

In addition to the direct benefits that tourism brings there are other, and at first less obvious, benefits, particularly for London. First, there is the expenditure of tourists in shops. As was noted in Chapter 3, this means that certain shops in the area of Bond Street and Regent Street earn several millions of pounds from tourists. In 1977 it was estimated that overseas visitors spent approximately £250 million on footwear and textiles, a figure which was about a quarter of our exports of this type of goods. A further £250 million was received by customs and excise from overseas visitors in the form of VAT on the purchases made by these visitors, and local authorities may also gain rates income from business premises which serve the tourist industry.

The tourist industry is at its most evident in London, and here tourism helps to subsidize the services available to Londoners. The London Transport Authority estimated that in 1979 the overseas visitor paid over £65 million in bus and underground fares; without this income fares would have been even higher if existing services were to be maintained. The dependence of theatres on the tourist industry is well known. In a survey of Londoners' attitudes towards tourists in 1978 by the English Tourist Board, it was found that over 70% of Londoners questioned had not visited a West End theatre for over 12 months. Likewise, museums and art galleries are heavily dependent on visitors for revenue they gain through the sale of miscellaneous items from postcards to replica Roman jewellery or Norse chessmen; for again over 70% of Londoners had not visited museums such as the British Museum, the Victoria and Albert Museum or the National Gallery. The very opportunity for Londoners to enjoy these facilities is, therefore, dependent on the trade generated by the overseas visitor.

11
Agencies Involved in the Hotel and Catering Industry

Introduction

As the industry's importance has come to be recognized, so too have the number of advisory, government and trade committees increased. Some are trade associations representing the interests of the companies and acting as pressure groups. Others are government-funded and serve to help the industry and act as an interface where government, employers and trade unions may meet, or they serve to promote British tourism. Under this chapter one may also mention the trades unions who represent employees in both their place of work and in the other committees. Whatever interests the various parties represent, all have the common concern of the hotel and catering industry.

The Catering Industries Liaison Committee (CILC)

The CILC was set up in October 1979 and potentially could be the main body representing the industry in its relations with the Government. This potential exists because of the demise of the Hotel and Catering Economic Development Council, and in understanding the CILC it is necessary to consider its predecessor.

In 1962 the National Economic Development Council was founded under the chairmanship of the Prime Minister to coordinate and formulate national economic policy. From 1964 it began to create a number of committees for particular industries, known informally as 'Little Neddies', and on 20 June 1966 the Economic Development Committee for the Hotel and Catering Industry first met. It was the twelfth of these 'Little Neddies' to have been set up, and with regard to its membership followed the same general principles that characterize all the committees. Since the committees are seen as primarily a means of communication between all interested parties, each consists of representatives from management organizations, the trades unions and the appropriate government departments, with perhaps some members drawn from universities and similar bodies who can contribute a specialized knowledge. It is the committee that chooses the chairman, who is drawn from outside the industry. The task of the body is to examine the industry and its economic progress, and to evaluate the whole area of its activities and encourage improvements in efficiency. To that end the committee undertakes enquiries and research into the industry, trying to assess its growth, identify the problems and suggest possible solutions. This information is made available to the industry, and to the NEDC for incorporation into planning economic policy.

However, the EDC for Hotels and Catering, like other 'Little Neddies' and the NEDC itself, had no executive power; it could persuade and cajole but not compel action. In consequence, it had influence only in as much as its reports and services were respected by the industry, and thus the working groups of the Committee that undertook the research carried a heavy responsibility. It was made all the more responsible by the fact that often the EDC reports were the major, if not the only, source of information on many aspects of the industry, and consequently incorrect data would adversely prejudice the way the Committee was regarded.

The Hotel and Catering 'Little Neddy' established working parties on Economics and Finance, Manpower, Marketing, Statistics and Forecasting, whilst it also had ad hoc working parties on particular projects. This is not to say, however, that all its publications were aimed at large-scale business and government departments, for some were deliberately published for the small concern. An example is *Marketing in a Small Business* (1970) which included examples for small restaurants based on case studies. The Hotel and Catering EDC was influentual in a number of fields, and was certainly active in creating the Hotel Development Incentive scheme which ran until 1973. It also made an impact on the industry by encouraging the use of a standardized accounting system, and was also instrumental in creating computer reservation systems. It, in many ways, helped with the BTA to create a government awareness of the significance of tourism to the UK.

Its membership consisted of 19, with trades union representation drawn from the General and Municipal Workers' Union, the Transport and General Workers' Union, the Union of Shop, Distributive and Allied Workers, the National Union of Public Employees, and the

National Union of Railwaymen. The Government members came from the NEDC, the Ministry of Agriculture, Fisheries and Food, the Department of Education and Science and the Department of Trade. The management side came from firms associated with hotels, restaurants, contract catering and the breweries. The two largest firms in the industry happen to be represented in that two members came from Trusthouse Forte and Grand Metropolitan, but those members were representative of the management side generally and not of those particular firms.

In part, the final ending of the Hotels and Catering EDC in October 1979 was due to its membership. After the promising beginning in the heady days of the 1960s the Committee became increasingly troubled by poor relations between the employers and trades union representatives. For the trades unions, from the very beginning, the Committee was important because it implied a recognition of their importance, and because membership gave them a source of information as to management thinking. From the management side, once the early projects were completed and, particularly after the ending of the Hotel Development Incentive Scheme, it became apparent that there were few major projects being envisaged, partly because the industry was increasingly being looked upon to finance any work undertaken. However, the increasing division between the employer and employee sides was due to a suspicion by some that the trades unions had an influence on the Committee out of proportion to their actual influence in the industry. By 1979 relationships had become strained, and the immediate cause of the 'Little Neddy' being disbanded was a dispute over the setting up of a tourism strategy group. Set up in April 1978, this subcommittee never began work due to a policy of non-cooperation by the British Hotels, Restaurants and Caterers Association, who did not nominate representatives to sit on the subcommittee. Simultaneously, bitter relationships between the two sides was also evident when the Committee attempted to set up a survey into manpower planning. Nor was the position aided within the last three years of the Committee's life by the resignation of some of its senior staff. Consequently, in spite of official union support for the body, it had come to be seen as, at best, dormant, at worst, moribund, and in the final degree an area which exacerbated bad relationships between the two sides of the industry. By 1979 the NEDO considered that the future prospects of the Hotel and Catering EDC being able to achieve positive action on behalf of the industry was negligible and thus in October of that year the Committee was wound up.

Perhaps ironically, one of the last actions of the 'Little Neddy' was to provide for its own possible successor. A sub-committee, the Catering Industries Liaison Committee was established to discuss the common problems of the industry. As the cynic may say, it was a case of one talking shop setting up another talking shop to which further talking shops joined, to talk about problems which the talking shops had originally been set up to talk about—but not apparently to solve! The membership of the CILC underlines the breeding habits of committees. Foremost amongst the members of CILC is the National Catering Federation, which itself had been formed from eight other associations in 1972 to discuss common problems and to act as an advisory group representing hotels and caterers. Other members include the HCIMA, the Catering Manufacturers' Association, the Automatic Vending Association, the Restaurateurs' Association of Great Britain, the Industrial Catering Association and the Hospital Caterers' Association. However, the BHRCA, the HCITB and the Brewers' Society are not among the 14 members of CILC. (Such a rich array of associations must be indicative of something!) The observant will also note that neither the Government nor trades unions are members of CILC.

The aims of CILC are to represent the interests of the industry to government departments and all other appropriate bodies. It also wishes to act as a medium of exchange of ideas and information, and to act as a meeting place for the different interests which comprise its membership. In addition, it aims to continue, to whatever possible degree, the research functions of the old 'Little Neddy' and consequently may continue the manpower surveys that that Committee had started. Certainly, CILC does have the advantage that it has a comparatively broad basis, for not only does it include the various forms of catering but also the manufacturers of catering equipment, and, in the HCIMA a body concerned with education and training.

The British Tourist Authority and the Regional Tourist Boards

The British Tourist Authority was established under the Development of Tourism Act 1969, taking over from the British Travel Association. Under the Act the BTA has certain statutory responsibilities, which are:

(i) to promote tourism to Britain from overseas;
(ii) to advise the Government on tourism matters affecting Britain as a whole;
(iii) to encourage the provision and improvement of tourist amenities and facilities in Britain; and
(iv) to prepare, after consultation with the English, Scottish and Welsh Tourist Boards, general schemes of assistance for tourist projects.

Subsidiary to this the BTA has established a set of marketing aims, which are:

(i) to earn for Britain as much foreign currency as possible from overseas tourism;
(ii) to increase the overall amount of travel throughout Britain, with an emphasis on traffic, to the Development Areas in England, Scotland and Wales;
(iii) to increase the proportion of traffic arriving in off-peak months from October to March; and
(iv) to work in partnership with the trade and to encourage support from the trade for the BTA's promotional work overseas.

The BTA is funded from two sources. The main one is government funding through the Department of Trade and Industry, and in the financial years of 1973/4–1978/9 this financing has grown from £5.6 million to £11.08 million. This last figure represents 82% of the BTA's revenue, the remainder coming from private industry in the shape of joint promotional activities. The trade contribution to the BTA has grown rapidly, by some 300% in the period 1974–77 from an initial sum of £275 000 in 1974. In the joint promotions, the partner concerned is not necessarily a British company, for TWA, WARDAIR and KLM have, in 1978, been involved in a 'come to Britain' campaign in the USA, Canada and Mexico, respectively.

The size of the BTA's overseas operations can be gauged by the fact that it distributed about 20 million pieces of literature with nearly 300 titles overseas in 1977–78 and has 24 overseas offices in places such as New York, Tokyo, Copenhagen, Frankfurt and Sydney. The BTA produces films, has produced reports on spa towns, patterns of demand and has contributed to enquiries into waterways, a new London airport, quotas of foreign workers, and made recommendations about such things as notices to guests about telephone charges. As this list shows, its activities are myriad and diverse. The BTA is organized into a series of subcommittees which deal with marketing, camping and caravanning, infrastructure, hotels and restaurants, and the British heritage. In many ways the BTA can be regarded as an active and successful body, but of late it has come under strain as its government financing has not expanded with Board's activities. Consequently, in 1978 it found itself cutting its publications by about 8% and reducing staffing levels, so creating longer response times in dealing with enquiries. In 1979 the BTA was to have had an original budget of nearly £13 million, but following the 1979 budget its finances were reduced by £200 000. None the less the 1979 budget did represent an increase in real terms after having had a stationary budget, and it is hoped that the past success of the BTA will enable it to attract higher degrees of industrial financing than in the past. The Government's attitude is, in part, one of trying to ensure that some of the beneficiaries of the increased trade pay a greater share of the cost of promoting that trade, and consequently the willingness of the industry to pay will be based on whether the BTA is successful in generating that business. Generally speaking, the fact that industrial financing is increasing indicates the success of the Board.

The same confidence, however, is not felt about the regional Tourist Boards, which in 1979 were being reviewed by the Department of Trade as part of its review of tourism. In that year the department reduced the budget of the English Tourist Board by £300 000, £200 000 of which was available for assistance under Section 4 of the Development of Tourism Act. Like the BTA the regional tourist boards are financed from two sources, the Government and the industry, but the regional Tourist Boards are more dependent on government than the BTA (Table 11.1). The English Tourist Board, in 1978–79, raised only 3.5% of its revenue from industry, and the continuance of the boards

TABLE 11.1 **Government funding of the regional tourist boards (£)**

	1973–74	1978–79
English Tourist Board	1 500 000	5 014 000
Scottish Tourist Board	711 000	2 154 000
Welsh Tourist Board	537 000	1 685 000

will depend greatly on their ability to increase this percentage. Certainly, the regional boards are facing severe financial difficulties. For example, the London Tourist Board is having to cut its marketing staff by half, and others are making similar economies. The problems may arise from an ambivalent attitude by the industry towards them, in part a heritage from 1978 when the English Tourist Board was strongly advocating a compulsory registration scheme which was rejected by the industry and particularly by the British Hotels, Restaurants and Caterers' Association. Also, because under the 1969 Development of Tourism Act (which set up the boards), part of the role of the English Tourist Board is to act as an agent in the distribution of development funds, many hoteliers view the ETB as a bureaucratic arm of the Department of Trade and Industry. Thus, its existence is seen as absorbing money in administration which may be allocated to the industry direct by the government, though such an attitude may be naïve. In addition, the research activities of the board may also be suspected by an industry which at times has tended to be lukewarm towards an academic tradition. Consequently, the boards were criticised by some resort directors of tourism for not getting down to the commercial 'nitty-gritty' of the job and for being too involved in 'non-contributory up-market peripheral promotions' and for having an 'over-inclination towards planning'. Such strong feelings engendered considerable column inches in the trade press (see, for example, the issues of *Catering Times* dated 14 and 18 October 1979).

On the other hand, the regional tourist boards have done much to create an awareness of the importance and the needs of tourism and have provided a means of publicity for hotels and restaurants. Of great importance to the independents and smaller chains has been the English Tourist Board's *Let's Go* which has done much to foster and promote the concept of the bargain break holiday. For reasonable rates it has meant national publicity for hoteliers who previously could not have afforded such a promotion, and, as seen on page 210 it has possibly been the smaller hotelier who has gained most from these promotions. In addition, all the regional boards print and distribute promotional literature, some free, some of it sold, and much of it funded by the travel trade itself. It is a valid question to ask if, in the absence of these boards, such promotional activity would have taken place. In as much as about half of the English Tourist Board's budget and more than half of that of the regional boards has been spent on advertising, it is probably naïve to think that government would have provided similar funds to other bodies. The politics and costs of sharing such finances between (say) competing resorts, would have been an exercise of stress. At the time of writing, it is uncertain what the result of the government review of tourist strategy will be, but if the boards were to disappear the industry might lose certain services or else not receive them free. It could be argued that a publication such as *Let's Go* could be a commercial proposition, and the specialized management consultants could provide the research at present provided if the industry were prepared to pay. Such factors would tend to favour the larger company rather than the independent proprietor. An alternative would be for the boards to increase their charges to lessen their dependence on government funding; yet perhaps the smaller unit could still be served at not too great a cost because local contacts could be used to acquire economies of scale in distributing promotional activity. Certainly, the boards are making every attempt to widen the base of their revenues with an increasing practice of selling services direct to the customer, while continually assessing the effectiveness of their expenditure in terms of its generating trade.

The Hotel, Catering and Management Association

Set up in 1971 through a merger of the Hotel and Catering Institute with the Institutional Management Association, the HCIMA is probably best known for its educational work as an examining body for qualifications recognized as suitable for management within the industry. Since 1978 its new syllabus has set new standards of training with a carefully considered mix between management principles, background knowledge, scientific knowledge and awareness of marketing, accommodation needs, accountancy, and the like. At the same time, the setting up of a research register, annually updated, has provided an important source of cross-fertilization of ideas and an avenue for the exchange of information.

Membership of the association through examination confers a prestige upon the membership. The association also provides advisory services, meetings, publications and represents management to others in the industry, as can be seen from its membership of CILC.

The British Hotels, Restaurants and Caterers Association

This too is a body formed from the merger of previously existing associations. In 1972 the British Hotels and Restaurants Association (itself the result of an earlier merger in 1948) joined forces with the Caterers Association of Great Britain to form the BHRCA as it is known today. A trade association with a membership of about 8000, it represents the firms in the industry and seeks to promote their interests. Consequently, the BHRCA has not only represented the industry on bodies such as the Hotels and Catering EDC but also directly approaches government in its own right as a pressure group. As a trade association, the BHRCA also promotes meetings and undertakes publicity. For example, its hotel guide is sold to the public, and, in the past it has organized the obtaining of work permits and the provision of jobs for foreign workers brought into the country to ease the labour shortage—a phenomenon which is less important than before due to a growth in the domestic labour force (so that, in 1979, only just over 1000 work permits were issued for foreign workers). The BHRCA has also followed the example of many other trade associations in the promotion of exhibitions and, for example, supports Hotelympia, as do many other associations including one of the sponsors, the Catering Equipment Manufacturers Association of Great Britain.

The Hotel and Catering Industrial Training Board

In 1962 a White Paper was published which expressed concern about the uneven standard of industrial training in the UK. Indeed, it stated that 'much (training) is barely adequate and some definitely unsatisfactory.' As a result, the Government passed legislation in 1964, the Industrial Training Act, seeking to fulfil three main objectives:

(i) to ensure an adequate supply of properly trained men and women at all levels in industry;

(ii) to improve the efficiency and quality of industrial training; and

(iii) to share the costs of training more evenly between firms.

Two years later, on 18 November 1966, the Training Board for the Hotel and Catering Industry was established, although it was not until later that contentions as to the range of its activities was clarified by an amendment to the original legislation which allowed employees in institutional and local authority sectors to be covered by the Board's activities.

Essentially the Training Board provides training courses at all levels or arranges for other organisations to do so. It has a stick-and-carrot approach to this in that the Board can impose a training levy on firms to finance training in the industry, whilst it can also give grants to firms providing training. Initially it was rumoured that firms could gain more in grants than they paid in levies by instituting some, possibly questionable, training schemes on their own premises, but subsequent alterations in 1973 in the regulations as to levies and grants have made this extremely difficult. Later, in 1976, the HCITB reviewed its procedures as to levies and grants in a five-year provision which remains in effect until 1981. Under this format the levy is imposed on the largest 1500 employers—which is determined by the size of payroll—at a rate of 0.7% of the payroll, although exemption is granted if companies are undertaking satisfactory training schemes of their own. Such employers may, in addition, be eligible for grants if they are offering training in designated key areas, which grants are also available in addition to the normal grants given to levied firms by the HCITB. Additional training for newcomers to the industry is now available through the Training Opportunities Schemes (TOPS) which are run by the Manpower Services Agency, usually at Technical Colleges and Colleges of Further Education. These were instituted in 1974 as a result of the Employment and Training Act of the previous year, as part of the programme to combat unemployment by giving people new skills. Such schemes are often run in close conjunction with the Department of Employment to give a reasonable chance of jobs being available in which the newly learnt skills could be used. The hotel and catering industry, being one where labour was being taken on, was seen by the Government as an industry that could absorb this pool of labour. The TOPS schemes are open to anyone who has not been in full-time education for three years and who, it is felt, can benefit from the training.

In addition to its training role, but arising out of it, the HCITB has also undertaken a research role into manpower supplies, the degree of labour movement in the industry, and the qualifications and training staff have received. In part, this research is to provide basic data on the pattern of manpower in the industry, but it is also important to the

TABLE 11.2 **Students studying in hotel and catering trades in 1975 (with 1969 figures in parentheses)**

	Full-time	Sandwich	Part-time	Evening
Professional qualification	215	212	159	14
	(436)	(—)	(—)	(—)
Advanced college diplomas and awards	26	77	—	—
	(20)	(—)	(—)	(—)
All advanced courses	380	2 460	159	14
	(522)	(337)	(—)	(—)
OND	3 412	181	—	—
	(1 294)	(85)	(—)	(—)
City and Guilds	12 570	83	13 268	1 287
	(5 419)	(230)	(11 765)	(1 339)

(Source: *Statistics of Education*, DES)

effectiveness with which the HCITB can carry out its role since it needs to identify the training needs of the industry.

In the training of personnel, schemes are aided by the existence of well-established examinations of skills provided by bodies such as City and Guilds, and consequently many firms can let their employees go to colleges on a day-release or block-release basis and obtain the training grants. Thus employees gain nationally recognized qualifications from experienced teachers, and the firms themselves are freed from the expense of creating their own training premises and staff. This can be particularly advantageous to the smaller business units, although many of the larger firms conduct their own training, especially from first-line management onwards. Increasingly, entrants to the industry voluntarily undergo some training prior to entry, and the number of full-time OND students in catering and institutional management rose from 1294 in 1969 to 3412 in 1975 (Table 11.2). At most levels, advanced and non-advanced, there has been an increase in training, and the total number of students pursuing hotel and catering courses has increased by 61% to over 35 000 in the period 1969–75.

The Wages Council

As has already been noted, the industry is one where wage levels have tended to lag behind average levels, perhaps due to the practice of 'wages in kind' (which are subject to severe limitations) and to tipping. At the same time, and it may not be coincidental, the industry is one where trades union organization is weak, due probably to many factors: no one union is uniquely concerned with the hotel and catering industry; the individual units of work tend to be small; there is a rapid labour turnover; and part-time working is commonplace. On the other hand, it must be pointed out that unions such as the Transport and General Workers' Union do have separate committees associated with the industry, and branches are often firm-based and/or industry-based. In addition, ownership of hotels and restaurants is highly fragmented, and consequently it would be extremely difficult for any union to negotiate with all employers, particularly with such a large number of self-employed businesses with only one or two employees who may be part-time workers.

Consequently, the Government saw fit to include the industry in its structure of Wages Councils by the Catering Wages Act 1943. The Wages Councils cover industries where pay tends to be low and minimum wage levels are established and enforced. Initially, a Catering Wages Commission was established to make enquiries into the industry and make recommendations, and on the basis of those recommendations, five wages boards were established between March 1944 and December 1945. Subsequently, the boards were changed when the 1959 Terms and Conditions of Employment Act repealed the original 1943 legislation and Wages Councils replaced the boards. The powers of the Wages Councils are determined by the Wages Councils Act 1959, a piece of consolidating legislation, and they can make recommendations not only in the matter of wages but also in questions of conditions of employment, health and welfare. If these suggestions are accepted by the Minister, he will then give them legal force by issuing a Wages Regulation Order, and it is these that lay down the minimum requirements of employment terms.

The Wages Councils covering the industry are:

(i) The Licensed Non-Residential Establishment, which covers those working in public houses, clubs and other licensed premises with accommodation for less than eight guests.

(ii) The Licensed Residential and Licensed Restaurants Council, which covers licensed restaurants and those licensed premises that have accommodation capacity for at least eight guests.

(iii) The Unlicensed Place of Refreshment Wages Council, which caters for workers in unlicensed businesses, contract catererers, and cafés, snack bars and the like.

The functions of the Wages Councils are:

(i) to fix the statutory minimum remuneration for any particular work;

(ii) to fix other terms and conditions of employment.

Since the 1975 Employment Protection Act, the Secretary of State for Trade and Industry may also set up a Wages Council to give effect to a recommendation by ACAS (the Advisory, Conciliation and Arbitration Service). The Wages Councils have an equal number of employer and employee representatives with no more than three additional independent members, one of whom is the chairman. In addition to powers to fix minimum wages and conditions of employment, they can make recommendations to any government department. To enforce their orders, the appropriate legislation demands that employers must keep records of hours worked and wages paid, that these records must be kept for three years at least, and that the notices of the Wages Councils be displayed at the place of work. Failure to keep records or place the notices makes an employer liable to a fine of £100, while a false entry in the records can mean a £400 fine or three months imprisonment or both. A wages inspectorate is appointed to enforce the law, and in its surveys of the industry it is finding consistently that at least 20% of catering establishments are paying below the statutory minimum wages, while many more do not display the Wages Councils' notices.

In 1976 the Wages Councils came under some criticism due to the extremely long negotiations that preceded the new rates of pay at the end of November, partly because of the differing interpretations of Government income policy by the employer and trades union representatives. As a result, alternatives were mooted: having a joint industrial council; having resort to the Advisory, Conciliation and Arbitration Service; a national minimum wage level for all employees; or the creation of yet more wages councils looking after smaller areas.

The criticisms made of the Councils are many. First, on the employers' side it has been argued that there was an under-representation of the smaller employers, while difficulties in getting agreement between the employers themselves meant that they tended to adopt a rigid stance in negotiations. At the same time, they tended perhaps to have an ambivalent approach since, for some of the large organizations, they were already paying above the minimum wage levels, certainly in London, yet would argue that the industry could not afford higher wage increases. On the union side it is always a moot point as to how representative they are of employees in the industry. They were open to the criticism of gaining recognition without mass membership, and P. Mitchell and G. Aston in the *HCIMA Review* of 1974 also argued that skilled workers in the industry were not attracted to general unions more concerned with representing the unskilled and the semi-skilled in manufacturing industry. Whatever the problems associated with negotiations—problems which mean that the independents are often in the decisive position and are 'shot at' by both sides—the fact does remain that the Wages Councils have not effectively raised the level of wages for male employees in line with other industries. Partly, one suspects the problem lies with enforcement procedures, and partly because for the large organizations the decisions of the Wages Council are peripheral to their thinking. Some choose to ignore unions; others negotiate directly with the unions in their own organizations and so bypass the Wages Councils. This implies a role for the Wages Councils only for smaller employers and their workers. Certainly, many from both sides of the industry are unhappy about the Wages Councils, and perhaps their survival is due to a lack of consensus about what to put in their place. As it is, one of the Councils, the Industrial and Staff Canteen Undertakings Council, has ceased to function, though as yet there is little evidence as to how its absence has affected the position of the workers employed in this sector.

Trades Unions

The position of trades unions within the hotel and catering industry has been a contentious one with considerable argument over the exact size of membership within the industry. The main unions involved are the General and Municipal Workers' Union (GMWU), the Transport and General Workers' Union (TGWU), and the National Union of Railwaymen (NUR). A smaller union, which made news in 1977 for its motion expelling the TGWU from the Trades Union Congress, is the National Association of Licensed House Managers (NALHM) with a membership of 14 000. It has always been difficult for the unions to make headway in the industry because of its atomistic structure. A very large number of small units (31% of the industry's labour force work in units employing less than nine people according to the HCITB surveys), a higher than average turnover, a preponderance of female labour, and the incidence of shift work are all factors that have made trades union organization comparatively weak in the commercial sector of the industry. Perversely, the amalgamation of companies and the creation of larger units has thereby slightly eased the task of union organizers. In 1977 and 1978 the unions made a determined attempt to win more membership with a sustained recruitment drive. The GMWU claimed a doubling of its London membership in this period to 12 000, which constitutes its largest geographical concentration of membership with a total membership of over 25 000 in the industry. Similarly, within the same period the TGWU built up its membership in London from 1500 to over 6000. But such membership figures are a small percentage of the total number employed in the industry, and a study by the Department of Hotel, Catering and Tourism Management at Surrey University (February 1979) estimated that perhaps only 5% of the industry's labour force belongs to a union. Two other reasons for the lack of union progress may also be important. The first is that many within the industry do not want to be members. Proprietor-managed units are more common in this industry than in many others, and possibly a more entrepreneurial spirit exists in its staff than in other industries. Second, there has been employer opposition and distrust of unions. Certainly, of the main hotel companies, Trusthouse Forte has been the most reluctant to recognize trade unions, and the company has adopted a policy of not negotiating with unions unless the unions can attract a 50% majority of those working in any one of their units. Such a position, it is argued, is not an 'anti-union' position but one of allowing employees to make their own decision about union membership. The company in fact once owned Terry's of York for a period of 17 years, and although Terry's was entirely unionised it never had any strikes or industrial stoppages. In contrast, Trusthouse Forte has been involved in long disputes at the Talk of the Town, London, at Grosvenor House, Sheffield, and some other units. At present, it estimates that its level of union membership has actually fallen in the period 1978–79 with present levels at about 8% of employees, as against 10–14% in 1977–78.

Not all companies have adopted the same attitude towards trades unions. Grand Metropolitan, Embassy Hotels and Thistle Hotels all have recognition agreements with the GMWU, and in these companies union membership is about 20% of the labour force. At Rank Hotels the figure is about double that at around 40%. One implication of a recognition agreement is that it usually means the installation of a complaints and grievances procedure, and the companies involved believe that this creates a degree of certainty and order in a situation where confusion over rights might exaggerate the sense of wrong-feeling. In May 1977 the personnel and training director of Grand Metropolitan, David Hutchins, produced a report arguing that commercial and social benefits could be gained through the involvement of both union and non-union labour in the decision-making process. On the other hand, unions have been accused of bullying tactics and of refusing people the right to resign membership.

Whatever the truth of particular instances, it can be argued that here, as in other industries, the important element is the motivation of those involved. If each party sees the other as offering a cooperative and supportive aid, less problems are likely to emerge than if they are suspicious of each other. Certainly, with the year-long action over Garner's steak houses and the disputes at the Randolph Hotel in Oxford and Claridges, the unions have shown persistence and endurance, but such disputes have also shown loyalty by other staff towards the employers. It is unlikely that this position will change considerably over the next few years, and existing low levels of union membership can be expected to continue even though the GMWU created a new union, the Hotel and Catering Workers' Union in February 1980. At that date the GMWU claimed a membership of 30 000 in the industry and with the HCWU hopes to achieve a membership of 60 000 by 1981—a modest target compared with the 2 million who work in the industry.

12
Future Trends: A Brief Note

More than once in this book I have made mention of the difficulties that the industry is facing as it moves into the beginning of a new decade. Higher wage costs, rentals, and equipment costs, combined with a resistance to too high a tariff increase all present problems, particularly for some of the resorts where demand has been falling. The growth of overseas visitors has slowed down in 1979, and there are fears about London becoming over-priced. Yet I think it is important that these factors be placed in context, a context that 1977 was an exceptional year

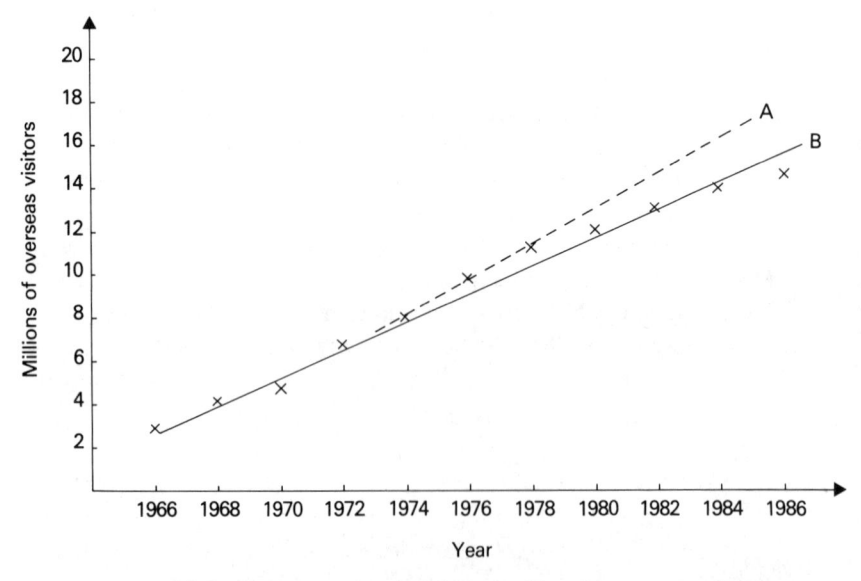

FIG. 12.1 **Estimated trend in growth of overseas visitors: A, trend if growth of 1975–77 was maintained; B, trend if growth of 1975–77 is seen as exceptional**

(Source: *British Home Tourism Surveys*)

due to Jubilee celebrations and, for tourism, a year with a favourable exchange rate. The underlying trends for tourism in the foreseeable future continue to be favourable (Fig. 12.1). There are signs that while 1980 will not see the past rapid growth sustained, hotels and caterers will certainly not be in the unprofitable positions of 1974–75, and on an extrapolated trend of growth 1980 may represent a return to the underlying rate of growth present since the early 1970s, rather than the accelerated growth of 1975–77. This is not to say, however, that all sectors of the industry will gain equally. There is a consensus of opinion that for hotels the main sources of growth in demand will continue to be overseas visitors and businessmen rather than domestic tourism, although an expansion of short holidays involving the use of hotel accommodation by British tourists can be expected. One of the fastest growing sectors is expected to be the self-catering area; nor is this simply an expression of cost. In many ways the tourist is increasingly looking for freedom of action and does not wish to be tied to particular meal times and particular menus. Indeed, the holiday-maker in a self-catering unit may often choose to eat out at least once a day, thereby increasing demand for restaurant facilities. This growth in demand could be shared by both the foreign and domestic tourist.

On one thing all forecasts are agreed: that the potential for underlying tourist demand growth is present (Table 12.1). Although the UK may have suffered from recession, other countries have suffered less, and with an increase in disposable income the wish to travel will likewise grow. By 1990, 21 million overseas visitors are expected to come to the UK. For these reasons the major groups are investing in hotels. The major threat against this growth comes from two areas, one more immediate than the other. The first is the impact of increasing fuel costs. In the face of fears of a possible energy shortage there are many long-term alternatives to petroleum products for domestic and industrial use. One may point to gas, coal, nuclear power and hydro-electric power, all of which will be increasingly used. At present there is no immediate alternative to petroleum for transport, and hence the cost of transport will depend to a large extent on how quickly other fuel-users switch to alternative energy sources. Unfortunately, such switches are time-absorbing. However, rapidly increasing fuel costs would probably speed such changes allied with energy-saving devices such as proper insulation and electronically controlled rates of fuel usage; and the faster such changes occur, the quicker is the easing of demand,

TABLE 12.1 **Forecast summary**

	Trips (% change 1978–95)		
	GB	Non-GB	Total
Short holidays			
Serviced	49.3	18.8	47.5
Self-catering	26.5	11.1	26.1
Visiting friends and relatives	34.9	—	34.8
Total	35.2	15.4	34.9
Long holidays			
Serviced	−1.0	33.4	11.0
Self-catering	8.6	43.8	12.1
Visiting friends and relatives	−13.4	5.9	−10.9
Total	−1.0	29.7	4.9
Business and conference			
Serviced	17.1	21.8	18.1
Self-catering	8.2	6.2	7.9
Visiting friends and relatives	−19.7	—	−19.5
Total	11.7	18.8	12.5
Others			
Visiting friends and relatives	19.0	30.0	19.1
Total	14.6	7.7	15.7

(Source: *English Tourist Board,* 1979)

thereby reducing the pressure on increasing prices. The second change is more uncertain. Much of business travel arises from a need to communicate, and increasingly, use is being made of electronic means of communication. The microcomputer already gives 16 k of usage for sums of about £600 for ready-made units (less for kits), and long-term futurologists envisage progressively less need for business travel. If the period since the Second World War has taught us anything, it is that for the advanced industrial nations the time gap between the vision and the reality in the field of electronic and other advancement has increasingly diminished, even as visions become more ambitious. Computers play chess; lasers are aimed at the moon and used in eye operations; calculators are the norm; heart transplants achieve increasingly greater success. All around us we see signs of increased technology. The impact of technology upon tourism is diverse. It may adversely influence business demand for travel, but it seems unlikely that *homo sapiens* will ever be happy with simply a picture (however created) of the person with whom he is negotiating. Certainly, computer technology will increasingly be used for reservations, automatic order levels, and accounting and forecasting.

One implication of all this is that manpower demands will be influenced. But in an industry with the emphasis on personal service it may be that numbers employed on the accounting, costing and marketing side will not increase, even if demand increases, but that numbers in the 'contact' side of the industry will, even if there are many more technological aids. As yet, there does not seem to be an automatic way of making a bed!

A potential growth area is the 'thematic holiday'. People may seek to combine an interest with a short break away from home; and this is why, for instance, major hotel groups are already marketing holiday packages involving theatre visits (including trips backstage). For a long time people have combined artistic or sporting activities with holidays. Today, painting, rambling, and lectures on Shakespeare, are possible package holiday pursuits. Increasingly, as such activities are integrated into holidays, hoteliers and caterers must consider themselves as part of a leisure services industry. The science fiction film *Westworld* was based on an idea of people holidaying in a facsimile of another period. Like much science fiction, it was an extension of trends already occurring. People enjoy the fantasies of Disneyland, but actually partake in the fantasy of Elizabethan banquets, or holiday in a dude ranch situated outside Paris. The Butlin's holiday camp of the future may be based on simulated living in another age. Already in the United States colonial towns such as Williamsburg exist to take people to such an age. All these holidays require accommodation.

The ability to provide this new type of package requires an integration between different organizations rather along the lines of the more traditional package holiday. Consequently, we can expect the selling of package holidays in Britain through travel agents on a much greater scale than before, with possibly even closer links between agents, transport companies and hotel and restaurant chains. We can expect to see an expansion of companies outside their traditional spheres of interest into connected leisure areas, but this is nothing new. The travel agents Thomas Cook's is also a package holiday company. The Thompson Organisation includes its package holiday company, its airway (Britannia) and its own hotels overseas. Airways such as British Airways launch their own package holidays under the trade name British Sovereign. Obviously, owing to licensing procedures as well as costs it would be unlikely for a hotel company to launch its own airline, but certainly airlines may consider an extension of their hotel-owning roles. Partially to offset this and similar trends, companies may have to prove that cooperation is more beneficial than competition, and so one can expect hotel companies to try and become larger so as to offer a wider choice and better packages to airlines and travel agents while hoping to achieve a parity in negotiations. Ally this to the advantages of central purchasing systems, promotion and marketing advantages and advantage of size in negotiating more favourable financial terms, and one can expect to see a continuation of mergers in the industry. Within the last half of the 1970s groups such as Mercury Hotels, Adda Hotels, and Myddleton Hotels have been taken over. For the independents to compete an answer appears to be the marketing consortium. In principle, this is akin to the development of voluntary trading groups such as Mace and Spar that have been resorted to by independent grocers as a means of survival in the face of supermarket growth. The equivalent to Mace and Spar in the hotel industry would be organizations such as Best Western. The advantages are primarily marketing ones in that a coordinated campaign on a national scale can be achieved by reason of their accumulated resources in a way that could not be achieved by any one of the independent hotels themselves. Such groupings also possess a potential for bulk buying with the discounts that may be gained.

Yet, in spite of the advantages of standardization, which perhaps reach their epitome in the fast-food trade, there is unlikely to be, at least in the immediate future, a risk of the deadening hand of sameness throttling the industry. Dealing as it does with a market comprising many individual tastes, and of such a size that it is a commercial proposition to cater for such diversities, the industry can expect a multitude of activities. We have already mentioned thematic holidays. The 1970s also showed how vegetarian restaurants can prosper. Another example of a minority interest with a growth market is that of nudist holidays. Increasing income is not only confined to those working. New pension schemes offering inflation-proofed salary-indexed pensions will mean increasingly that an older age group will not only have the leisure time but also the income to enjoy that time. Thus, assuming that a major economic catastrophe is avoided, the extended holiday of the pensioner may become more commonplace.

Any forecast as to future trends is only as good as the assumptions upon which it is based. None of the above trends are particularly revolutionary; they are but extrapolations of present occurrences. Whether these occurrences are significant or but temporary phases leading nowhere but to their own demise, is for you, the reader, to judge. Time will tell. If you are optimistic the energy problem may be, for you, but a problem that, given time, will be solved. The population pressures upon food may also be solved. If, on the other hand you are pessimistic, then the 1980s may begin to confirm your worse fears. The energy problems may lead to increasing travel costs that will reduce tourism, and competition for food may strain international relations, thus creating, in the fullness of time, divisions within societies. Technology and computers may create centralized systems that will threaten individual freedom. At present our society contains all these themes. It is, perhaps, at a crossroads, but then every writer often conceives of his age as being at such a junction in time and development. The hotel and catering industry exists within a framework of such changes and is not isolated from its context. The patterns of costs and revenues referred to earlier in the book are but the indicators of such changes, and yet are the causal agents of how the industry reacts. Of one thing we can be sure. The 1980s will perhaps provide stronger indicators of whether optimism or pessimism is the right attitude for a longer time span.

Questions

1. What is a demand curve, and what application has the theory to the hotel and catering industry?

2. What factors have caused the development of fast-food catering in the commercial sector?

3. What is the importance of the hotel and catering industry to the UK?

4. What are economies of scale? Give examples of economies of scale in the hotel and catering industry.

5. What considerations might a hotelier take into account when deciding his tariff?

6. What changes have occurred in the hotel and catering industry since 1946? What factors account for those changes?

7. What are the main determinants of profitability for a hotel? How might a hotel improve its profitability?

8. How competitive is the hotel and catering industry?

9. What are the determinants of a good location for a hotel or a restaurant?

Outline answers follow.

Outline Answers

1. I Define the demand curve.

   II List the determinants—i.e., price, income, taste, fashion.

   III Adopt a macro-economic approach.

   National levels of demand rest on:

   (a) income movements and inflation;

   (b) rates of exchange and thus prices for overseas tourists;

   (c) increases in leisure time;

   (d) movements of 'discretionary income' resting on prices of other items.

   IV Adopt a micro-economic approach.

   (a) identify market by taste, income, etc.;

   (b) adapt decor and menu to that market;

   (c) advertise;

   (d) price accordingly;

   (e) use differential pricing (elasticity).

See pages 32–43 for further details.

2. I Discuss the following:

   (a) labour costs;

   (b) food costs and portion control;

   (c) available technology;

   (d) acceptability to the market:
   (i) age distribution;
   (ii) work patterns;
   (iii) use of convenience foods;

(e) availability of right size sites with high pedestrian flow;

(f) variations on a hamburger theme;

(g) franchising as a cheap means of achieving national sales.

Give examples of the above factors.

See pages 162–170 for further details.

3. Discuss by:
   I   Establishing criteria of importance.

   II   Introduction of main themes by general comments, e.g.:

   (a) export earner;

   (b) import saver;

   (c) creates employment in Development Areas;

   (d) has multiplier effects.

   III   Enter details relating to:

   (a) tourism:
   - (i) size of domestic demand;
   - (ii) size of overseas demand;
   - (iii) tourism contribution to the balance of payments;

   (b) employment:
   - (i) total size of employment;
   - (ii) geographical spread of employment;

   (c) source of revenue for local and central government:
   - (i) rates;
   - (ii) tax payments by overseas visitors on purchases;
   - (iii) income tax from employees;
   - (iv) corporation tax;

   (N.B. There is little state aid to the industry);

   (d) importance of its services:
   - (i) need for accommodation;
   - (ii) need for eating outside the home—mention types of catering— especially institutional and welfare.

IV Summarize by reference to:
  (a) turnover as a percentage of GNP;
  (b) employment as a percentage of the UK labour force;
  (c) tourism payments as a percentage of the balance of payments.

V Draw a conclusion!

See pages 23–30 and 222–239 for further details.

4. I Define economies of scale.

   II Give examples of economies of scale in the industry:
   (a) financial economies:
       (i) large companies like THF have access to the stock exchange;
       (ii) large companies have securities for loans;
       (iii) large companies can achieve lower interest charges;
   (b) purchasing economies:
       (i) bulk purchase discount (on frozen food);
       (ii) preferential treatment by suppliers;
       (iii) ability to negotiate terms (e.g. with tour operators);
   (c) marketing economies:
       (i) ability to afford national advertising; THF note existence of marketing consortia for independents and association schemes, e.g. Best Western, Centre Link;
   (d) risk diversification:
       (i) diversifying into other leisure activities, e.g. Ladbrokes, Grand Metropolitan, Rank;
   (e) finances available for technical advantages:
       (i) buying modern equipment, e.g. computers for forward booking, accounts, stock control and ordering;
       (ii) building larger hotels, so reducing cost per room built;
   (f) managerial economies:
       (i) using specialised and skilled staff;
   (N.B. Problems of coordination, possible loss of motivation, and friendly touch; on the other hand, delegation);

(g) large companies form large pressure groups:
   (i) representation on various national bodies;
   (ii) direct access to bodies like BTA and 'Parliamentary Tourism Committee' (unofficial).

N.B. In questions like this avoid simply 'listing' items. Rather, try to introduce an element of discussion by comparing and contrasting. If time allows, give any cases you know.

See pages 188–192 for further details.

5. Type of hotel:
   (a) its grade and facilities offered;
   (b) sales mix—ability to gain revenue from guests in bar and restaurant;
   (c) location, e.g. a London hotel can charge higher tariffs.

II Objectives:
   (a) maximising profit(?);
   (b) providing a good service;
   (c) providing work and revenue in off-peak periods;
   (d) need to generate investment capital.

III Market:
   (a) ratio of private residents to businessmen;
   (b) ratio of domestic to overseas visitors;
   (c) socio-economic groupings;
   (d) existing occupancy levels.

IV Costs:
   (a) ratio of fixed to variable costs;
   (b) ratio of full-time to part-time labour;
   (c) amount of capital and interest repayments on borrowed funds.

OUTLINE ANSWERS

V   Approach to pricing policy.

VI   Promotions: is tariff part of a promotion?

VII   Groups:
- (a) is hotel an independent; or
- (b) part of a group; or
- (c) part of a marketing consortium?

VIII   Summary and conclusion:
not a simple process;
tendency to charge what market bears.

See pages 192–206, 211–216 and 175–183 for further details.

6. The changes:
   1. greater diversity of eating out establishments;
   2. emergence of large groups;
   3. greater use of technology;
   4. more people employed;
   5. growth in size and importance;
   6. greater government interest.

   Give examples of each of the above points; for example:
   - (a) development of fast-food outlets, institutional catering and ethnic restaurants;
   - (b) decline in formality of eating out;
   - (c) THF, Grand Metropolitan developing from mergers and takeovers (e.g. Ring and Brymer, Travel-lodge, Bateman's etc.);
   - (d) microwave, cook-freeze and cook-chill;
   - (e) employment of 2 000 000 people;
   - (f) contribution of balance of payments;
   - (g) setting up of tourist boards.

Incorporate these examples in the outline of changes.

The causes:

1. increases in (a) income and (b) leisure time;

2. development of foreign tourism;

3. increase in costs of labour creating greater use of capital;

4. need for economies of scale, and national promotions;

5. increasing contribution to the economy;

6. importance of holidays in today's society;

7. growth of business creating growth of business demand for accommodation.

N.B. This is not a story of unbroken growth. Note the problems of the middle 1970s and early 1980s.

See pages 1–5, 47–71, 211–216, 222–226 for further details.

7. Determinants of profitability. Note that it is difficult to be precise.

   I   Each hotel is in a different situation; e.g. an important burden for new hotels is repayment of borrowed investment capital; older hotels that have belonged to the same group for a long time will not have this problem.

   II   Sales mix:

   (a) accommodation, the most profitable sector;

   (b) drink sales;

   (c) food sales;

   (d) sundries.

   III   Use of labour important:

   ratio of part-time to full-time staff, and flexibility to reduce labour costs when occupancy rates at their lowest.

OUTLINE ANSWERS

IV Average length of stay:

Longer stays:

(a) reduce administrative costs per guest;

(b) can cause less uncertainty over restaurant usage, depending on location of hotel.

V Ability to obtain discounts on purchases:

(a) but for food this may mean over-dependence on convenience foods;

(b) a hotel group has greater ability than an independent hotel;

(c) apart from food and drink, there are few large regular purchases;

(d) one could consider leasing fixtures;

(e) there is a need to be aware of bank overdraft interest rates and trade suppliers' discounts.

VI Ability to raise tariffs over and above cost increases:

(a) ability rests on guests seeing the hotel providing value for money;

(b) also on guests' elasticity of demand.

VII Ability to promote extra revenue raising activities:

(a) conference business: has the hotel the facilities?;

(b) weekend and 'thematic' breaks—problem of occupancy levels, facilities and ability to advertise effectively;

(c) banqueting seasons;

(d) dinner and dances: are they compatible with other business?

VIII Need to identify present sources of business.

IX Location of the hotel.

X   Competition: are there other hotels of similar grade in the immediate vicinity?

Means of improving profitability

I   Increasing revenue:

(a) effective advertising;

(b) good selling e.g.:
- (i) listing facilities available to guests in rooms;
- (ii) clear, attractive menus complete with wine lists—ask if wine wanted;
- (iii) clear pricing;

(c) offering schemes to local companies for their visitors;

(d) adding to facilities suitable for clients for which charges can be made, e.g.:
- (i) squash courts;
- (ii) booking facilities where commission is gained.

(e) increasing tariffs.

II   Controlling costs:

(a) recording costs;

(b) effective ordering and stock control;

(c) reducing use of trade credit if possible;

(d) insulation to reduce heating costs;

(e) effective use of labour;

(f) considering an 'on-premises' laundry;

(g) effective design and layout of kitchens and rooms for:
- (i) easy cleaning;
- (ii) easy access for equipment, etc.;

(h) use of self-service where appropriate;

(i) paying reasonable wages for honest staff!;

(j) creating good working atmosphere to reduce labour turnover.

OUTLINE ANSWERS

Summary

Obviously the above is not an inclusive list, and much depends on each hotel's own situation. And, of course, the above points may be in vain if the hotel has a poor location. Basically, profits rest on a relationship between costs and revenues, and it is easier to raise tariffs than cut costs, but the market structure may restrict increases in tariffs, whereas some of the determinants of the cost structure are under the hotel's own control.

See pages, 177–183 and 208–216 for further details.

8. I   Establish the need for criteria of 'competitive'.

    II   Distinguish between:

        (a) local conditions, e.g. only hotel near a firm;

        (b) national conditions.

    III   Distinguish between markets, e.g.:

        (a) business;

        (b) tourist;

        and link with previous point.

    IV   Indicate concentration ratios by differing criteria for:

        (a) hotels;

        (b) restaurants.

    V   Indicate that restaurants only form a part of catering services and list other outlets, e.g. pubs, institutional, etc.

    VI   Indicate concentration ratios may underestimate influence of leading hoteliers.

VII Discuss the importance of national promotions and competition by:

(a) tariffs;

(b) advertising;

(c) selling to:
   (i) travel trade;
   (ii) incentive schemes organisations;
   (iii) business.

VIII Conclusion:

(a) note the ambiguity of the term 'market';
   (i) a hotel serves an area and it may have area monopoly, but it still competes with other areas;
   (ii) a restaurant may have different lunch-time and evening trades;

(b) one can argue that this is indicative of a degree of competition not truly indicated by concentration ratios;

(c) on a national basis concentration ratios imply an 'imperfect competition' type.

See pages 143–150 and 153–155 for further details.

9. *Hotels*

I For hotels location relates to market, therefore indicate types of demand.

II For business demand:

(a) nearness to centres of industry;

(b) nearness to exhibition centres;

(c) ease of transport and access.

III For tourist demand:

(a) nearness to tourist centres;

(b) ease of transport and access.

IV Site considerations:

(a) size, drainage, load-bearing abilities of soil;

(b) car-parking facilities;

(c) environment;

(d) rates;

(e) freehold or leasehold;

(f) access to main road system.

V Labour force:

(a) ease of obtaining employees;

(b) skill of those employees;

(c) competition for labour and effect on wages.

VI State of competition:

(a) nearness of other hotels;

(b) grades of those hotels;

(c) relate to size of market.

Restaurants

I Identify different types of trade in restaurants, e.g.:

(a) lunch-time;

(b) evening;

(c) urban or rural;

(d) casual or party bookings.

II Ease of access to the restaurant:

(a) public transport may be of some little importance;

(b) road system;

(c) for lunch-time trade, pedestrian flow.

III Compare sites:

for rural areas:

(a) relation to roads and centres of population;

(b) number of competitors;

(c) ease of obtaining labour;

for city centres:

(a) if in shopping centres—first or second floor;

(b) car-parking facilities;

(c) rates in different parts of town;

(d) access for deliveries.

IV Other site considerations:

(a) size:
   (i) for number of covers;
   (ii) space for good kitchen layout;
   (iii) space for storage;
(b) leasehold or freehold.

V State of competition:

(a) number of competing restaurants;

(b) style of cuisine of competitors.

For both hotels and restaurants it is valid to discuss importance of location. Can problems of location be overcome by:

(a) advertising and promotion if (say) little pedestrian flow?;

(b) providing carefully specified needs not otherwise met (say vegetarian)?

See pages 62–67, 122–125 and 153–157 for further details.

Appendix on Sources of Statistical Information

Naturally, any book will become dated as to its factual content, and you may want to update the statistics given in this book. In which case the most easily available statistical reference works do give some information about the industry. Probably the handiest are the *Monthly Digest of Statistics* and the *Annual Abstract of Statistics*. The following indicates the information they give.

The Monthly Digest of Statistics (HMSO)

(i) *Turnover statistics*
These are given in a section entitled 'retailing and catering' and will give the turnover of the industry for hotels and holiday camps; restaurants, cafés etc. and fish and chip shops; public houses; canteens; and the total industry. The statistics are in index form with 1969 the base year, with 1969 data also being given in full at current prices.

(ii) *Employment statistics*
The total employed in the industry, without any breakdown by sex or sector, is to be found in the table *Employees in employment: all industries*, which is useful for comparative purposes.

(iii) *Other statistics*
General statistics as to national income, investment, profits, employment, etc. are to be found, but unfortunately the hotel and catering industry is not separately itemized, and is usually included in a composite 'other services' sector which encompasses hairdressing, laundering and one or two others as well.

The Annual Abstract of Statistics (HMSO)

(i) *Unemployment*
Statistics on the total number of workers unemployed, broken down between five sectors of the industry, including: hotels and licensed residential; public houses, contract catering; clubs and

restaurants, cafés and snack bars are to be found in the tables headed *Numbers unemployed.*

(ii) *Balance of Payments*
This, and other trade figures can be found in the sections on visible trade and the balance of payments. The *Monthly Digest of Statistics* will also give the same figures on a monthly basis. In the *Annual Abstract* the table *Private services: travel—geographical analysis* will indicate the tourism balance.

(iii) *Other statistics*
General economic data on a yearly basis will be given as to the major flows of money, investment, employment etc. within the economy.

National Income and Expenditure Income Tables ('The Blue Book') (HMSO)

(i) *Consumers' expenditure*
This table will show the expenditure on food and drink along with other consumer expenditure. Search into the Appendix at the end of the book and a table showing caterers' expenditure on food will be found.

(ii) *Other statistics*
General data as to national income, company investment, input and output data are also available.

The British Home Tourism Survey (BTA)

This contains statistics relating to holidaying by domestic tourists.

British Industry (HMSO)

This is the new title of *Industry and Trade Gazette.* It has a statistical appendix and publishes all the Business Monitors and thus contains:

(i) *The International Passenger Surveys.*
(ii) *The Business Monitor* (SDS) which gives catering turnover figures.

Index

ABC tea shops 1
Accommodation—see Occupancy rates
Allied Breweries 159, 161
Alveston Kitchens 21
Associated Fisheries 171

Backward pricing 203–204
Balance of payments 28–30, 218, 234–237
Bank loans—see Sources of finance
Bass Charrington 159, 161
Bateman Catering Organisation 22, 157–158
Beer, consumption of 75–79
Berni Inns 166, 167
Bird's Eye 20
Break-even points 187, 202
Breweries 159–161
British Hotels, Restaurants and Caterers Association 17, 242, 243, 248
British Tourist Authority 29, 243–245
Building societies 98
Burger King 166
Butlins 11

CAMRA 77, 159, 161
Capital 89, 91–92
  rates of return on 92–93, 184
Capital costs 175
Catering
  costs of 185–188
  expenditure on food 75, 80–81
  industrial and welfare 139–141
  investment in 95
  types of outlet 18, 80
Catering Industries Liaison Committee 240, 243
Catering Wages Act 251
Centre Hotels 213
Clarksons 3
Competition types
  duopoly 147–150
  imperfect competition 147
  monopoly 147–150
  oligopoly 147–150
  perfect competition 143–147
Concentration ratios 151–153
  of breweries 159
  of contract caterers 157
  of hotels 153–155
Conferences 58–61
Contract catering 13, 141–142, 157–158
Contribution analysis 204–206
Convenience foods 104
  advantages of 106–107
  costs of 105–106
COSIRA 99
Costs
  capital costs 175–177
  definitions of 193, 196, 197
  fixed and variable 178, 187
  operating costs of catering 185–188 (see also Pricing)
  operating costs of hotels 177–183, 185
Cost-plus pricing policies 200–203

Da Costa 168
Debentures 96
Demand
  curve 32–36, 145–146
  determinants 36–39
  elasticity 39–43, 68–70
  statistical demand curves 69
  types of 15–18, 47–48
  (see also Occupancy rates, Expenditure)
Dennys Inc. 167
Dunkin Donuts 167

Economic growth 219
  contribution of the industry 237
Economies of scale 188–192
Elasticity
  in catering 87
  of demand, income and cross-elasticity 40
  (see also demand)
Employment 20, 109, 110
  categories of 114–118
  patterns of 110–114
  regional quotients of 223–224
  (see also labour)
English Tourist Board 9, 69, 71, 100, 233, 245–247
European Economic Community 101
Exchange rates 67, 235–236
Expenditure
  on drinks 77–79
  on food 74–75, 80–81
  general 31
  on tourism 29, 48, 52–53
Export, tourism as an 235–237
  (see also Balance of payments)

Factors of production 89–90

Fast foods 105, 162–170
Finance
  sources of 95–102
  (see also Capital)
Fire Precautions (Loans) Act 1973 100
Foreign visitors—see Overseas visitors
Franchising 170–174
Fringe benefits 126

Gardner Merchant Food Services 157, 158
Good Food Guide 1
Government
  and the hotel and catering industry 21, 100, 222–226, 233
  policy objectives 217–222
Grand Metropolitan 6, 22, 153, 156, 172, 209, 254

Hamburgers 163
Holiday camps 10–11
Holidays—see tourism
Hotels
  number of 135
  definitions 7–8
Hotel and Catering Economic Development Committee 7, 21, 67, 83, 84, 180, 240–242
Hotel and Catering Industry 18–19, 22–31, 153–158, 162–174
  (see also under separate categories)
Hotel and Catering Industry Training Board 248–250
  labour surveys of 108–110, 116, 117, 254

INDEX

Hotel Development Incentive
  Scheme 100–101, 225–226

Imperfect competition 147
Industrial and Commercial
  Finance Corporation 99
Industrial Training Act 1964 248
Industrial and Welfare Catering
  13, 139–142
Inflation 218, 220
  and tariffs 211, 212
Investment 91, 93, 102

Kentucky Fried Chicken 155,
  164, 169–71

Labour
  costs of
  turnover 122–125
  (see also Employment)
Ladbroke Hotels 205
Lager 76, 77, 160
Legislation
  Development of Tourism Act
    81
  Finance Act 1978 101
  Fire Precautions (Loans) Act
    100
  Hotel Proprietors Act 1956 7
  Industrial Training Act 1964
    248
  Wages Councils Act 1959 251
Let's Go 205, 210, 246
Little Chef 171

Manpower 24–25
  (see also Employment, Labour)
Marginal cost 193–194, 197–198,
  201, 208
  revenue 195

Market structure 143–150
  measurement of 151–153
  (see also Concentration ratios)
Mark-ups 202, 212
McDonald's 162, 164, 165, 166
Mercury Motor Inns 205, 260
Midland Catering 157, 158
Monopolies Commission 173
Monopoly 149
Motels 10
Multipliers 228–232

National Income 26–27

Occupancy rates
  definition 61–62
  patterns of 61–67, 69
Overseas visitors 3, 28–30, 50–53

Pay 126–129
Perfect competition 143
Pizza Hut 164, 166, 171
Pizzaland 168
Pricing systems
  contribution pricing 204–206
  cost-plus pricing 200–203
  marginal costing 192–200
  problems in 211–216
  target rate of return 203–204
Profitability 181–182, 211

Rank Organisation 153, 155
Regional location
  quotients 223–224
Regional policy 221–222, 230
Registration of hotels 8–9
Restaurants 11, 18, 81
  patterns of activity 82, 84–85

Sales maximisation 148
Sales mix, importance of 180

Scottish and Newcastle 159
Self-employed 117–118
'Shrinkage' 185
Small Industries Council for Rural Areas 99
Standard industrial classification 5–7
Statistical sources 262
Supply
  curves 130, 133, 145–146
  determinants of 131
  elasticity 134
Supply of hotel accommodation
Sutcliffe Catering 157, 158

Target rate of return pricing 203–204
Tariffs 63–68, 211–215
Tipping 124, 126
Tourism
  domestic 48–50, 53–58, 61–71
  forecasts 71–73, 256–261

overseas 28–30, 50–53
types 47
Trades Unions 242, 253–255
Trusthouse Forte 2, 153, 169, 172, 173, 254
Turnover
  —see Expenditure, Labour

Unemployment 118–121
United Biscuits 167, 168, 171

Value Added Tax 212–213

Wages 127
Wages Councils 72
Watney-Truman 159, 160
Weekend breaks 202, 205, 208–211, 213, 259
Whitbread 159
Wimpy's 1, 155, 168, 171